Training Without Jobs:
New Deals and Broken Promises

£8.95

POB

YOUTH QUESTIONS

Series Editors: PHILIP COHEN and ANGELA McROBBIE

This series sets out to question the ways in which youth has traditionally been defined by social scientists and policy-makers, by the caring professions and the mass media, as well as in 'common-sense' ideology. It explores some of the new directions in research and practice which are beginning to challenge existing patterns of knowledge and provision. Each book examines a particular aspect of the youth question in depth. All of them seek to connect their concerns to the major political and intellectual debates that are now taking place about the present crisis and future shape of our society. The series will be of interest to those who deal professionally with young people, especially those concerned with the development of socialist, feminist and anti-racist perspectives. But it is also aimed at students and general readers who want a lively and accessible introduction to some of the most awkward but important issues of our time.

Training Without Jobs:
New Deals and Broken Promises

*From Raising the School Leaving Age to the
Youth Training Scheme*

Dan Finn

**MACMILLAN
EDUCATION**

First published 1987

Published by
MACMILLAN EDUCATION LTD
Houndmills, Basingstoke, Hampshire RG21 2XS
and London
Companies and representatives
throughout the world

Typeset by Wessex Typesetters
(Division of The Eastern Press Ltd)
Frome, Somerset

Printed in Hong Kong

British Library Cataloguing in Publication Data
Finn, Dan
Training without jobs: new deals and
broken promises: from raising the school
leaving age to the Youth Training Scheme.
—(Youth questions)
1. Youth. *Training of*—Great Britain
2. Unemployed—Training of—Great
Britain
I. Title   II. Series
331.3'42592   HD5715.5.G7
ISBN 0–333–36508–9 (hardcover)
ISBN 0–333–36509–7 (paperback)

Series Standing Order

If you would like to receive future titles in this series as they are published,
you can make use of our standing order facility. To place a standing order
please contact your bookseller or, in case of difficulty, write to us at the
address below with your name and address and the name of the series.
Please state with which title you wish to begin your standing order. (If you
live outside the United Kingdom we may not have the rights for your area,
in which case we will forward your order to the publisher concerned.)

Customer Services Department, Macmillan Distribution Ltd
Houndmills, Basingstoke, Hampshire, RG21 2XS, England.

Mr Rowley, much enthused, came and set the first moot point, chalking it up on the board – 'Children should go to school until they are fifteen' . . .

Mackie chose me at once as a protagonist. Unfortunately, in spite of threat or cajolery, he couldn't find a single other pupil willing to stand before the class and put the opposing, or indeed any, point of view, and this not for want of ideas but through fear alone. Free speech didn't come easily to children kept down at home and in the classroom. Just before the time for the debate arrived, however . . . the teacher dragooned a terrified girl off the back row . . .

I got on the box provided and did my three minute stint without trouble. Rich people, I remember saying, sent their children to schools and colleges until they were twenty-one, so there must be something good in it. We would become doctors and teachers and chemists and explorers – things like that, if we went to school until we were fifteen. I was all for it.

Although Mackie had informed us that the audience was quite free to heckle or clap, they heard me out in dead silence. But both adult listeners seemed very pleased; the Head even patted my shoulder . . . My opponent, Lily Weeton, a pallid girl with plaits, came out and stepped on the box. Her words were few but explosive, 'I think', she said, 'we should gerrout to work at fourteen and fetch some money in for us parents'. Then she stepped off the box to a thunderclap of applause, cheering and clog-stamping that rocked the school. Bubbling excitement, our 'electorate' now went to the poll, and the headmaster, acting as returning officer, announced the result in professional style:

Roberts, Robert   2
Weeton, Lily   48

Storming cheers again for the victor. Eddie Franklin and a girl friend had given me a sympathy vote, but nevertheless admitted to being intellectually with the opposition. (*A Ragged Schooling: Growing Up in the Classic Slum*, Robert Roberts, Manchester University Press, 1975, pp. 151–2)

Contents

List of Tables

List of Statutes

List of Abbreviations

AMB	Area Manpower Board
ATS	Adult Training Strategy
CACE	Central Advisory Council for Education
CBI	Confederation of British Industry
CEP	Community Enterprise Programme
CP	Community Programme
CPRS	Central Policy Review Staff
CPVE	Certificate of Pre Vocational Education
CSE	Certificate of Secondary Education
CRE	Commission for Racial Equality
CTC	Central Training Council
DE	Department of Employment
DES	Department of Education and Science
DHSS	Department of Health and Social Security
EEC	European Economic Community
FEU	Further Education Unit
GCE	General Certificate of Education
HMI	Her Majesty's Inspectorate
IDS	Income Data Services
ILO	International Labour Organisation
ITB	Industrial Training Board
IMS	Institute of Manpower Studies
JCP	Job Creation Programme
LEA	Local Education Authority
MSC	Manpower Services Commission
NAS/UWT	National Association of Schoolmasters/Union of Women Teachers

NATFHE	National Association of Teachers in Further and Higher Education
NEDC	National Economic Development Council
NTI	New Training Initiative
NUT	National Union of Teachers
NYEC	National Youth Employment Council
OECD	Organisation for Economic and Co-operative Development
OTF	Occupational Training Family
OFV	Opportunities for Volunteering
RSLA	Raising of the School Leaving Age to Sixteen
RSSL	Recruitment Subsidy for School Leavers
STEP	Special Temporary Employment Programme
TES	Times Education Supplement
TOPS	Training Opportunities Programme
TUC	Trades Union Congress
TVEI	Technical and Vocational Education Initiative
UVP	Unified Vocational Preparation
VPP	Voluntary Projects Programme
WEP	Work Experience Programme
WEEP	Work Experience on Employers Premises
YES	Youth Employment Subsidy
YOP	Youth Opportunities Programme
YTS	Youth Training Scheme
YWS	Young Workers Subsidy

Acknowledgements

I would like to thank the young people and teachers who have given me their time and helped with the research which I draw on in this book. I would also express my gratitude to Richard Johnson and Simon Frith for the early help and advice they gave me, and to Paul Willis, Chris Griffin, Dave Carter, Bob Holland, and especially to Fran McCabe for their constructive criticisms.

D.F.

Foreword
Paul Willis

Since the early 1970s when I did the research for *Learning to Labour* (Gower, 1977) the transition from school to work of minimum age school-leavers has changed unrecognisably. Then all sixteen-year-olds could get a job if they wanted one. There were plenty of jobs but not much training. The worries concerned the quality of jobs, the lack of training and the lack of provision for continuing education for most young workers. Now there aren't any jobs but plenty of 'training'. The deadest of dead-end jobs are presented as the new youth Eldorado, and the obscenity of mass youth unemployment has been met with the promise of work in the ever-delayed future along with near compulsory training/work experience and massive regulation of the transition by a newly ascendant and assertive state apparatus – the Manpower Services Commission.

But what is the quality of what happens in these two years? Does the Youth Training Scheme represent the long overdue reform and equalisation of provision between the social classes over which the left and labour movements have been campaigning for fifty years, or is it simply another diversion or oppression for the young working class?

The 'training' bit of the education and training couplet always seems to pose problems for progressives and socialists. Whereas employers and industrialists warm to their contradictory platitudes, the left seems bored or reticent. That is one of the reasons why the right has claimed the field as its own in the era of the new realism and the vocationalisation of everything for working-class students. It is also why the persistent and well-informed work of Dan Finn in documenting and exposing the rise of 'MSC-dom' has been so important over recent years. He brings to the training debate the qualities of seriousness, attention to detail and the impulse to practicality which usually characterise only the right's and employers' perspectives, and which, in their hands, help to render the whole area so impenetrable and eye-glazing. But Dan Finn brings those qualities to bear from a progressive viewpoint and shows both that training matters, and that it links up with other areas of crucial concern. This book is the culmination of his recent work. It provides us with a firm framework both for the critique of current tendencies and for the discussion of the alternatives which must come.

Why is Dan Finn so unusual? Why don't progressives and socialists get properly stuck into the training debate? In my view the problem of entering the whole debate from a progressive viewpoint is that 'training' at once concretely presupposes what it is that is to be trained for – working-class destinations structured by division and hierarchy. It cannot be avoided that 'training' not only helps to reproduce but is explicitly addressed to reproducing the existing divisions of labour.

Training is always to some degree about class (and other) reproduction – bottom end up – but the current trends seem to be making it exclusively so. The whole massive apparatus of the MSC and its training programmes have hardly been set into place for the middle-class young! For the middle class and mobile working class it is still 'Education' – now separated more than ever and with a vengeance from the new menial tracks of the 'new realism'.

There may be a crisis in higher education and some interruption in privileged transmission, but this is nothing like the attempted wholesale restructuration downwards of opportunity for the young working-class which the MSC and the penetration of the 'new vocationalism' even further back into the working-class school curriculum are bringing about.

'Training' is now coming to stand for the reversal of decades of concern with educational equality. Structural inequality is now back on the agenda – but in a different column. Now it is what is to be promoted rather than what is to be eradicated. The more the school curriculum is vocationalised, the deeper and earlier will class reproduction take root.

Of course this new obsession with training might have been acceptable in a genuinely mobile and 'equal opportunity' society where, for instance, a similar proportion from the different classes and races entered the different education and training routes. But, actually, it has never been more true than now that it is 'education' for the middle class and 'training' for the rest. YTS membership is overwhelmingly working class. The middle-class young are still six times as likely to go into higher education as are the working-class young. Within YTS itself – reflecting the hierarchy which locates it – there is a class, race and gender hierarchy which mirrors and reproduces inequality *within* the working class.

Dan Finn shows how the Tories were originally hostile to the MSC which they saw as a Labour-inspired QUANGO and a fetter on free-market relations and forces. They were converted to a belief in its usefulness by two possibilities it offered: firstly, to throw up a smokescreen around the obscene and unacceptable facts of youth unemployment; secondly, and under the cover of this screen, to shift the whole education/training complex – ideology, institutions, curriculum, resources – firmly on to the applied training terrain defined exclusively in terms of employers' needs. The education 'bit' could be finally dropped from the education/training couplet and the remainder subsumed as never before to the needs of capital and industry. What a prospect! As Dan Finn so clearly shows, achieving the aims of a century of reform aimed at limiting the exploitation of young workers and extending educational provision has been purchased at the price of handing the whole thing over to those from whom the young were to be protected: the employers.

For all of these reasons it is only too easy to see the training issue and recent developments as serving dominant interests only too well. Many feel that to enter the debate and to assume its definitions necessarily is to collude in the operation and success of those interests.

But there is a whole other side to the training debate which Dan Finn rescues and brings into focus for us – though it is usually forgotten in fashionable left debates. This is quite simply that there is a real working-class stake in training. It is in their main material interest for the young working-class to gain access to wage labour.

They must negotiate whatever framework is put in their way to reach wage labour. Their 'good sense' and practical cultures are organised around the getting and giving of wage labour and the spending of its rewards. Despite forty years of the welfare state, it is still fundamentally the case that 'the labourer into the market place naked goes'. The young working-class person without capital, without income guarantees and without income support from parents if forced (with the partial exception of young mothers), for all practical purposes, to seek out wage labour as the only means of decent survival and as the only access in this society to the future possibilities of dignity, consumption and separate independent living. If training increases the possibility of individual or collective access to the wage, or brings greater individual or collective bargaining power to make it bigger once possessed, then training is a good thing and, of course, a central trade-union issue. After all, from a practical working-class point of view, it may well seem that, short of the millenium, there will always be social classes and they will always be reproduced somehow. Meanwhile the problem is how to find the best personal and collective terms of accomodation and settlement *now*. So long as the wage is the universal target for the working-class young – and what other 'clothes' are we offering? – so long will there be a central, perhaps excluding, working-class interest in training. Now that the MSC has all but destroyed other kinds of access to wage labour, YTS has become of paramount importance to the working class. It is their only access to the wage, quite apart from its pretensions to provide quality skill training. Putting aside the confusing, contradictory and masking ideological debates concerning 'quality of labour supply' and 'national economic interests', the fundamental question which Dan Finn's book poses is this: how is it, and is it, possible to reconcile the tensions between training as class reproduction and training as working-class interest more in favour of the working class? It is a scandal that, so far, there has been no effective response – ideologically or politically – to this question from the labour movement.

In working through our positions on this question we should not overlook the vigour and autonomy of the material cultures of the young working class and of their likely reactions and resistance to the new vocationalism and its institutioned bridges and compulsions. This can alert us to some deep-seated and intractable contradictions in the new vocationalism which ensure its longer-term failure – in its own terms at least – and which gives some footings to a more rational and hopeful view of the training question.

In *Learning to Labour* I argued that the dominant teaching

paradigm in schools, locating and underlying actual teaching relationships, concerns the 'fair exchange' of knowledge for respect. In theory, students get the knowledge; the teachers get the respect. Knowledge is the basis for gaining qualifications which is the basis for getting a job. Respect is the basis for the teacher's moral and social control of the classroom (gaining obedience from students). This paradigm was in trouble when I wrote *Learning to Labour*. Now it is in tatters. Many working-class students, especially through the expression of their collective cultures, cannot see the point of yielding their obedience for inflated or worthless 'qualifications' followed by no jobs anyway. YTS makes a valiant post-school attempt to reinstate the teaching exchange for its 'trainees'.

In one way this new relationship is more tangible for 'trainees' than the old one was for its 'students'. 'Trainees' receive a document setting out rights and obligations in quasi-contractual and legal forms. The difficulties arise, however, as before in finding a meaningful equivalent to offer the trainee in return for attendance and good behaviour. Many 'equivalents' have been used up or discredited already – especially in the vocationalisation of everything in the school – or are simply plainly valueless in relation to the future. But the new training schemes are finding ingenious though tautological ways of scraping the barrel of vocational relevances. They are offering (institutionally) to the kids what they have (culturally) already: detailed knowledge of work; motivation to work; skills to deal with working with others – in short the capacity to labour itself. One might say that the curse of the working class – work – has been taken from the working class, repackaged, and given back to them as a 'blessing'. It seems that it is now necessary to provide for the working class remedial learning in order for it to be properly working class! The next step may be vocational certificates to prove that future workers are human at all – measured by the employers' template of course.

As Dan Finn shows it is, of course, the working class which knows and knows intimately most about the world of work, about boredom, about compulsion, about coping on low pay, about the compensations of camaraderie, and about the faceted deflection of unreasonable authority. It is these things which constitute the daily fabric of production. And the working class know about work from *their* point of view through 'useful knowledges' derived from and addressed to survival as the weaker party in continuous struggle. Such knowledges are passed to the new generation through shared cultures, shared stories, shared conditions and through the massive working-class experience of child labour.

Of course there may be a more Machiavellian point in the new training schemes. It may be that the aim is to make institutional additions to, and work insidious reformations of, *recognised* existing working-class material cultures and *in situ* knowledges to make them more consonant with employers' views of the basic qualities necessary to worker humans.

In some ways such an explicit cultural offensive would be more acceptable. It would perhaps provide the terms of a real and critical exchange within which 'really useful' working-class knowledge would have a meaningful role – no matter if contested. The 'world of work' might then signify something of the real complex of interests and conflicts involved in production rather than simply the crass class interests of employers in the fullest domination of their workers. As it is, the crucial point here, it really does seem that the current tendency of the vocational approach – especially social and life skills and transferable skills for the YTS bottom track – is to assume a cultural vacuum amongst students: that they know nothing about the world of work or that what they do know is completely invalid. This is remedialism for an imagined deficit. Effectively it constitutes a cultural insult to 'trainees' – an insult which is going to be at the heart of likely future resistances and disorders (in newspeak, motivational and behavioural problems) amongst trainees.

But there are also and will also be inevitable responses from trainees to the other more blatant contradiction of YTS – the use of massive doses of work socialisation as an antidote to mass youth unemployment: often mindlessly applied manual training for precisely these jobs which are disappearing. Training for what has disappeared or does not exist actually doubles the cultural insult. The reality of a future of poverty and unemployment faced by many trainees will be lived through their own material cultures and practical social relations and knowledges – precisely those resources which are ignored or devalued on training schemes.

My point is simply this: that those subjected to the new, narrow and 'realistic' training will not be without their own collective and cultural reactions. Those capacities insulted or denied in industrial remedialism will strike back here and in many other sites, with their own forms of life: cultural, social, political and practical.

It is this life which must in some sense be grasped and dialectically developed in alternative models of post-school education and training if we are not to be left gasping embarrassing reflections of the 'new realism' at young workers and non-workers across incomprehending cultural and economic divides.

Dan Finn concludes his book with a discussion of the many reforms necessary to tilt the training apparatus more towards the interests and definitions of the young working class. It is clear that there has been enough of training aimed at increasing *individual employability*. What is needed now is *employment*, or at least honesty about (un)employment. Genuine training (for jobs, not the smokescreen) must be part of a total package which includes economic and employment development and vigorous equal opportunities policies – training should be part of a larger process of a wider public policy aimed at breaking down rather than reproducing the division of labour and its associated hierarchies and ideological dualisms.

I endorse Dan Finn's shopping list, but would like to add two further points relating directly to that wider 'life' of young workers and non-workers that goes on, now, despite rather than because of current training schemes.

The first is the importance of maintaining, and opening up, in all possible ways – institutionally, formally, financially, culturally – broad and life-long working-class, female and black educational interests and opportunities in ways that are not mugged all the time by the dull thud of employers' views of characteristics appropriate to be developed in worker Eor non-worker) humans. The crisis of mass unemployment does not lessen the importance of this – it adds, immeasurably, to it.

My second and final point concerns the urgency of making real progress in the long overdue task of developing a strategic and integrated policy for youth, for youth emancipation and for youth autonomy which is way beyond our current *de facto* youth policy of 'MSC-dom'. My recent work (*The Social Condition of Young People in Wolverhampton in 1984*, Information Centre, Wolverhampton) has been exploring the new social condition of young people and the ways in which a variety of state forms are, and are perceived to be, oppressive and/or infantilising rather than emancipatory for young people. Our inner cities are developing bureaucratic walls of containment to go along with the economic, social and policing ones. In a whole variety of areas – including social services, careers work, housing, planning, finance, urban programmes – we should be looking to, and *involving* as contributing partners, young people as the nucleus of a developing society rather than as a social problem for the old static society requiring hard policing or soft welfaring, or as, at best, peripheral material to be moulded in narrow and contradictory ways to suit the self-interests of small dominating groups. It is high time that we offered more to our young than being sent 'naked into the market-place' – even if it takes the disappearance of the market to make us act.

There have been enough empty and repetitious promises for a new deal. Let's really use some imagination. Let's take and make a political will. Let's take the force of the crisis to put some real guts into the rhetorical shell of the next 'new deal'.

Wolverhampton   P. W.
August 1986

1

Introduction: New Deals and Broken Promises

For more than a century the state has prohibited children from obtaining full-time employment and it has assumed increasing control over the conditions awaiting school leavers in the labour market. This book traces these developments from the introduction of compulsory schooling to the creation of the two-year Youth Training Scheme (YTS). It describes the ways in which the experiences and possibilities of minimum age school leavers have been actively transformed as successive governments have attempted to structure the transition into work.

The major reforms introduced have all, in their turn, been attractively presented and justified as meeting the needs of the young people affected. However, by concentrating on what happened when the school leaving age was raised to sixteen (RSLA) and on the subsequent introduction of YTS, it will become clear that the motives of the policy-makers have never been that straightforward. Both changes were also justified by claims that in producing more effective and efficient workers the reforms would, in their different ways, resolve some of the political and economic problems created by changes in the labour market.

All major structural reforms of schooling and of the juvenile labour market have involved costs as well as benefits for the young working class. For example, the exclusion of young people from work may have protected them from exploitation, but it also stopped them getting a wage, delayed their 'growing up', and made them dependent on their families. Training schemes may stop school leavers sinking into long-term unemployment, but as trainees many have found themselves in workplaces on low

1

allowances doing the same work as others who received a full wage. It is this dynamic tension, and the contradictions of reform, which have frequently provoked an ambivalent response from the school leavers involved.

In Chapter 2, I examine how some of these contradictions surfaced in the period between the wars 1918–39. As successive governments resisted pressure to extend educational opportunities to the young working class, and created temporary schemes for alleviating juvenile unemployment, an increasingly broad-based opposition denounced the waste and inequality involved, and called for a school leaving age of sixteen as a key part of their overall demand of secondary education for all.

RSLA was not to be implemented, however, until the early 1970s. This was after the particular combination of political forces and intellectual assumptions which made up the social democratic consensus on education gave a higher leaving age a renewed priority on both social *and* economic grounds. As I show in Chapter 3, by then RSLA had become inextricably connected with the comprehensive reorganisation of secondary education.

This connection is highlighted in Chapter 4, when I assess the impact that RSLA had on a particular comprehensive school in the mid-1970s and analyse how a group of pupils and teachers experienced a higher leaving age as an everyday reality. In the final four chapters of the book, I describe and assess the transformation that has taken place in the lives of the young working class brought about by unemployment and the activities of the Manpower Services Commission (MSC), and draw some conclusions.

The debate about the political success and consequences of what is called 'Thatcherism', and about its popular appeal, has often been characterised by abstractions, generalisations and sophisticated theoretical appraisals. In this book by contrast I draw on a wealth of empirical studies of education, young people and the labour market both to illustrate the failures of social democratic reform and to reveal how, since 1979, the Conservative government has attempted to restructure the relationship between education, training and work.

Through a detailed examination of the development and politics of the MSC, and by assessing the specific impact of its training schemes and the reactions of young people to them, I want to show how the monetarists have used the power of the state to manage the continuing crisis of youth unemployment and create the institutions and schemes through which they wish to remake the young working class. I want to reveal the contradictory and fragile base upon which the success of their schemes depends, and in the conclusion I outline some of the key elements required of a progressive strategy for change in education and training in 1980s Britain.

Before commencing this analysis I want to consider briefly the social construction of youth, and why the young working class has been the focus of so many policy initiatives and interventions in the postwar period. I also want to stress that despite expansion and reorganisation educational institutions continue to reproduce the major inequalities which characterise British society.

Most importantly, I want to look at how working class families and their children first reacted to the imposition of compulsory schooling. The forms of education which emerged in that period set the pattern for subsequent events, and the conflicts which erupted graphically illustrate the contradictions which have since bedevilled attempts to secure real improvements in the educational condition of young workers.

From RSLA to YTS

Following the commitment given in the Education Act 1944, the school leaving age was finally raised to sixteen in 1973. A large cohort of young people were permanently excluded from the labour market, in return for which they were promised the benefits of a reformed and comprehensive secondary education. On leaving school, however, an increasing number of young people did not make a transition to full-time jobs and careers, but experienced extensive periods of unemployment. By the summer of 1984 it was anticipated that without training schemes over 400,000 school leavers would have been unemployed.

The escalating crisis of youth unemployment has been punctuated by a succession of politicians and bureaucrats proclaiming 'new deals' and solutions for the young unemployed.[1] These proposals, however, have never addressed the obvious material needs of the young for adequate housing, leisure facilities, a reasonable income or even conventional wage labour. Instead, a series of *ad hoc* and temporary measures evolved which were designed to make the young more competitive in the labour market. In 1983, these were replaced by the one-year YTS which became a two-year scheme in 1986. Geoffrey Holland, Director of the MSC, yet again described this traineeship as a 'new deal', which he assured us would 'begin in school and end in the workplace' (1984b).

With a million unemployed under-twenty-five year olds such ambitions should be regarded with considerable scepticism. In contrast with the images of Saatchi and Saatchi advertising campaigns – which have depicted the arrival of a virtual new 'golden age' for youth – the evidence shows that a very different, hidden agenda was set for training policy early in 1981. These objectives emerged in the 1983 General Election campaign when confidential government papers were leaked to *Time Out* magazine. They showed that as far as Mrs Thatcher's government was concerned the purpose of YTS was to act as a mechanism for removing young people from the collective bargaining process, for depressing their wage levels, and for relocating them in a new dependent status suspended mid-way between school and wage labour. The introduction of a training year would also 'massage' the unemployment statistics, and it was hoped, reduce crime and social unrest.

Assessing the political success of this process requires an analysis of the rise to power of what has been called 'manpower-servicedom'. The MSC, which came into existence in 1974, has actively participated in defining the political and ideological response of the state to youth unemployment. Since its creation, its activities have affected millions of people, kept thousands off the dole queues, and structured the initial labour market experiences of the vast majority of school leavers.

The MSC's budget grew from £125 million in 1974 to £2.5 billion in 1986–7, when some 2.5 million people were expected to use its services and participate in its schemes. Throughout the 1980s the MSC has been involved in a *qualitative* and *quantitative* expansion of its activities, and in the process has been redefining the nature of education and training. In the midst of the worst unemployment levels since the 1930s, the Commission has helped persuade public opinion that the young working class now need lengthy periods of training before they can even enter the labour market.

'Youth'

Such transformations of working class life are by no means unique. The history of industrial capitalism has been characterised by a complex interplay of economic development and state intervention which has extended the period between working class childhood and adult maturity. The most obvious aspect of this process has been the introduction of compulsory schooling and the gradual increase in the minimum school leaving age.

Although the transition to adulthood is most dramatically experienced through the individual processes of physical maturation, it has always been characterised by important social and economic changes as well. Alongside compulsory schooling a whole complex of institutions and social practices have been created which both define and control young people and at the same time attempt to meet their needs. These can range from the direct control exercised by parents or the courts, and the controls and freedoms offered in the sponsored leisure activities of voluntary organisations and youth clubs, through to the freedoms of consumption offered to young people by modern leisure industries. Within these freedoms and constraints a multiplicity of 'class-specific' youth cultures and transitions have emerged.

Especially in postwar Britain, debates and controversies about young people have become powerful metaphors for arguments about society in general. 'Youth', as it has been socially constructed, can conjure up a set of menacing and largely masculine images which in various moral panics[2] have defined young people as a threat – from the connoted black face of the mugger to the closely-cropped hair of the neo-nazi skinhead and the loose virtues of the single parent family. On the other hand, youth has itself been seen as threatened and at risk. It is a fragile, vulnerable stage of physical and personal development through which we must pass to independence and maturity. Its disruption could pose threats to an individual's subsequent social and economic development.

Working class youth has thus been consistently understood as a potential threat to the social order, yet at the same time – and partly as a consequence – as in need of special provision. Policies around the young working class have always displayed a Janus face, where what is altruistically proclaimed to be meeting their developmental needs contains within it the means for controlling and directing their activities.

In this book however, the focus will not be directly on the patterns of leisure and stylised consumption of working class youth – in response to which so many scenarios around their imminent descent to barbarism have been constructed, and from which so many 'law 'n order' policies have been derived. The starting point will be that most mundane of working class concerns, the experience of compulsory schooling and the transition to work.

My object is to explore the relationship between the interventions of the state and the material realities which have confronted different generations of working class school leavers. This analysis will concentrate as much on the condition of the youth labour market and the contradictions of government policy, as it will on the capacities and aptitudes that young people first bring to work. Lifting some of the ideological fog which obscures these connections should help us understand why it is that young school leavers are unlikely to become the perfect model workers, complete with employability and social and life skills, that the MSC would like them to be.

Schooling and inequality

This book will not announce, once again, the 'failure' of comprehensive schools, by detailing their inability to have a dramatic impact on class-related social and economic inequalities. Within capitalist societies the existence and character of social classes is not an outcome of a differentiated education system, but precisely the opposite. The educational system may have some degree of autonomy, but its key features of selection and hierarchy derive from the character of the social division of labour. This is no simple reflection, or reflex response, but is achieved through the complex translation of economic and social privilege into educational attainments and the subsequent retranslation of those educational credentials into renewed forms of privilege.[3]

Nevertheless, my concern with the working class experience of schooling should not obscure the continuing material and social inequalities that are a marked feature of the British education system.[4] Nor should it diminish the important ways in which educational practices and assumptions can be challenged and transformed to provide young people with skills and experiences which can ease the transition to adulthood. Schools have always prepared pupils for an unequal future but the demand for a common, broad-based education for all is reinforced rather than diminished by that reality.

The transition to work and the school leaving age

Within a class experience there have always been a complex variety of transitions from school to work. The diverse regional and occupational forms these transitions take are structured through the divisions of gender, class and race. Young women have made short-term job choices within the long-term context of marriage, and have confronted a labour market which by and large exploits and confirms that choice. Children of the unskilled or irregularly employed have rarely had the resources or contacts to obtain and complete apprenticeships. Black youngsters have been confronted by institutional racism, and by the direct and indirect discrimination which characterises patterns of recruitment.

The juvenile labour market has also been complex and volatile, and has reacted dramatically to structural and cyclical variations in the economy. Traditionally, it has been characterised by numerous 'blind alleys', where young people are employed in short-term unskilled jobs because of their inexperience and cheapness. In response to these conditions reformers and progressive organisations called both for a higher school leaving age and for young workers to be given some systematic access to continuing forms of education in their first years in employment.

Most educational histories which have considered the raising of the school leaving age record a tale of progress from the dark ages of industrial capitalism to the enlightened practices of the modern state, extolling the virtues of enlightened reformers who rescued children from the rapacious grasp of employers and the avaricious ignorance of their parents. In contrast, I want to suggest that the complex legal and practical controls imposed on youth employment have created a particular kind of labour power which can be drawn on both whilst children are at school and in their early years on the labour market. An extended period of compulsory schooling and now a two-year period of initial training have been presented as the political achievement of new rights for young people, but in reality they have had a *contradictory* impact on the experience of growing up working class.

Compulsory schooling and the working class

The Education Act 1870, which introduced a national system of elementary education, did not enforce attendance but left it to the discretion of local School Boards, which were empowered to supplement the provision of the earlier voluntary denominational schools. By 1876 about half of the child population were in areas of compulsory attendance. In that year legislation was introduced requiring attendance from all children up to ten years of age, and for those between ten and thirteen who did not satisfy certain attendance requirements. It enabled local boards to set up School Attendance Committees. In many areas, these committees were responsive to the demands of mill and land owners who were anxious not to lose the cheapest segments of their labour force. In 1880, compulsion was enforced nationally, though it was still possible for eleven–thirteen year olds to be employed in factories. The Factory and Workshops Act 1878 complemented school attendance requirements by raising the minimum age of employment to ten and by limiting the hours of children under the age of fourteen to half the normal working day.

These legislative enactments and new demands for attendance encountered much opposition. In some areas they were fiercely resisted by employers and workers alike. As late as 1881 children still constituted 5 per cent of the working population, and as E. J. Hobsbawm points out, child labour 'remained surprisingly important . . . showing no significant tendency to diminish in important industries until very late in the century' (1968, p. 293).

Increases in the leaving age were persistently undermined by the half-time exemption system which lasted into the 1920s and enabled pupils who satisfied minimum attendance requirements to leave school anything up to two years before the official leaving age.[5]

In the period before compulsion, schooling remained a marginal experience for many working class children. They attended irregularly, left early and rarely stayed at the same school for more than two years. This instrumental behaviour was not simply the product of greedy parents and employers setting children to work as soon as they were able. It reflected, in the absence of general compulsion, the way working people used schools, by taking from the system what they wanted – especially the acquisition of literacy – and withdrawing from school once those skills were acquired.

In working class communities the imposition of compulsory schooling created important conflicts. The school imposed a series of demands on children and their families. They had to attend regularly, be classified by age and ability, learn a given curriculum in a given order and a given way, be periodically examined and display their new 'knowledge' for the annual inspections. These expectations directly contradicted the rhythms and priorities of working class life, where domestic duties took precedence over school attendance; family groupings were more important than age classifications; school was a waiting period before employment and then marriage, to be abandoned as soon as there was a job going, rather than a preparation for it (Frith, 1977a). Resistance to attendance, particularly for poorer families, was reinforced by their reluctance to pay school fees – which were not abolished for elementary schools until 1892 – and by their inability to forego the meagre earnings that their children could generate.

The compulsory schooling of the working class involved far more than filling up gaps in provision. It involved establishing and enforcing definitions of what did and did not count as 'education'. The educative value of the family and of wider forms of popular culture were undermined and the educative value of what took place in these new, redbrick institutions – the schools – systematically enhanced. For Stephen Humphries the battle over school attendance was no simple exercise in philanthropic salvation, but represented a protracted struggle:

The authoritarian and bureaucratic form taken by the emerging state schooling system was clearly instrumental in perpetuating, reproducing and legitimising capitalist social relations. Some of the key elements in this process were the enforcement of a time-orientated and depersonalised organisation of work, regular and punctual attendance, obedience to authority and the severe punishment of any form of behaviour that did not conform to the demands of the regimented school routine. When viewed from this perspective, the occasional or persistent truants, the children who disrupted lessons and protected classmates from punishment and the parents who threatened or assaulted teachers must be seen to have been involved in a fierce class–cultural struggle over the form of social relationships that were to prevail in schools. Their resistance was rooted in a powerful residual tradition that . . . clung to the belief that learning and work should spring from the needs of the individual, the family and the community, not the authoritarian demands of an essentially bureaucratic institution (1981, p. 89).

In the final analysis, the imposition of compulsory attendance was secured through the coercive power of the courts and the activities of the School Board men. Working class families and children were 'disciplined' to the demands of the school. In the area administered by the London County Council almost 30,000 formal summonses for truancy were issued each year around the turn of the century, 90 per cent of which led to convictions and fines (EWO, 1971, p. 4). Between 1888 and 1916, truancy was the second most common offence, and in peak years there were as many as 100,000 prosecutions of working class parents (Hutt, 1972, p. 203). Average attendance rates increased from approximately 60 per cent in the 1880s to over 80 per cent from 1906 onwards (Humphries, 1981, p. 63).

The developing system of elementary schooling was to offer a newly-created working class some concrete material and social benefits. It could help the family by removing children into a different form of custody and care, relieving the mother in particular from some of the brunt of child care. Given the new employment disciplines and restrictions on the time and energy of the working class family, schooling of various forms could also achieve the learning of elementary skills. It offered some the chance of social mobility, and for many parents became the repository of all their hopes of a better life for their children.

From this progressive side of the institution schooling became associated with all kinds of benefits – real and imaginary – and organised popular pressure for the expansion of provision has since the 1850s played an important part in the growth of schooling. Nevertheless, the elaboration of working class political demands for more access to education went hand in hand with a localised resistance and hostility to the demands of compulsory schooling.

By the end of the nineteenth century a specifically working class programme of educational reform was emerging. In the struggles to abolish school fees, extend medical and welfare services, end child labour, humanise school discipline and establish a secular education, the conditions were laid for the demands that became central to the educational programmes of the new socialist parties. At the heart of these programmes was the fundamental requirement that all working class children should have access to secondary education within a school life that lasted until they were sixteen. These demands were to dominate educational politics between the wars, and were to set the framework for many contemporary changes.

2

'Secondary Education for All': Raising the School Leaving Age and Juvenile Unemployment Between the Wars

The creation of YTS is often presented as the realisation of proposals first outlined in the Education Act 1918, which suggested that all young workers should be given a right of access to day release education. Despite the enormous differences between then and now, it is still useful to examine the period when both the call for day release education and the demand for a school leaving age of sixteen were first formulated. In contrast with the contemporary YTS, both these demands were concerned with *protecting* young workers from exploitation, and with encouraging their broader intellectual and social development.

During the interwar period the arguments for these reforms evolved in response to the changing economic and social plight of the young working class. On the one hand, the increasingly complex relationship between science, industry and higher education was to create a new generation of working practices which deskilled certain areas of craftwork and facilitated the exploitation of cheap juvenile labour. On the other, escalating unemployment – especially in the distressed areas – was to intensify the long-term employment problems associated with the 'blind alley' dead end jobs which were the short-term destiny of most school leavers. In showing the effects that these changes had on the situation of young workers, it will become apparent that the major government response of introducing special schemes for the young unemployed was viewed as an unacceptable palliative which took attention away from the reforms needed to secure real change.

Throughout the 1930s a broad-based alliance, spearheaded by the Labour Party, was to win increasing popular support for a progressive agenda for educational reform. Its primary objective was the introduction of secondary education for all with a compulsory school leaving age of sixteen. There was a convergence between the groups making up this alliance, although fundamental differences were evident between those socialists who wished to use educational change to challenge the class structure and those reformers who wanted educational change to alleviate its worst effects. Significantly, as the argument for RSLA developed, what was originally demanded as a way of protecting the young from the recruitment and employment policies of important sectors of industrial and commercial capital became increasingly interpreted as a problem *about* the young and their exposure to a 'natural' process of elementary and secondary education. This specifically educational rationale for RSLA enabled its supporters to cultivate the broader support of teachers' organisations, educational administrators and other political parties, but it served to deflect critical attention away from what happened to the young at work.

It was to these problems that the call for day release education was addressed. This proposal, however, did not arise from any desire to challenge the exclusion of the young working class from secondary education; it was concerned instead with alleviating the problems associated with the initial employment experiences of many young workers. Not surprisingly, as the elements making up the progressive alliance battled with the government over expenditure cuts and a higher leaving age, they regarded this demand as a diversion and gave it little priority. Before analysing these political and educational developments, it is worth looking in more detail at why the state had become interested in day release education, and what was to become of the proposals for its introduction contained in the Education Act 1918.

Day continuation education and educational politics between the wars

Before the First World War, the economic changes being generated by a second industrial revolution were actually increasing the demand for juvenile labour of both sexes. In 1909 the educational consequences of these developments were pointed to in a Board of Education consultative paper which recommended the introduction of what was to be called day continuation education:

> Certain branches of machine production are being so organised as to make profitable the employment of boy and girl labour in processes, which, while demanding some intelligence and previous school training, are in themselves non-educative and deadening to the mind . . . organised efforts are needed to counteract the hurtful effects of these new economic developments (quoted in Gollan, 1937, p. 226).

The subsequent impact of the war, with conscription and full employment, enabled young people to experience a period of high wages and unparalleled prosperity. Many girls entered 'men's' jobs, and fewer went into domestic service. The affluence and autonomy of this new generation of young workers were regarded with some apprehension, and its consequences were assessed in the Lewis Report, published in 1917.

This report drew attention to the upheavals in family life, and to the chaos that surrounded juvenile employment and apprenticeship training. It proposed the introduction of a school leaving age of fourteen with no exemptions, followed by attendance for not less than eight hours a week or 320 hours a year at day continuation classes up to the age of eighteen. These proposals were not just a response to the problems experienced at work by young people. Underlying them was an expressed concern about the independence given to young people by the wage and full employment:

> Their economic value in the home renders them largely independent of parental control, just as the law of school exemption renders them independent of social control. At the mature age of 14 they have become free competitors in the labour market, and they use their freedom to the full (van der Eyken (ed.), 1973, p. 210).

The impulse was not to extend secondary education to all but to create a new form of social control. For the report, the dominant influence on young people aged between twelve and eighteen should be an educational one:

Can the age of adolescence be brought out of the purview of economic exploitation and into that of the social conscience? Can the conception of the juvenile as primarily a little wage earner be replaced by the conception of the juvenile as primarily the workman and citizen in training? (van der Eyken (ed.), 1973, p. 211)

It seemed that these questions would be answered positively within the terms of the Education Act 1918. The subsequent fate of these proposals, however, served as an early illustration of interwar educational politics. The leaving age was raised to fourteen, and the half-time exemption system was finally ended in 1922, but the other proposals were quickly embroiled with the economy drive initiated by the Geddes Committee in 1921. The £6.5 million savings in education – achieved mainly at the expense of teachers' salaries and school meals – signalled the abandonment of the plans for major reconstruction suggested by the 1918 Act. The proposed introduction of nursery schools, day continuation classes and the raising of the school leaving age to fifteen were abandoned.

Between 1919 and 1939, the progressive alliance of forces who argued – often unsuccessfully – that working class children should be provided with the necessities of life and be given access to secondary education was always confronted by more powerful forces who resisted these demands. Frequently it appeared that educational advances had been won, only to evaporate in the next round of expenditure cuts. In 1922, in 1925–6, in 1931–2 and in 1936 – all periods of severe financial retrenchment – Conservative or National governments faced the outrage of teacher unions, local educational administrators, and the whole range of national and local working class organisations (Simon, 1974). Since government measures were solidly supported by business and since on two occasions the committees recommending cutbacks were actually staffed by leading businessmen, the politics of education were often and overtly a politics of class.

Nevertheless, the debate about a higher leaving age grew in intensity as the distressed areas began to be wracked by the effects of long-term mass unemployment, and as the nature of juvenile employment continued to change.[1] Alongside traditional areas of blind alley work the semi-skilled jobs created by the new mass production industries now emerged. In these sectors, the proportion of skilled workers was much smaller, factories were larger, relations between employer and employees more impersonal, and they employed many more women and 'dexterous' youth, who could shift with relative ease from one job to another (Stevenson, 1984).

Education, science and employment

These new industries and their technical innovations were the product of an ever more intimate relationship between scientists and employers. Technical advances in the electrical and chemical industries, for example, required a knowledge of developments in pure science and a consistent process of experiment and testing for their development. New relationships were created between industrialists, technologists, professional scientists and scientific institutions. Employers became involved in the systematic organisation of science, paying for scientific research, education and laboratories.[2] This shift of science from being incidental to being fundamental to the process of production represented, according to Harry Braverman (1974), the contrast between the industrial revolution which occupied the last half of the eighteenth and the first third of the nineteenth century, and the 'scientific/technical revolution, which began in the last decades of the nineteenth and is still going on'.

Just as the first industrial revolution involved more than the creation of new technical processes, so too the period of the scientific–technical revolution inaugurated further changes in the organisation and experience of work. In many cases this consisted of the extension of the factory system to areas hitherto untouched by it, but the most important development was the application of science to the organisation of labour as well as to the creation of new products and processes. For Frederick Taylor, the apostle of 'scientific management', the labour process and organisation of the work were to be broken down into their component elements. The exercise of skill and judgement and the coordination of different activities were to be the prerogative of a management which was to ensure that industrial workers behaved as much like machines as possible. As the relationship between higher education and industry became more productive, one fruit was the creation of jobs which required fewer skills from manual workers.

Other changes in the division of labour resulted in the creation of new layers of intermediate workers who required technical and commercial skills which could not be provided through the older forms of apprenticeship training. One consequence was mass participation in part-time education, predominantly in the evening. By 1934 over 2 million students were registered on part-time courses, which were largely concerned either with filling in gaps in formal education or obtaining qualifications relevant to their occupations.

For the Coles, writing in 1937, this phenomenon was 'one of the most important and least noticed facts of the modern world'. By the late 1930s there had been a:

> great increase in the number of persons who possess minor technical qualifications which are enough to raise them, both in their estimation and in their earning power, above the ruck of the unqualified or of those whose sole qualification is based on manual apprenticeship. The 'black-coated' proletariat consists to an ever increasing extent of these qualified workers who have laboured away in the evenings to advance themselves, and by that means have in most cases raised themselves a step up the social ladder (quoted by Stevenson, 1984, p. 253).

Despite this increasingly complex relationship between industry and education, and between class position and educational level, the mass of working class children left school at the earliest possible moment. In a not untypical year – 1934 – of 555,000 new recruits to employment of all ages, 85 per cent came from elementary schools, 70 per cent having left at the earliest possible age of fourteen. Only a tenth of those entering employment were aged over sixteen (Stevenson, 1984, p. 257).

Leaving school and blind alley employment

Many working class families were less than enthusiastic about the prospect of an extended period of compulsory schooling. After bringing children up under the strains of poverty, many parents wanted them to enter employment as soon as they could. Even where working class youngsters were educationally successful, the force of economic circumstance would usually require leaving school at the earliest moment, or a withdrawal from secondary education after a short period. The painful contradiction between the promise of secondary education for the most talented, and the reality of enforced withdrawal from school through economic hardship was frequently experienced by girls and by children from large and unskilled families (Humphries, 1981, p. 57). These problems were exacerbated by the reimposition of school fees in 1932, and by restrictions on the scope and number of free places.

Nevertheless, most school leavers eagerly anticipated the transition to work. Many experienced an education and school routines which offered them little. Fed a diet of 'religion, imperialism and competitive individualism', and housed in inadequate buildings in large classes, they encountered a harsh regime deemed appropriate for their station in life. In making each school day pass as painlessly as possible they created complex and subterranean means for negotiating the demands of the school.[3]

Starting work marked the awaited transition from the enforced dependence of schooling to some of the freedoms of the wage and adulthood. By the 1920s these 'freedoms' were giving access to new and attractive forms of consumption for both boys and girls. After meeting the costs of their upkeep, they could when in work get access to the new commodities that mass production and costcutting was making available. For John Stevenson, this led to clear 'manifestations' of a distinct teenage culture before the Second World War (1984, p. 246). The 'affluent' young could buy cigarettes, go to dances, enjoy music and above all, go to the cinema: 'the essential social habit of the age' (Taylor, 1970, p. 237). They may have had few future prospects, lived in a slum dwelling, and worked long hours, but with money in their pocket they enjoyed some freedom. To a contemporary observer – A. E. Morgan – it seemed that the young had 'watched [this freedom] enviously through the school bars and [were] now . . . free to expand in it like a butterfly in the sunshine' (1943, p. 20).

These realities could undermine the confidence of progressive reformers. For George Orwell, on his journey to Wigan Pier:

The time was when I used to lament over quite imaginary pictures of lads of fourteen dragged protesting from their lessons and set to work at dismal jobs. It seemed to me dreadful that the doom of a 'job' should descend upon anyone at fourteen. Of course I know now that there is not one working class boy in a thousand who does not pine for the day when he will leave school. He wants to be doing real work, not wasting time on ridiculous rubbish like history and geography. To the working class, the notion of staying at school till you are nearly grown up seems merely contemptible and unmanly (1970, p. 130).

Although many young people were glad to leave school, the experience of both girls and boys could be grossly exploitative, labouring for long hours for low pay only to be confronted by the sack when they became entitled to adult wages.

In contrast with the failure of attempts to raise the leaving age, agitation around limiting the working hours of children was more successful, at least legislatively. In the 'regulated' trades the hours of youngsters were legally controlled, but in 1932 it was established that over a quarter of school leavers entered 'unregulated' trades. In these sectors over 80 per cent of fourteen year olds worked more than 48 hours per week, over 20 per cent were doing more than 60 hours, and 10 per cent over 66 hours (Tawney, 1934b, p. 7). As a result of these revelations substantial additions were made to the controls already established.[4] These defined the terms under which the young could sell their labour, and controlled the uses to which employers could direct it. Regulations limited the total spread of the working day of anyone aged under eighteen; the total hours they could work; their rest breaks and holiday periods; the substances and processes they could work with; and excluded them from night work (Morgan, 1943, p. 48). The impact of the legislation was constrained by the material realities of working class life and by inadequacies in enforcement. The adaptability of capital, the collusion of parents and the 'liberation' of children, ensured the survival of outlawed working practices both before and after children left school.

Many industries depended on a continual supply of inexperienced and cheap juvenile workers, and this was one of the major constraints on increasing the leaving age. As early as the 1890s, social investigators and reformers were pointing out that this short-term market for juvenile labour created blind alleys for young people. In particular, boys who entered jobs between the ages of twelve and fourteen, tended to lose them between the ages of eighteen and twenty-two, or else left them to secure jobs paying adult rates. That a proportion got regular work subsequently was, according to Charles Booth in London, largely accidental. It was in response to this problem that reformers advocated the specific creation of a juvenile employment service, alongside the demand for day release education or a higher leaving age.

Predictably, the patriarchal assumptions which underlay the anxieties of the reformers marginalised the experiences of girls whose future domestic role precluded any concern with their long-term economic prospects. There were moral panics about their sexuality, about promiscuity, pregnancy and prostitution, but the exploitation of girls in blind alley work was held to be less serious because there was a 'constant stream of girls passing out of employment into marriage', and because they were 'not faced with the same need for an increase of wage to enable them to marry and support a home' (Morgan, 1943, p. 22).

In the blind alley debate, the objects of anxiety were the social and economic transitions of young men. For many commentators, who rejected the shortsighted exploitation of juvenile labour, the central issue was whether young unskilled men could become the 'breadwinners' of future families and the responsible citizens of a social order which was experiencing fundamental tensions. Girls were to remain locked in the vicious circle where their low wages forced them into marriage and financial dependence on men, and that position was then used to justify their low wages and lack of training opportunities.

The blind alleys of juvenile employment were not confined to the 'sweated' trades, or to the hidden labour markets of the informal economy, but were characteristic of most sectors of the economy, from the most advanced to the most backward. The 'eagerness to obtain juvenile labour was such that boys and girls were often engaged by employers prior to their leaving school' (Gollan, 1937, p. 228). They were wanted in the declining textile industry of Lancashire and in the new engineering industries of the West Midlands. School leavers were used for carrying messages, doing menial work in offices and shops, and for performing simple mechanical tasks in factories and small workshops. In addition many girls, and some boys, had the option of domestic service.

In the distributive trades, which were the largest employer of juvenile labour, over 20 per cent of the insured labour force was aged under eighteen in 1935. The conditions of this sector were characterised by low wages, poor conditions of service, and patterns of overworking which eventually precipitated the Shops Act 1934. John Gollan summarised the evidence:

So now we have a picture of the greatest paradox of all industry – distribution, the greatest single occupation for youth and the industry containing the greatest proportion of youth. The greatest opportunity for youth leaving school is also the most tragic blind alley . . . They crowd into distribution, one of the few jobs open in many places, suffering long hours, low wages, sweated conditions, hundreds of thousands of them to be unemployed by the age of 25. What a prospect for youth labour is the country's most rapidly expanding 'industry' (1937, p. 140).

Young workers did not merely rely on the support and goodwill of adults to secure changes in their conditions of labour. Although the odds against them were prodigious, late in the 1930s young workers in the engineering industry embarked on a series of strikes which swept the country. The cause of this unrest was the low wages paid to apprentices, the absence of proper training and their exclusion from collective bargaining and negotiated wage rates. The strikes started on the Clyde in 1937 and involved 15,000 apprentices in 60 firms. Subsequently, the unrest spread to many engineering towns and cities in the North and West Midlands. The Clyde Apprentices Charter was formulated. It demanded adequate pay and training and a reasonable ratio of apprentices to skilled workers. The apprentices forged an alliance with adult workers, over a 100,000 of whom came out for a one day strike. The result, apart from better pay, was the formation of Apprentices Committees in many skilled unions and the achievement of the right of trades unions to negotiate on their behalf. These negotiations may have subsequently enshrined adult differentials, but they established clearly that apprentices and other young workers were part of the collective bargaining process. Especially in organised industries youth wages rates and conditions were to be removed from the arbitrary control of employers, and attached to negotiations about the conditions and wages of adult workers (Gollan, 1937, Appendix II).

These changes in the legal regulation of youth labour, and in their collective bargaining position at work, took place in a context where their job prospects were disproportionately affected by the growth of unemployment. It would be difficult to understand the arguments that were to rage about the school leaving age without appreciating the impact that mass unemployment had on working class parents and their children.[5]

Response of the state to juvenile unemployment

Between the wars, the state was preoccupied with cutting the cost of poor relief and with making the national insurance fund solvent: between 1920 and 1934 there were twenty-one Insurance Acts. The final Act, introduced by the National Government in 1934, introduced labour camps for some of the unemployed,[6] and made attendance at Junior Instruction Centres compulsory for the young unemployed. It also introduced the infamous Means Test, which in its own way had a dramatic impact on those young people who were living with their parents.

Over a million of the registered unemployed were immediately affected by this inquisition, with its complex questionnaire designed to expose every detail of a worker's individual and family position. Through the agency of the means test the unemployed were deprived of nearly £30 million a year. In its first year 50 per cent of all those coming within its scope were granted benefit only below the standard rate, or else were refused benefit entirely. These cuts gnawed away at meagre family budgets, forcing those in work to support unemployed relatives. Families broke up as young people left home to avoid their parents being means tested on their account. The means test redefined the legal relationships within and between working class families and hit the young in two ways. If out of work, the chances of drawing any benefit were very slender; in work, it was highly likely that they would be expected to support workless parents on a sweated wage. In the worst of the distressed areas the average age of the population rose steeply as the young left *en masse* in search of work. Behind them a generation of undernourished and unhealthy children were growing up – and infant mortality reached levels which were often four times higher than those in Southern Home Counties towns (Friend and Metcalfe, 1981, p. 76).

The full extent and duration of juvenile unemployment is difficult to quantify, especially before more comprehensive registration was introduced in 1934. Nevertheless, contemporary estimates suggest that from the late 1920s up to 1938 there were at least 100,000 unemployed fourteen to seventeen year olds each year (Gollan, 1937, p. 157), fairly evenly distributed between boys and girls (Morgan, 1943, p. 32).

The structure of juvenile unemployment was to reflect the impact of technical change, the cyclical variations of the economy as a whole, and the complexity of local and regional employment conditions. The decline of staple industries and the emergence of the distressed areas was to shape the nature of the state's response. This involved the creation of Junior Instruction Centres and a Juvenile Transference Scheme. These responses were bitterly criticised by proponents of a higher leaving age.

The transference schemes aimed to remove juveniles from the depressed regions of the North East, South Wales and Scotland to the new manufacturing industries and prosperous residential and recreational centres (such as seaside resorts) in the Midlands and South East. Started in 1928 (and expanded in 1934), the scheme was responsible for thousands of youngsters being shipped into domestic service and wage labour in a form reminiscent of the reverse journey forced on the pauper apprentices of the early nineteenth century.

The meagre wages paid to juveniles were actually subsidised to enable them to survive in the new area, provoking the cryptic observation: 'that while maintenance grants could not be provided for keeping juveniles at school . . . money was readily forthcoming to provide employers with cheap sources of labour' (Gollan, 1937, p. 176). The transference scheme was deeply unpopular, and many of the young people affected returned to their home

areas. In 1944, Beveridge estimated that a total of 190,000 young
people had been transferred between 1928 and 1937.

Juvenile instruction centres

Although the proposals for day continuation education outlined
in the 1918 Act had been eclipsed by the expenditure cuts of the
1920s, one of the less noted proposals to emerge from the 1917
Report on Juvenile Employment was the establishment of Juvenile
Unemployment Centres (subsequently to be renamed Juvenile
Instruction Centres). These were initially expected to cope with
the problems generated by the transition to a peacetime economy,
especially for those school leavers entering the labour market at
the end of the war. By April 1919, there were over 24,000
youngsters attending 215 centres. Between 1918 and 1934 there
were seven separate schemes introduced, and in that time over a
million young people passed through the centres (Gollan, 1937,
p. 177), for stays lasting on average between five and eight weeks
(Pope, 1978, p. 17).

In January 1934, there were 72 Junior Instruction Centres for
boys, 26 for girls and 26 mixed ones, catering for roughly 17,000
youngsters. Under the 1934 Act the centres were reorganised
and given a comprehensive structure. Attendance was made
compulsory but the impact of the means test and disqualifications
from benefit undermined the ability to enforce such a requirement.
Without a financial penalty the state reverted to other means and
in many districts 'School Attendance Officers were kept busy
chasing up non-attenders' (Pope, 1978, p. 18).

The aim of these centres, popularly called the 'dole schools',
was to keep the young occupied and expose them to the 'healthy'
atmosphere of something like work discipline for a number of
sessions each week. The National Advisory Council for Juvenile
Employment argued that the centres should be established with
'the object of preventing deterioration and of facilitating the
reabsorbtion of the boys and girls into industry'. The centres
should, according to the Ministry of Labour:

give the boys and girls a real interest in life, to keep their minds and fingers active and alert, and their bodies fit, to teach them something which will be of real use to them whether at home or at work, and without trying to train them for specific occupations to give them the type of mental and manual instruction which will help them to become absorbed or reabsorbed into employment (quoted in Gollan, 1937, p. 178).

The curriculum provided would contain some school subjects, such as rudimentary arithmetic and English, but the main content was handicrafts for boys and domestic subjects for girls, and physical training for both. The quality of provision varied enormously. In 1937, Wal Hannington had heard:

reports from many of the centres . . . that the juveniles spend most of their time in physical drill and community singing. At some centres well-advanced children have been expected to sing nursery rhymes for hours on end (p. 88).

Normally housed in disused elementary schools or in old commercial premises, the young unemployed were far from enamoured with the provision on offer. When attendance could be enforced, it was far from clear that they would simply subordinate themselves to the requirements of the institution. Many of the centres achieved some success, particularly where they acted as a conduit for job vacancies. But there was a hidden internal history of conflict and resistance. J. B. Mays of Liverpool University, when writing about the impact of the centres on working class areas of the city, pointed out that:

internal discipline was based on the mark system. A lad received an attendance mark, which, if he was sent out for indiscipline, could be cancelled and the result of such a cancellation could reduce the amount of benefit he would receive . . . Life in these old 'dole schools' resembled an inefficient penal institution more than anything else. Staff and pupils alike existed in a state of anxiety, misery and depression which, on some occasions, developed into physical outbursts of temper and rebellion. There were occasions when the blood flowed freely, times when knuckledusters were used on teachers

. . . and when by way of retaliation and self-protection, the staff used their fists on the boys (1962, p. 171).

Although such outbursts were a limited, if sporadic, occurrence the centres were the focus of sustained criticism up to their eventual disappearance. Not only was working class youth a reluctant recipient, and their parents decidedly ambivalent (Hannington, 1937, p. 89), but the schemes were also criticised by the labour movement and savaged by individuals such as R. H. Tawney, who saw in them something 'designed not to provide efficient education for children who are unemployed, but to use the pretence of providing it as one more excuse for refusing to do justice to all children by raising the school leaving age' (1934c, p. 16).

Demand for a higher leaving age

It was to take another world war before many Conservatives and employers accepted the need for reform, but the argument for a higher leaving age and restrictions on juvenile employment was to attract broader political support in the 1930s. The Liberal Party and other political forces, such as 'The Next Five Years Group',[7] were to take up these demands as they constructed new political and economic strategies appropriate to the turmoil of the period. In the famous 'Yellow Book' where the Liberals embraced the interventionist strategies outlined by Keynes, it was argued that for Liberalism 'The purpose of education is not to provide industry with amenable or even efficient human material' (quoted in Gollan, 1937, p. 288). The utilitarian view of schooling as a servant of industry was condemned as politically counter-productive. Education was to be the vehicle for creating new citizens, no longer susceptible to the influence of political 'extremism'. As part of this common citizenship it was accepted that all children were entitled to a secondary education up to sixteen years of age, with day-release classes for all young workers up to the age of eighteen.

Despite these conversions, it was undoubtedly the alliance created through the Labour Party's policy of 'Secondary Education for All', inspired by R. H. Tawney, which was to lead the struggle for a higher leaving age and for an extension of opportunities in education. For this political alliance, schemes for the young unemployed, and even day continuation education, were palliatives. At best they would ameliorate the excesses of capitalist employment, at worst they would perpetuate them. For Tawney and his allies, the remedy was obvious:

> What then should be done? The answer is simple . . . It is not to throw children into the water at 14, and then, when some of them are so careless as to show signs of drowning, to toss them straws to keep afloat with. It is to keep them on dry land. It is to retain them at school, where, both for their own sake and the nation's, they ought in any case to be, till they are mature enough to enter industry without risk of injury. It is, in short, not to improvise a makeshift in the shape of part-time instruction for boys and girls who are unemployed. It is to continue till 15 the moral progress of education, and thus to save them from unemployment (1934b, p. 16).

In acknowledging the leading role of this alliance, it is important to probe its assumptions a little more deeply.

Secondary education for all

Working class children had been excluded from secondary education at the turn of the century. In the 1890s what were called higher grade elementary schools had undermined the institutional and curricular monopoly of fee-paying secondary schools. The conflict that resulted ended with the Education Act 1902 which abolished School Boards and integrated both systems under the new County Councils. The Act institutionalised the dominance of secondary schools and introduced a watered-down version of their curriculum into the elementary schools.

Because secondary education was – and remained – predominantly concerned with preparing pupils for university entrance, one consequence was that technical and practical subjects were taken out of the mainstream curriculum (NEDC, 1982, p. 3). A 'free place' system allowed some transfer from the elementary school, but only a small proportion of working class children – hardly more than one in twenty – were ever able to get access to secondary education (Bruce, 1972, p. 150).

First articulated by the TUC in 1897, the demand for a leaving age of sixteen and secondary education for all were prompted by the objectives of extending educational opportunities and protecting the young from exploitation. As the progressive alliance was constructed, however, the demand for RSLA became increasingly justified in terms of its being a necessary part of an autonomous *educational* process. For R. H. Tawney, by the 1930s an extended period of schooling was necessary to facilitate what was seen as an organic process of adolescence and natural growth – 'each state of education must be guided by canons of its own, appropriate to the stage of life for which it is designed, not distorted by . . . the demand of the practical world for serviceable employees' (Tawney, 1934a, p. 45).

This assumption provided a rationale for a higher leaving age which stitched together the disparate elements making up the progressive alliance. It provided a hardheaded response to the shortsighted exploitation of youth by employers; it gave teachers an important position in designing and implementing this education; and it provided a justification for removing children from the labour market, and located that decision in the 'educational' needs of the young.

A key moment, when the demand for a higher leaving age was given a direct educational rationale, was in the publication of the Hadow Report on the 'Education of the Adolescent' in 1926. The committee, of which Tawney was a member, commenced work two years after the school leaving age had been increased to fourteen and, when it recommended a further increase to fifteen years, this was tightly related to a redefinition of the process of schooling. This new definition was based on a number of psychological assumptions which had become ever more prominent in educational debates. Instead of just adding an extra year to elementary schooling, the essential recommendation was for a major reorganisation to be constructed around a transition at the age of eleven between a primary and secondary education. While many of the report's concerns were to be eclipsed by economic crisis, it gave a particular definition to the organisational changes which had been occurring haphazardly since 1918, and set the pattern for future reorganisations.

In correspondence with its psychologistic assumptions, the report went on to argue for different *forms* of secondary schooling. There may have been a new consensus in the educational world about secondary education for all, but it was to be a form of schooling appropriate to the 'natural' aptitudes and abilities of different groups of children. Even for Tawney:

> Equality of provision is not identity of provision. It is to be achieved not by meeting different requirements in the same way, but by taking equal care to ensure that varying requirements are met in the ways most appropriate to each (Tawney, 1934a, p. 48).

'Grammar' schools would be appropriate only for certain categories of children (who could now be discovered 'scientifically'), and the subsequent pattern of reorganisations in those areas which undertook them began to lay some foundations for the tripartite system.[8] It was the TUC which was to push the case for multilateral or common schools, arguing that 'real parity in education and equality of opportunity in after life' could not be secured if secondary schools were segregated (Bernbaum, 1971, p. 65).

Provision in many areas was, however, to remain dominated by the all-age elementary school up to the 1940s, and by the large classes and inadequate resources which characterised them. School fees were charged throughout the 1930s and never more than 14 per cent of elementary pupils in England and Wales went on to receive a secondary education. Only four or five out of every thousand elementary pupils ever reached the universities (Stevenson, 1984, p. 255).

Control of the curriculum

The theories of psychological development upon which the educational consensus around secondary schooling was constructed were also to have a direct impact – through testing and child-centred learning – on teaching methods and the content of the curriculum. Control of the secondary school curriculum had been relinquished by the Board of Education in 1917, when effective control passed to the examination boards. These institutions ensured that the secondary school curriculum was appropriate for university preparation and – since the boards determined syllabuses – their control might have been indirect but it was absolutely effective. Likewise in the elementary schools after 1907 the concern to transmit basic skills and instil good conduct and discipline was increasingly subordinated to winning the maximum number of 'free' places.

This had a dramatic impact on the internal organisation of elementary schools, which introduced streaming to get as many pupils as possible through the selection tests which controlled intake into secondary education. Although no formal prescriptions existed about what had to be taught in the interwar years, a very real set of determinations operated on the teaching situation through the elementary and secondary stages. Indeed these indirect constraints and requirements were to bedevil subsequent attempts at reform and reinforced the hold of the academic and elitist model of education favoured by the universities. Politically, however, the curriculum became a 'secret garden' into which politicians entered at their peril, since any incursion could now be represented as totalitarian in nature and intent.

For teachers one of the main sources of dissatisfaction with the education practices of the period was this indirect control of the curriculum exercised through external examinations. The pervasive influence of the examination boards, and the effects on the elementary and secondary schools of streaming and selection, created support for institutional arrangements which would give greater freedom within the curriculum. In those areas of the schools least affected by external determinations – the lower streams of elementary schools and some pioneering independent schools – experimental curricular reforms demonstrated the viability of alternative modes of teaching. The elementary school curriculum could begin to develop in a child-centred, enquiry-based direction, but the traditional conservatism of teachers and the pressures to prepare pupils for the selection exams inhibited the spread of these methods.

By 1931 a Consultative Committee of the Board of Education was arguing that 'the curriculum is to be thought of in terms activity and experience rather than of knowledge to be acquired and facts to be stored' (HMSO, 1931, p. 93). They pointed out that the transformation of social life created by industrialisation, whereby children no longer grew up experiencing 'a gradual apprenticeship to the discipline of the house, the farm, the workshop', required schools to take on a new role. They now 'have to teach children to live'. The report noted that this 'profound change in purpose' was hampered by a 'slowness of adaptation', and was constrained where 'the curriculum is distorted and the teaching warped from its proper character by the supposed need of meeting the requirements of a later educational stage' (HMSO, 1931, p. 92).

Within the education system the struggle for reform was intended to change both the formal organisation and duration of schooling *and* the external control exercised over the curriculum by selection procedures and the examination boards. By 1946, the NUT was demanding the abolition of external examinations; teachers had a combination of educational *and* professional motives for supporting the arguments for reform.

Raising the leaving age

By the mid-1930s, with some recovery in the economy, there was a reawakening of interest in educational reform. The National Government committed itself in the election campaign in 1935 and introduced legislation in 1936. Amongst other things this provided for the leaving age to be raised to fifteen in 1939. However, it also provided for a system of 'beneficial exemptions' where children could be removed from school when they were fourteen if it could be shown that the employment for which they were destined was 'beneficial'.

This reduced the proposal to a sham. There were already ten local authorities which had a leaving age of fifteen, but each operated a system of beneficial exemptions and had exemption rates between 79 and 96 per cent. It was estimated by the Education correspondent of *The Times* that the 1936 Act would lead to a national proportion of exemption amounting to 85 per cent: the leaving age for most children would remain at fourteen (Bernbaum, 1971, p. 63). This provoked the government's parliamentary critics who denounced the legislation as 'founded upon the principle of cheap labour and blind alley occupations', which was intended not to raise the school leaving age but to regulate 'the entry of children to employment' (Bernbaum, 1971, p. 63).

The government justified its position by arguing that it would take three years to make the necessary arrangements, and that parents and employers would encounter real problems if some children were not granted exemptions. Most importantly, they pointed to the central ambiguity in the argument for reform, in that there was no widespread public demand for the measure, and government had therefore to move cautiously. Oliver Stanley, President of the Board of Education, pointed out that:

The possibility of the success of the scheme depends on being really able to convince the parents of what I do not believe at the moment they are convinced, that in many schools with many curricula . . . that extra year between 14 and 15 is really worthwhile . . . Many people must know schools in which the education is such, in which the facilities are such, that they would not conscientiously go to a parent and tell him that an extra year in that school was going to be of lasting benefit to the child (quoted by Bernbaum, 1971, p. 61).

He responded to those calling for immediate action by pointing out that the result would be 'children in schools, kept there by school attendance officers and magistrates'. This procrastination, and the disaster of world war, stopped any increase in the leaving age before 1945.

By the late 1930s the demand for a higher leaving age had been politically accepted and had become synonymous with secondary education for all. Without a higher leaving age of at least fifteen years, ultimately sixteen years, opening up access to secondary schools would be useless. The provision of day continuation classes or centres for the young unemployed were seen as diversions. They may have ameliorated some of the problems confronting young workers, but they presupposed their early entry to the labour market. For Tawney and the political alliance constructed around the demand for educational reform the issue was no longer about the young at work. It was to do with the exposure of young people to an organic process of education which was separate from their potential future employment. It was a new democratic right to be extended to all potential citizens and was not to be subordinated to the 'vulgar commercialism which conceives of the manufacture of efficient typists and mechanics as the primary object of adolescent education' (Tawney, 1922, p. 11).

This anti-capitalist stance was to define education as a space that should be preserved against economic considerations and the 'vulgar' intrusions of class. This definition, however, had a double logic which was not perhaps altogether intended. On the one hand, it separated (and made it difficult to talk about) the actual relationships that linked the two worlds; subsequently arguments for a higher leaving age were less related to the problems confronted by young people at work and defined more in relation to their assumed educational needs. On the other hand, it tended to exalt the experts and the forms of knowledge indigenous to education as the only arbiters of what occurs there.

This deference may have been a necessary condition for winning support from constituencies in the educational world, and may also have been the source of an argument against a pure subordination to employers' requirements, but it was to result in a differentiated and highly academic form of education which imitated and gave legitimacy to the independent schools. However, it was *organisational* issues rather than curricular concerns which dominated the postwar politics of education. As the differences between types of secondary schools emerged, it became apparent that most working class children were still not receiving equal treatment.

3

Raising the School Leaving Age to Sixteen: School and Work in the 1960s

Enshrined in law by the Education Act 1944, the commitment to raise the school leaving age to sixteen proved to be the most elusive objective of the educational agenda constructed in the 1930s. It was not until the 1960s, when RSLA was identified as a social *and* economic imperative, that it was given a renewed priority. Its final implementation in 1973, some thirty years on, was to mark the watershed of postwar consensus and educational expansion. After 1944, the creation of the tripartite system was to provoke a controversy which dominated educational politics. Initially fought out within the Labour Party, the campaign for comprehensive reform was to attract increasing support in the 1950s. In practical terms, the introduction of RSLA in many areas became inextricably connected with comprehensive reorganisation.

After the austerity of postwar reconstruction working class youth received the rewards of full employment. 'Affluent' youth and their parents were to enjoy the fruits of an explosion in consumption and they experienced a complex cultural reorientation towards the pursuit of leisure, holidays, enjoyment and recreation. Having left school, with rising disposable incomes, what was called the 'teenage ball'[1] appeared to give rise to new ways of growing up working class. Leisure-based youth cultures, from the Teddy Boys to the Mods, were to act as important metaphors and reference points in educational debates. Fears were expressed about the impact of mass culture, lawlessness, promiscuity, and the new freedoms of teenage life; and in many ways educational reform was seen as a response to these problems.

But it was the educational consequences of *economic change*

35

which became the driving motor behind reform. In a succession of government reports it was assumed that a general process of 'upskilling' was taking place: new technologies, the rapid transformation of many jobs, and the rise of service industries were seen to require a higher level of skill and better education from *all* workers. Coupled with a concern to promote equal opportunities and realise individual potential, a distinctive argument was to emerge for an extended and reformed period of secondary schooling. It was this particular combination of motives which was to be the Labour Party's contribution to the creation of a period of social democratic consensus around educational policy.

To explore the postwar relationship between school and work we have to assess some of the dramatic changes taking place in the juvenile labour market. The state became more active in post-school education and, for the first time, became directly involved in employers training practices through the Industrial Training Act 1964. Nevertheless RSLA was given priority over securing day-release education. Before assessing the preparations made to secure RSLA's success and examining its immediate impact on schools in the early 1970s, it is worth finding out what happened to 'secondary education for all' after 1944.

Education Act 1944: Labour Party policy and secondary education

The end of world war in 1945 had been preceded by intense debate about the nature of any peacetime political settlement. It was anticipated that securing victory abroad would yield greater social equality at home, and freedom from the mass unemployment and privation which dominated the lives of many working people before the war. In short, in return for the imposed obligations of the war effort a new set of rights for the citizen was to be created. Full employment and the construction of the Welfare State were to be the central pillars of this new settlement.

Labour's election to office in 1945 took place within these changed definitions. In place of the political polarisation that characterised the 1930s, there was a fundamental shift in legitimate political conflict – both sides were to accept that the solution to old problems were to be found within a reformed (now mixed) market economy. The experience of war, its collective planning, mobilisation and necessary political consensus, provided the groundwork for the reforms which were acclaimed as ushering in a new era of capitalist development.

Nowhere was this clearer than in the achievement of secondary education for all: a new democratic right, which being introduced by a Conservative minister removed the most controversial educational issue from any electoral debate between Conservative and Labour. The Education Bill was introduced into the House of Commons in December 1943 and became law in August 1944. Its major provisions involved the abolition of tuition fees at all state-maintained schools. It ended the old distinction between elementary and secondary education, and replaced it with a continuous system of provision divided into three stages of primary, secondary and further education. The specific form which secondary school reorganisation should take was not prescribed in the Act, though it was evident that the Board of Education favoured the tripartite recommendations of the Norwood Report (Simon, 1974, pp. 323–37). The leaving age was to be increased – initially to fifteen, and then sixteen – and all young workers were to be given day-release education up to eighteen. The Board of Education was to become a Ministry, and the new minister was charged with overseeing the work of the local authorities which were responsible for carrying through the main provisions of the Act.

In implementing the Act, the new Labour Minister of Education did so on the basis of a separation in types of secondary schooling. Controversy raged. On the one hand, the minister and officials emphasised the 'parity of esteem' between grammar, secondary modern and secondary technical schools. On the other hand, successive Labour Party conferences rejected the tripartite system and called for the rapid development of comprehensive schemes. In Labour's period of office only a handful of new comprehensives were established, and many other provisions of the 1944 Act were postponed.

Notwithstanding a massive rebuilding programme and other material improvements, there were actually very few technical schools established. Over 40 per cent of LEAs did not provide any at all (CACE, 1959, p. 22). In practice a rigid bipartite system developed, selective grammar schools for the few (about

20 per cent), and modern schools for the rest. Only the former opened the way to the universities, colleges and professions – in 1952 only one pupil in 22,000 proceeded directly from a secondary modern school to a university (Simon, 1971, p. 227).

Within the Labour Party, support for the tripartite system declined, particularly as the accuracy of the 'eleven plus' was persistently called into question (Barker, 1972). Even under Conservative administrations the number of comprehensive schemes increased substantially in the 1950s. The emphasis of Labour's educational policies were to be affected by the party's electoral fortunes after 1951. The party helped to construct the postwar consensus, but it was Macmillan's conservatism that completed it. Between 1951 and 1960 Conservative success, under the banners of affluence – 'you've never had it so good' – and political consensus precipitated Labour's revisionism. Due to full employment and the operation of the Welfare State it was argued that old sources of class conflict were being progressively eliminated or rendered irrelevant, and society was being recast in the privatised forms of the middle class.[2]

The most significant Labour theorists of the 1950s – like Tony Crosland (1962) – accepted much of the argument and sought to provide political programmes acceptable in 'present-day, as opposed to capitalist, society'. From this perspective, educational expansion and comprehensive reform became identified as a prerequisite for sustained economic growth and social harmony.

The secondary moderns

The tripartite system was justified with reference to the division of labour and class system, but there was no simple subordination of secondary moderns to the needs of employers. The terms of the relationship were spelled out in the first report of the Central Advisory Council on Education, established under the 1945 Act to advise on educational policy. This 1947 Report, on 'School and Life', explicitly rejected the employment of juveniles in blind alley work and asserted that the educational needs of young workers should be dominant in their formative years.

The period of employment up to the age of 18 must be

regarded as primarily one of learning . . . The employment of juveniles as cheap labour can no longer be tolerated; in the long run it has not been to the advantage of industry itself (CACE, 1947, p. 49).

This was not to exclude vocational relevance from the curriculum, but to argue that it was subordinate to 'the prior claims of the full development of individual personality' (p. 56).

When examining the impact of technological change and 'the deadening routine of much industrial work' (p. 58), and in pointing to the rapidity of occupational change and job turnover, the Council distanced the schools from any obligation to serve industry directly. Schools were to develop the tastes and habits which could compensate for 'deadening routine', and should cultivate the social dispositions, adaptability and responsibility upon which employers would increasingly depend.

The educational requirements of the young extended beyond the need for specific academic skills or vocational guidance. Secondary schools and sponsored leisure activities were now expected to prepare the young working class for their emergence into the profane world of wage labour and youth culture:

It is not to be expected that a change so big, both from the economic and from the social point of view, can be gone through without difficulty. This new freedom is often a heady drink, and some young heads cannot take it . . . It is not enough to prepare the young people scholastically, technically, vocationally, for their work in the world while neglecting to prepare them socially, personally and emotionally. For this will lead to tension, dissatisfaction and discontent, and finally, either disillusioned apathy, or breakdown and revolt. To prepare boys and girls for the revolution in their personal lives is no less an educational problem than it is to make them into efficient bank clerks, engineers or builders (CACE, 1947, pp. 67–8).

Meanwhile, within their new secondary schools the mass of working class children were experiencing the parity of esteem which they were supposed to share with the selective schools. Many secondary moderns were organised on the house system, had prefects, adopted school uniforms and, after the mid-1950s, entered a small – though growing – proportion of their pupils for the same examinations as the grammar schools. Paradoxically, the 'very attempt to win prestige drew attention to their lower status' (Musgrave, 1972, p. 114). Many modern schools created extended courses and participated in external examinations, and throughout the 1950s 'staying on' rates increased by about 1 per cent a year, reaching 25 per cent in 1958. Nevertheless, as the Crowther Report pointed out: 'among families of manual workers it is still the exception for a child to stay at school after he is legally free to go' (CACE, 1959, p. 8).

By the late 1950s experience and research began to expose the inadequacies of the bipartite system. Psychological research questioned the whole basis of selection at eleven, and detailed investigation showed that many secondary moderns were under-resourced, inadequately staffed and, as the Newsom Report discovered in 1963, only 21 per cent of them were 'generally up to present standards', and as many as 41 per cent were 'seriously deficient in many respects' (CACE, 1959, p. 258).

The Newsom Report showed that secondary moderns were short of ideas as well as resources. They persisted with unimaginative curricula that were completely out of touch with the experiences and interest of the boys and girls for whom they were supposed to have been designed:

The fascinations of science are made mundane by the repetition of uncomprehended formulae; history is churned out in the form of dates and mixed with improbable stories; English is reduced to verbs and antonyms; and literature is debased as children are called upon to chant sonnets in unison or to do some compulsory reading of classics that abbreviation has rendered meaningless (Carter, 1966, p. 18).

Earlier, in a survey of schools in Liverpool, J. B. Mays (1962) found that a higher leaving age of fifteen had not produced a new, integrated process of secondary education, and few schools had rethought their syllabus. The existing three-year course had been stretched to cover the extra year with the addition, perhaps, of some visits to industry or other contacts with the outside environment.

The reason, according to Mays, was the system which enabled a young person to leave at the end of the term in which they became fifteen. Although not as crude a device as the earlier exemption system it still made the extra year 'largely illusory' as anything up to a third of the class would leave school at Christmas or Easter, eager to get to work in the local juvenile labour market. In this situation, 'it is an impossibility to provide a course which in its final stages is anything more than a marking-time period in which pupils are kept as quiet and interested as possible, as they eagerly await the moment of release when they will be free to go out and earn their own living' (1962, p. 157).

In response to these problems, and to the growing demand for examination success, the Newsom Report and other educational bodies sponsored initiatives to broaden the curriculum. In addition, the Beloe Report on Secondary School Examinations (1963) recommended the creation of the Certificate of Secondary Education (CSE). This broke with tradition by creating an internal examination with external moderation, and permitted the inclusion of a large amount of course work. It was, of course, to be inferior to the more prestigious General Certificate of Education (GCE) which were intended to meet the requirements of university entrance.

These initiatives were not able to allay the disquiet about the inability of some schools to secure legitimacy and conformity from their assumed beneficiaries. J. B. Mays found a significant minority of working class parents in Liverpool who held 'the belief that school is not very important, that education is something imposed on them from above, with which they are forced to comply' (1962, p. 100). He concluded that in some schools the 'tradition of two nations lives on', and that the 'benign sunlight generated by the 1944 Act filters with difficulty down through the obscuring smoke and gloom of the older and less privileged neighbourhoods'.

So the experience of secondary education for all was not straightforward. Most working class children were arbitrarily excluded from the grammar schools and sent to under-resourced secondary moderns. For many the direct experience of schooling was both alien and irrelevant. The adolescent boys who talked to Peter Willmott in the early 1960s, for example, complained bitterly about an out-of-date curriculum that failed to connect with their interests or arouse their enthusiasm. Their main complaint against the modern school was 'that it was dull and uninteresting, sometimes that it was a "crap school ", inferior to others' (1979, p. 101). A substantial minority complained that 'school and teachers oppressed them' and that 'school could offer them little' (p. 91).

Inside the 'blackboard jungles', as some media portrayed them, many of these boys were to react with passive indifference or even overt hostility. This was as likely to be directed at girls or black youth as much as at the school. One of the first studies to examine the internal processes of a working class school noted that 'hostility was the key feature'. J. Webb described the forms this hostility could take:

> It is present whenever a teacher deals with boys but varies in intensity. At one extreme it can be almost ferocious, when for example an inexperienced teacher wrestles with a lad for possession of a flick knife, surrounded by cheering boys . . . At the other extreme, the hostility is so mild that it needs inverted commas. An example would be a teacher trying to make a class get on with a given task. They play him up by exaggerating the bluntness, or breaking the points of their pencils, or losing rubbers or complaining loudly that they cannot see the blackboard, no matter where he stations it (1962, pp. 264–72).

Subsequently, in a Manchester study, David Hargreaves was to find an anti-school subculture where boys rejected and inverted the conventional values of the school (1967). In a related study Colin Lacey also found a similar subculture amongst a group of working class boys in a grammar school (1970).

Whatever the causes or interpretations offered, qualitative attempts to investigate the working class experience of secondary education virtually ignored the situation of girls, and revealed an enduring contrast in boys' attitudes. For some working class families education created avenues for social mobility, but for many working class youngsters schooling offered little, especially as they got closer to leaving school.

Affluent youth

The attraction of leaving school was enhanced after the war by the vastly improved material prospects for the young working class. It was not that the actual work or jobs available had improved particularly, but that early leaving was eminently sensible in a context of full employment where education was of little relevance to their actual destinies. J. B. Mays described why it was that so many working class girls were eager to leave at the first moment, irrespective of the quality of work available:

> The girls know at a fairly early age exactly what they want to do with their lives. In the top classes . . . they are already going out with boyfriends and seriously considering marriage . . . These girls spend perhaps 5 shillings per week on their hair and make up . . . They are eager to get out to work so as to be able to earn more and save as much as they can (without curtailing pleasure of course) before matrimony . . . Thus a simple repetitive process job at a local factory, an opening at one of the big football pools firms or a chance to serve at one of the chain stores exactly meet their requirements . . . Marriage for the girl confers status. It is perhaps her only way of acquiring the outward signs of adulthood and a limited and temporary limelight. The engagement period is the golden age of her relationship with her future husband. For then she has a good time, spends money, has plenty of clothes, enjoys herself and stands high in the estimation of her peers and contemporaries (1962, p. 101).

With a higher leaving age and the postwar boom school leavers entered a buoyant labour market: between 1947 and 1957 the supply of young workers under eighteen was expected to halve (CACE, 1947, p. 64). Between 1945 and 1950 it was estimated by Mark Abrams (1959) that the average real wage of teenagers increased at twice the adult rate.

Before the war, severe economic pressures on working class families meant that young people were often required to start work as soon as possible in order to augment the family wage. The period between leaving school and gaining adult status was largely a time of assuming the responsibilities of adulthood in the role of auxiliary breadwinners, but with few of the material or social freedoms. With the financial security of full employment many working class families were able, for the first time, to allow their children to choose to start work at a later age and, more importantly, to allow them to keep a relatively large proportion of their wages for their own use. There can be little doubt that it was these changes in the family economy, creating a new role for young people as a *consumer* group, which brought about the great changes in their social role which were to follow.

Working class areas and communities were to be fragmented by redevelopment and rehousing, by changes in the structure of the family, and by significant changes in the relative status of work and leisure. This was the background to the emergence of postwar youth cultures (Cohen, 1972). Material changes in working class households, alterations in the organisation and duration of school and work, the growth of earlier marriage, the development of a teenage leisure industry, and the abolition of national service,[3] served to transform the lives of young people. When combined with the new signs and symbols of the mass media and advertising industry, they contributed to the emergence of a generational consciousness amongst the young. This was a class experience, but it was expressed in new ways, different from – and in some respects openly antagonistic to – the values and preoccupations of traditional working class communities (Hoggart, 1957).

The empirical and local studies of young people that were prompted by the moral panics around juvenile delinquency and the rise of the Teddy Boys were, in common with other contemporary social investigations, to emphasise the importance of social class (Downes, 1966; Willmott, 1969). These studies, which prepared the way for a distinct sociology of male youth, emphasised the continuing importance of class relationships and illuminated some of the new cultural forms and expressions these were taking. They paid less attention, however, to the ways in which the young working class made a living, and even less attention to the particular experiences of young women or black youth.[4]

The juvenile labour market

At the same time that the leisure activities of the young were receiving attention significant changes were taking place in the juvenile labour market. Most early school leavers were, by and large, getting access to jobs, but the nature of recruitment and training was changing. There was a buoyant labour market for unskilled juvenile labour (at least initially) but other sectors were bureaucratising their recruitment practices, especially in the much expanded service and public sectors.

Apprenticeship training was gradually reorganised after the war, and over the next two decades successive pieces of legislation laid down the hours and conditions of work for juvenile labour. In 1961, for example, the Factories Act restricted the hours of fifteen year olds to 44 a week and of sixteen year olds to 48 per week. It specified the duration of meal breaks and rest intervals and prevented young people working with or near certain processes.

Juvenile employment became part of an emerging dual labour market characterised by a division between different sectors of employment (Brannen, 1975). What was called the primary labour market offered job security, training opportunities, good conditions of service, and the possibility of some upward occupational or social mobility. A feature of many jobs in this sector was their explicit knowledge base, and access to them was expressed in levels of certification which employers could also use to filter out applications. The secondary labour market offered low pay, poor working conditions, unstable employment, limited job advancement and little provision for training. For young workers, the secondary sector retained many characteristics of blind alley work.

These different labour markets were structured through divisions of sex, age and race. It was no coincidence that many school leavers, working women and ethnic minority workers were confined to the secondary sector. Patterns of direct and indirect discrimination, the complex legal regulations and educational requirements which excluded many juveniles from the primary sector, and the dual role of many women as housewives and workers, all served to underpin the patterns of employment which thrived in the secondary sector (Loveridge and Mok, 1978, pp. 43–58).

To understand the destinations of school leavers and the forms of training then on offer, it is worth briefly examining what happened to school leavers in a not untypical year, 1964 – the year in which Labour returned to office. Of the 608,000 school leavers starting work, 425,000 were fifteen years of age. Thirty-seven per cent of boys and 35 per cent of girls entered manufacturing; 17 per cent of boys entered distribution and 33 per cent of all girl leavers were employed as shop assistants. Twenty-five per cent of the girls entered clerical work. In terms of access to training 35 per cent of boys went into apprenticeships, 16 per cent had training other than apprenticeships, and 4 per cent entered clerical work. Six and a half per cent of girls became apprentices (mainly in hairdressing), 15 per cent had training other than apprenticeships, and 27 per cent entered clerical work. Forty-five per cent of boys and 51 per cent of girls had no access to formal training at all, because as Michael Carter found, 'numerous children are in jobs for which training simply is not necessary – it is pointless to pretend otherwise' (1966, p. 189). Furthermore, even where it was offered many questions were raised about the quality of the training provided.

In the early 1960s a panic emerged about youth unemployment as the postwar baby boom started to enter the labour market. Haunted by the spectre of a trade depression and the end of National Service, the Crowther Report warned that 'there could be a million young people on the streets with no work, nowhere to go and nothing to do' (CACE, 1959, p. 4). In some of the old industrial areas, such as Newcastle, Sunderland, Liverpool and Fife, special schemes were established to help unemployed school leavers (Carter, 1966, pp. 124–7).

However, there was to be nothing like the crisis which confronted the young in the late 1970s. This was due to two main factors. In the first place, the expansion of the service and public sectors increased employment for young workers, mitigating the worst effects of the shake out taking place in manufacturing and the staple industries. The second factor was the expansion in the numbers of young people staying on in full-time education. From just under 30 per cent in 1961, the number of fifteen–seventeen year olds staying on voluntarily increased to over 50 per cent by 1971.

In this context, the labour market behaviour of young school leavers in making the transition to work became the object of increasing concern. Research was to focus on the assumed culture shock experienced when starting work; on the influence of schools on job choice; on the process of induction into work; on the role of the Youth Employment Service (YES) and the efficiency of other methods of obtaining work; and above all on patterns of job satisfaction and job changing. Linda Clarke, in a comprehensive review of this literature, concluded that about 50 per cent of early school leavers changed jobs at least once in the early years at work; and between 10 and 18 per cent changed jobs frequently (1978, p. 21). Job changers were typically employed in 'low levels' of work. She also found that about half of early school leavers did not obtain the work they wanted and ended up in jobs at a lower level than they had aspired to.

Employers' complaints about job changing, poor attitudes, bad time keeping and attendance, were interpreted as a broadly educational problem (Bates, 1984). What seemed like the traditional reaction to blind alley work in a context of full employment was defined as a pathology which more relevant school provision or better careers advice would remedy.

Paradoxically, the research carried out found that most school leavers had little problem making the transition to work and expressed 'themselves as content or satisfied in their jobs' (Clarke, 1978, p. 22). It was to be another decade before researchers pointed to the rationality underlying job changing in an unskilled labour market (Roberts, 1975). Needless to say Linda Clarke found there had been 'little effort to examine the particular experiences and difficulties of girls in the transition period' (1978, p. 3). The focus of concern, as in the blind alley debate, was on the labour market behaviour of young boys. It was only towards the end of the 1960s that the wastage of girls' talents came on to the political agenda (Rauta and Hunt, 1975).

It was also in 1969, in a report on 'The Problems of Coloured School Leavers', that serious attention began to be paid to the situation of second generation immigrants, whom it was found were more likely to be unemployed, to be in unskilled jobs and to be dissatisfied with their work than were their white contemporaries.

Nancy Keene pointed to a Birmingham survey which showed that only 8 per cent of 'coloured' teenagers at work had skilled jobs, compared with 37 per cent of whites from the same district. She quoted one London employment office which found that half of the 147 firms offering vacancies would not take 'coloured' workers (1969, p. 175). Political and Economic Planning (PEP), the social science institute, revealed the widespread extent of racial discrimination in a study of employment in 1966–7 (Daniel 1968). The 1971 census showed that ethnic minority workers were twice as likely as white people to be unemployed.

A more complex understanding of divisions in the juvenile labour market emerged in the early 1970s, when they were dramatically emphasised by changed economic circumstances and the failure of reform. However, during the period of social democratic consensus such complexities were obscured by a series of overarching assumptions. Central to these was the belief that the labour market required a higher level of skill in general and that the education system could supply it.

Upskilling and Qualifications

The proponents of educational expansion argued that the growth of employment in the white collar and service sectors, and the increasing automation of manufacturing industry, were producing a situation where Britain's economic survival depended on a more generally skilled and educated labour force. Educational achievement, as measured by certificates, also became more important in determining at which point young people entered the labour market. Both changes fuelled a growing demand from parents, students and employers for more formal qualifications and a more extended period of education.

This had two vital consequences. In the first place, debates about school reform took place in a context where educational hierarchies were progressively related to economic ones. Secondly, irrespective of the changes that were taking place at work, as young people stayed on longer in education and obtained more qualifications the competition for places in the primary labour market ensured that there would be an increase in the formal requirements for particular jobs. A process of 'credential inflation' took place, confirming the view that jobs required higher levels of education (Berg, 1977).

Within the educational debate, the concern with skills never solely referred to the needs of employment. It also carried assessments about the forms of education which were required to cope with the other complexities of social life – from changes in the family and leisure through to education for citizenship. Nevertheless, government reports and inquiries were preoccupied with the inadequacies of the existing system to produce the types of labour power required for economic expansion. The Crowther Report, on policy for fifteen–eighteen year olds, made the point in 1959:

> The growth in the proportion of highly skilled jobs, and the decline in the proportion of unskilled jobs, imply a reassessment of what must be attempted by people of only average intelligence. That reassessment carries with it a fresh estimate of the length of time their education should last. It is not only at the top but almost to the bottom of the pyramid that the scientific revolution of our time needs to be reflected in a longer, educational process (CACE, 1959, p. 124).

The assumptions implicit in these reports tended to naturalise the class structure, which was viewed as somehow directly reflecting the technical requirements of the production process. The question this posed for educational policy was one of *access* to positions in the hierarchy of job opportunities. Equality of opportunity was interpreted in relation to individuals, as equalising their chances in the lottery of job allocation. The twin concern about wasted talent and equal opportunities dominated the emerging academic disciplines of the economics and sociology of education, particularly in those areas sponsored by official and semi-official agencies. Their findings were to amount to a damaging critique of the tripartite system on both economic and social grounds. Influential policy-makers, such as Lord Vaizey – the 'founding father' of the economics of education – interpreted changes in the labour market as reinforcing and justifying the need for egalitarian concessions (Vaizey and Debeauvais, 1961, p. 38).

As a description of labour market reality, these perspectives distorted the nature of the changes that were taking place. The application of science and new technologies to manufacturing industry may have produced a demand for more highly skilled specialists and managers, but it was also associated with the deskilling of areas of craft work. These processes produced a polarisation of skill requirements rather than a simple increase in the *average* skill required.[5]

The expansion of employment in the service sector was taken as proof of the need for a higher level of education and skill from workers. Yet the experience of women working in these industries was a far cry from that implied by upskilling. Expelled from the men's jobs they had been encouraged to do during the war, women were to return to the labour market in part-time jobs in the service sector. Between 1951 and 1971 the working population grew by over 2.5 million, and of this increase 2.2 million were women. By 1971 they formed 38 per cent of the labour force. Rather than increasing their range of jobs, this expansion compounded the tendency for women to work in very narrow sectors of the economy, irrespective of their educational qualifications. Women were also largely confined to jobs at the lower end of the service sector: in 1971 over 80 per cent of female sales workers were classified as 'sales assistants'.

The skill requirements of advanced technology certainly undermined traditional class barriers, but at the same time they generated new divisions and inequalities. Upskilling obscured the ways in which technological innovation was used to secure maximum control over labour as much as to maximise productive capacity (Zimbalist, 1979). It also disguised the ways in which skill is a *socially* constructed category. Skilled status is struggled over in the workplace and is used to legitimate social and sexual divisions which have little to do with technical competence. Phillips and Taylor have emphasised that:

> The classification of women's jobs as unskilled and men's jobs as skilled or semi-skilled frequently bears little relation to the actual amount of training or ability required for them. Skill definitions are saturated with sexual bias . . . Women workers carry into the workplace their status as subordinate individuals, and this status comes to define the value of the work they do. Far from being an objective economic fact, skill is often an

ideological category imposed on certain types of work done by virtue of the sex and power of the workers who perform it (1980, p. 79).

There were noticeable transformations in the division of labour and the class structure but their representation in the education debates of the 1960s distorted the nature of the impact they were having both on people's working lives and on the kind of schooling they required. Nevertheless, throughout the reports, policy documents and political speeches the belief that postwar capitalism required generally – and not merely for its elites – a wider diffusion of skill (and that the education system could supply it) was completely taken for granted.

Labour and educational expansion: the relative autonomy of schools

The upskilling thesis had a direct impact on Labour Party policy and provided the 'objective' rationale for its educational programme. It held together all the main elements in the political alliance which the Labour Party constructed in the 1960s. In the first place, it provided a thoroughly economic justification for egalitarian policies – ending or mitigating selection, comprehensivisation, and so on. Without this, the charge that such policies were doctrinaire and even 'socialist' was liable to stick. Secondly, the upskilling/more education/economic growth combination appealed directly to those constituencies which the Labour Party sought to woo: especially workers in new industries, professionals like the teachers, and the more progressive, modernising sections of management and national capital. Thirdly, it reconciled the inevitable tension between the humanistic ideology characteristic of educational practitioners – the importance of doing your best for the personal development of each child – and the world of work afterwards. Teachers were led to believe (whatever their direct experience might suggest) that there would be plenty of upskilled and interesting jobs for their pupils to enter. Finally, since the relationship between school and work was left extremely vague, teachers could conscientiously fill the empty spaces with stimulating and relevant activities, reassured by a sense of their usefulness, even though their pupils might appear inexplicably uninterested in what was on offer.

The relative autonomy of teachers and the education system in the 1960s was based on the idea that an educational expansion of a particular kind was essential for the British economy. The stress on organisational reform, on child-centred education, on classroom flexibility and on developing relevant curricula, stemmed from the theory that a vast untapped pool of ability existed among working class youngsters and that this ability had to be released to meet the needs of the economy for upskilled labour.

The twin problems of modernising the economy and overcoming working class failure required the abolition of the tripartite system. If working class failure could be overcome through comprehensive schools, more resources, better teachers, a relevant curriculum, and so on, and if at the same time a more educated labour force was an essential determinant of economic success, it was not only logical but politically and economically vital to call for more investment in education.[6]

Even when it was argued that the 'less able' would require a more relevant curriculum, the emphasis was on general education in opposition to training. For the influential Newsom Report vocationally biased courses were to be treated as 'vehicles of general education'. Alongside courses 'broadly related' to occupational interests, it suggested that equal attention 'should be paid both to the imaginative experience through the arts, and to the personal and social development of the pupils' (CACE, 1963, paras 110–16).

Throughout this period the relationship between school and work appeared to be largely harmonious. The organisational structure of schooling was changed in successive attempts to provide more people, particularly within the working class, with an education which economists, sociologists and politicians regarded, without question, as a 'good' thing. Protected by the argument that more education equals economic growth, the loose and relatively unstructured relationship between school and work seemed to be all that was necessary. It is not that there was an *absence* of a relationship with the economy, but that its particular political and ideological expression involved specific forms of educational reform and expansion, which in turn allowed educational practices to develop in certain ways. After the watershed of RSLA, it was this pattern of practices and institutional arrangements, particularly in schools, which was to come under attack.

It should also be added that while there was a distinctive social democratic 'moment' in the formulation of educational policy, it was always constructed within sharp limits. In many senses the 1960s was a period of educational consensus but there were many controversies and struggles around particular policies and their effects (Education Group, 1981, Chapter 5). In combination with the upheavals of local government reform, comprehensive reorganisation not only spawned a diversity of schemes, but through the 1970s they were in varied stages of completion: twenty-four local authorities in England had not even started reorganisation by January 1974 (Bellaby, 1977, p. 15).

More importantly, the fruits of reform were not distributed evenly, especially in access to post-compulsory forms of education. Educational expenditure expanded by 242.9 per cent between 1953 and 1972 (as compared with an overall increase in public expenditure of 82.9 per cent), but it was to be found by Vaizey (1968) and others that this had been disproportionately allocated to those staying in education beyond the minimum leaving age. So although there was an expansion and some opening of access, it was not straightforwardly 'for all'; and those who gained least were the young people who left school at the earliest moment and who by and large ceased to have any contact with the education system.

Post-school education

The relationship between school and work may have been vague, but the connections between further and higher education, vocational training and the requirements of employers became tighter and increasingly complex. A succession of major and minor reports, supplemented by a series of White Papers, analysed the entire range of post-school education, made sweeping recommendations and gave rise to government decisions resulting in an unprecedented expansion, reorganisation and capital investment in all these sectors.

In particular, the whole emphasis of the post-school sector was dramatically affected by an increase in the number of students on full-time and advanced courses in further and higher education, and by a shift in part-time education away from vocational evening work to part-time day release and sandwich courses. This expansion benefited certain groups disproportionately. Most working class school leavers and many middle class women were excluded, or could gain access only to less prestigious courses and qualifications. By 1967, for example, over 14 per cent of the relevant age group in England and Wales entered some form of full-time higher education (an increase of nearly 100 per cent in less than 10 years), but the proportions from different social class backgrounds had hardly changed (Banks, 1976, p. 20).

The diverse and complex stratification of the labour force was increasingly expressed in – and partly reproduced through – a new education and training hierarchy. Crudely, this involved apprenticeship or on-the-job training for skilled manual workers; technical colleges, sandwich courses and staff colleges for technicians, intermediate non-manual workers and state employees. The universities, especially Oxford and Cambridge, were largely restricted to the offspring of the elites, recruited from the public schools, who would go on to be future managers, members of the professions and the controllers and leaders of most British intellectual, political and public institutions.

It is possible to identify the new hierarchies and patterns of stratification emerging, but it would be simplisitic to see educational institutions as somehow mechanically responding to the demands of employers and the requirements of the class structure. Economic and social imperatives were articulated through a conflicting web of government departments, professional organisations, curricula and monitoring agencies, and employer and corporate bodies. Their many effects were translated into practice through the provision of resources for funding and staffing, and through forms of certification and assessment. The response of the education system has never been one-dimensional. Broader social and economic imperatives were translated and expressed in terms of its internal logic, priorities and conflicts (Bordieu and Passeron, 1977).

A major precipitating factor underlying these changes was fear of international competition and anxiety about shortages of scientific, technical and skilled labour. However, there was an associated assumption of an untroubled harmony between a *general* educational expansion and economic growth, notably in relation to the universities and the newly-created polytechnics. In response to the pressure on higher education and university places following the growth of secondary education, the 1963 Robbins Report proposed a large-scale general expansion of the university sector. Courses should be available to all who were qualified to pursue them, and higher education was encouraged to develop a diverse range of provision.

State involvement in training

With respect to industrial training the state was progressively – though reluctantly – forced to rationalise and impose some coherence on the training practices of industry and commerce. After the war the government encouraged employers' associations and trade unions to agree national apprenticeship systems and establish training standards. By 1950 33 per cent of boy, and 8 per cent of girl school leavers were being given apprenticeships. These figures, as Ken Roberts points out, 'subsequently fluctuated without changing dramatically' (1984, p.26). The largest sectors involved were the engineering and construction industries. Young apprentices were increasingly given access to day release provision: from just over 40,000 in 1938 the number of young workers on day release increased to 435,000 in 1959 (CACE, 1959). The Crowther Report, however, raised questions about the value of this off-the-job provision. The contradiction between a time-served apprenticeship at work and college qualifications which required annual success in abstract curricula and arbitrary tests was never confronted. Drop out and failure rates were chronic (Roberts, 1984, p. 27).

Attempts to improve the quality of training, and extend its scope, invariably foundered on the refusal of many employers to devote resources to an area of low priority. A 1964 DES study on 'Day Release' found that many small employers regarded day release as an interference with their business and thought that young people should use evening classes (Keene, 1969, p. 18). The Crowther Report concluded from the evidence that 'There could be no clearer indication of the basis on which the day release system stands. The structure of industry and the attitude of employers determine the issue' (CACE, 1959, p. 334).

Throughout the 1950s the government refused to become directly involved in industrial training, even when evidence suggested that Britain's sluggish economic growth was exacerbated by shortages of skilled manual workers and the archaic structure of apprenticeship training. Reaffirming this principle in 1958, the Carr Committee also pointed out that employers were overwhelmingly opposed to schools providing vocational instruction (NJAC, 1958, p. 23).

However, it was gradually accepted that if training was left to market forces skill shortages would be an inevitable consequence of the trade cycle, especially in the UK where employers regarded training as a disposable overhead (Perry, 1975). In periods of economic contraction, employers cut costs by reducing their training of apprentices and by laying off workers, including skilled ones. In periods of expansion the subsequent skill shortages led to bottlenecks in production. Employers' attempts to 'poach' other firms' skilled workers often provoked an upward movement in wage levels. Poaching and the cost of apprenticeship training, discouraged employers from investing resources in training workers who might not stay with them.

It was the shortage of craft and technical skills, especially at the peak of economic cycles, which finally precipitated direct state involvement. In 1964, the Industrial Training Act enabled the then Minister of Labour to organise Industrial Training Boards (ITBs), which were to be administered jointly by employers and trade unions and established in, and financed by, individual industrial sectors. The Boards were required to improve the quality of training, and to spread its costs more equitably by a system of grants and levies. By 1971, there were 27 ITBs covering employers with some 15 million workers.

These Boards were mainly created in those industries which had few women workers and as the ITBs did not consider it to be their role to encourage the training of women and girls their establishment did not help many women (Wickham, 1985, p. 98). Contrary to the expectations of educationalists the ITBs also failed to extend day release provision to unskilled and semi-skilled workers.

The activities of the ITBs were fiercely criticised by the small firms lobby which wanted the levies ended and training returned to market forces (GLC, 1984). The number of apprentices fell consistently after 1966 and (proportionately at its greatest in 1969) just about covered a quarter of all young workers, the vast majority of whom were male (FECDRU, 1980, pp. 34–5).

Within this process of decline the climate was created for developments witnessed in the 1980s. In particular, the activities of the ITBs led to a more direct and growing involvement of the Department of Employment in vocational training and its now associated relationship with the further education sector. A Central Training Council (CTC) had been established but it possessed only advisory powers. The TUC argued that this body should be given broader executive powers over the ITBs and national training policy.

In this period the role of training and employment services was understood to be a *reactive* one: they were mobilised in response to the independent regulation of labour demand at the macroeconomic level. Throughout the 1960s and early 1970s the statutory agencies placed great emphasis on careers information, guidance and placement (both occupationally and geographically) in a largely buoyant labour market characterised by high levels of employment. Subsequently, the growing crisis of unemployment alongside industrialists' complaints about the financing of the ITBs was to result in a comprehensive review and reorganisation of these agencies. It was from this review, in the early 1970s, that the MSC was eventually to appear (DE, 1972).

Despite these developments in industrial training, and in post-school education, there was no substantial progress on the clauses of the 1944 Education Act which had provided for the compulsory further education of all young workers up to the age of eighteen. This objective had been relegated to the sidelines for consideration only after that other commitment – to raise the school leaving age to sixteen – had been secured.

Preparing for RSLA

The introduction of a school leaving age of sixteen was consistently identified as an important way of preventing the wastage of working class talent. Although the number of fifteen year olds staying on voluntarily increased during the 1960s, by 1971 this still only accounted for just over half the age group. Nevertheless, the commitment given in 1964 to implement RSLA 'in 1971–2 was, as a response to developing expenditure constraints, deferred in January 1968 to 1973–4. As the date for RSLA drew closer, apprehension about its likely effects increased. It was anticipated with some foreboding in educational discussion – particularly in the threatening form of those identified as the 'reluctant stayers'. A Schools Council Paper of 1965 warned that 'for many, vocational motivation will be weak; it will be difficult to engage their interest and sense of relevance. Some will actively resent having to stay longer at school' (p. 1).

This anxiety was understandable, given the century-old tensions which had existed especially between working class boys and compulsory state schooling. John Partridge, writing about the secondary modern school in 1968, indicated the anxiety felt by many teachers who expressed 'great alarm' at 'the added difficulties which they can foresee when the most unmanageable pupils are forced against their will to remain until they are sixteen'. At sixteen these 'boys and girls will be far stronger physically and so even less controllable and altogether a greater source of mischief'. Many of the teachers dealing with difficult adolescents suggested 'this reform is being forced upon them by starry-eyed educationalists against all the evidence of common sense' (1968, p. 178). As late as May 1971, four-fifths of all Scottish secondary teachers signed a petition calling on the government to postpone RSLA.

To allay these fears, and in preparation for RSLA, considerable development work appeared to be taking place. The Schools Council Working Paper argued for a completely new approach to the curriculum as 'more of the same will not bring success'. They suggested that it was not the extra year itself that made the difference, but that the opportunities of a five-year course were totally different from those of a four-year course: 'they require new assumptions, attitudes and understandings . . . [so that curricula] . . . differ from the present approach more in the range and quality of the work that is attempted, than in its quantity' (1965, p. 8). The DES emphasised that:

RSLA ought not to consist simply of tacking on an 'extra year' but should include a review of the curriculum as a whole, so that the years up to 16 represent a coherent educational experience for all secondary pupils (Circular 8/70, 1970).

This desperate search for relevance, and experiments to fill the gap – increasingly, a yawning chasm – of the extra year, were to construct the reluctant stayers as peculiarly 'ignorant' and in need of a whole new range of developmental skills and experiences.

The direct involvement of many pupils in part-time work and domestic labour was it seems largely ignored, even though the Newsom Report conservatively estimated that at least half of school age boys were involved in casual work. The object of many development projects was one of introducing the young to the world of work, precisely the place they wanted to be had it not been for RSLA! Unlike the 1980s, however, the emphasis was on making schools more relevant to pupils rather on making pupils more attractive to potential employers.

The Schools Council worked with the CBI to organise 'introduction to industry' schemes to foster better relationships between teachers and employers. New forms of assessment and school organisation were experimented with. Work experience schemes organised by the schools, and approved by the local authority, were legalised through the Education (Work Experience) Act 1973.

Despite the preparations and the fear of the reluctant stayers, the evidence suggested that the initial response to RSLA consisted of little more than 'tacking on' the extra year.[7] Many local authorities, mid-way though comprehensive reorganisation and feeling the first chill winds of expenditure cuts, had not found resources for much more. There were also signs that young people ensnared by the extra year were voting with their feet. Coventry's truancy rate for fifth year pupils in 1973–4 was 'conservatively' estimated to have run at 30–40 per cent, rising to nearly 60 per cent in the summer term (Finn, 1975). Absenteeism, which is now largely a secondary school problem, steadily increases from the second year onwards, and since 1973 has peaked in the year group that would not have been included in the school population but for RSLA (Grimshaw and Pratt, 1984).

In more or less sensational fashion, the mass media were to

present 'evidence' from many sources of what appeared to be determined resistance to the extra year. The President of the National Association of Education Welfare Officers, at their annual conference, claimed that in his home town of Norwich there had been a 75 per cent increase in juvenile delinquency and about 80 per cent of it was caused by fifteen–sixteen year olds. School absenteeism among the age group was about 50 per cent, and 'there had been an increase in the number of disturbances in classrooms, and violence towards teachers' (*Guardian*, 19 April 1974). The DES's own report, 'The First Year After RSLA', noted 'a strong impression that misbehaviour had increased'. The teaching unions commissioned and issued a series of reports on the threats posed to discipline and authority in 1975 and 1976 (NAS, 1975, 1976; NUT, 1976).

In these circumstances it was not surprising when the media highlighted as 'news' problems which were in many respects extremely old. With suitable graphics, in dramatic locations, the *Sunday People* on 16 June 1974, was to report 'In our schools . . . defiance, gang war and mugging'; the *Sunday Times* colour supplement, on 17 November, was to headline RSLA as 'blamed for increased truancy, mass disruption and vandalism among bored and frustrated youngsters who complain that they are wasting their time'. This was something of the texture of education reporting by the media that was to be so important in subsequently shifting the whole debate about educational means and ends.

For the moment, the teachers themselves could provide the fiery language and emotive imagery. The following speech at the NUT Conference, calling unsuccessfully for RSLA to be abandoned, appeared in 1974. Pupils reached their last year:

> barely literate, in spite of the devoted attention of their teachers. These malcontents express their disapproval of their enforced incarceration . . . During lunch hour or break they roam the school or locality like the inhabitants of Dodge City on a Saturday night fling before the arrival of Wyatt Earp. These corridor cowboys think nothing of wrecking a locker door, smashing a few classroom doors or windows, or slashing new curtains in their form rooms (*Guardian*, 19 April 1974).

However, far from the imminent collapse of all moral standards;

far from the invasion of uncontrollable vandals in local shopping centres during school time; and far from the feared assaults on embattled teachers, what actually took place was the rapid eclipse of RSLA both as a political and educational issue.

This had a number of related causes. In the first place, the developing critique of the social democratic consensus by the New Right,[8] whilst focusing for a time on RSLA as a *cause célèbre*, was more centrally concerned with broader themes of standards, teaching methods, accountability, parental involvement, and so on, and was to be presented – in the form of the William Tyndale affair and other events – with much more productive metaphors for percolating its new common sense about education (Education Group, 1981, Chapter 9). In the course of a few years, the perception of schools as a source of solutions to social and economic problems was to be transformed to one which ascribed the blame for many of those same problems to precisely the reforms which had been pursued in the 1960s.

Secondly, the massive and sudden growth of youth unemployment, whilst partially deflected by RSLA itself, was to begin to bite after the summer of 1974. This reduced the pressure from RSLA pupils and their parents who were now confronted by a contracting labour market. Most important, however, was the ability of the new comprehensives, after the initial period of implementation, to adjust their internal processes to the acute – though clearly sensationalised – problems posed by RSLA. It is to an examination of that internal adaptation in a school in the West Midlands that I now turn.

4

The Impact of RSLA: Growing Up and Leaving School

Before assessing how RSLA and secondary education for all were finally made a reality in the lives of the young working class, it is worth considering what secondary schools appear to offer young people and their parents.

Through the transmission of facts, procedures, practices and judgements, schools offer access to bodies of knowledge which when assessed through the process of certification play a vital role in the allocation of individuals to particular occupational groupings. Schools are also involved in a process of character formation which they seek to achieve through rules imposing patterns of behaviour and regulating conduct.

The school secures its objectives through formal and informal processes, and through a hidden as well as an obvious curriculum. This hidden curriculum refers to the assumptions about authority and their own abilities which are absorbed by the young through the day-to-day activities associated with school routines. These assumptions are expressed in the expectations and the forms of organisation which shape the pattern of social relationships in the school. The assembly and the examination, the layout of the classroom and the sequencing of the school day, all provide the young with both a formal and an informal education.

Ideally, the school wants the complete consent of its pupils; it wants them to internalise the values and models of behaviour it attempts to transmit. More pragmatically, its modern legitimacy rests on the offer of what Paul Willis (1977) described in 'Learning to Labour' as an *educational exchange*. In return for conformity and obedience the school offers knowledge and qualifications which can be translated into occupational destinies. On this basis most people give legitimacy to the educational process. The reality for some pupils, however, can be very different.

The school is a *compulsory* institution and is legally empowered, *in loco parentis*, to enforce its rules and standards of behaviour. School regimes rest on elements of *coercion* as well as consent, and educational strategies display both features. Many working class youngsters experience school as an institution which pushes them about and tries to make them something they are not (Corrigan, 1979). They are sceptical about the educational rewards on offer.

The internal practices of schools are riven with hidden tensions as its rhythms and requirements conflict with the subterranean processes of growing up working class. This process can assume dramatic forms, resulting in physical violence or the destruction of property, but more usually is expressed through apathy and a lack of interest in what is on offer. Much of this disaffection and resistance is accepted by pupils and teachers as part of the reality of everyday life in school.

In this context, the concept of resistance is ambiguous. It has negative and positive features. Within schools there are many processes which generate resistance: from the authority and generational relationships which provoke a resistance to youthful dependence, to the ideological and educational relationships which provoke a resistance to penpushing and mental work. This resistance in school can be the source of real insights; it can also be the source of racist and other oppressive responses. Paul Willis (1977) has illustrated how this resistance can indicate a broader accommodation to – even a celebration of – a particular class destiny. It was this complex web of resistance and accommodation which was extended in the extra year of compulsory schooling.

It was to explore these dimensions of educational experience that I undertook research in a comprehensive school two years after RSLA was implemented.[1] I wanted to assess how an educational strategy for coping with it had been created, and to what extent the school had been able to integrate the 'reluctant stayers' into the educational exchange. I also wanted to assess the reactions of some young people to the extra year and explore the impact of a higher leaving age on the transitions involved in growing up working class. What did secondary education for all offer to the reluctant stayers?

The research and the area

Between November 1975 and May 1976 I was involved in an intensive period of research – using interviews, questionnaire and observation techniques – in a single comprehensive school. The choice of the school was not intended to be statistically representative, but was picked as typical of the area (if slightly above average), in discussion with LEA officials. For reasons of confidence, and brevity, I call the area Crowtherville and the school Newsoms.

The school was located to the north-west of Birmingham and its local economy was just moving into recession. Service sector employment was growing but the labour market was dominated by factory work in the car, car component and small metalworking industries. In 1970, just under 80 per cent of the working population was employed in manufacturing of some kind and 60 per cent of the total workforce were in firms employing over 1,000 people. Since the late 1940s Crowtherville had experienced very low levels of unemployment.

In the harsher conditions of the 1970s unemployment was starting to grow. Between early 1975 and April 1976 adult unemployment had doubled, with over 2,000 registered unemployed at the local Job Centre. The impact on school leavers' prospects had been equally noticeable. Of the 4,500 youngsters who left school in the summer of 1975 over 400 were still unemployed the following Easter.

Newsoms High School had been comprehensive since 1969, but full reorganisation in the newly-formed local authority was not completed until 1973. The school was an eleven–sixteen, eight-form entry comprehensive located in a predominantly white working class estate. It had been created out of three older schools – two single-sex secondary moderns and one girls' grammar. The school had just been consolidated on one site by the first year of RSLA and had about 1,000 pupils.

The school responded positively to my approach and after some negotiation accepted my research programme. Over the following two terms this involved participating for one full day each week in the classes of a group of fifth formers defined as the 'achievers' (varying, over the day, from four to six pupils) and those defined as 'reluctant stayers' (from eight to twelve pupils).

This was supplemented each week by interviews with both groups. I also used a questionnaire which was completed by 152 of the 187 pupils in the fifth form on a Monday two weeks before the end of the Easter term: a response rate of over 80 per cent. I talked extensively to the Head, a Deputy Head, and the teachers of the groups I was following, and recorded interviews with all of them immediately after the end of the Easter holiday. This was augmented by a questionnaire to all members of staff, but only 28 out of 57 completed it: a response rate of just under 50 per cent.

When discussing the pupils' questionnaires I differentiated them according to sex and the number of examinations the young person was entered for. Both these factors have a key influence on subsequent destinations in the labour market. For a number of reasons, I chose to distinguish between the 'academics', who were entered for four or more 'O' levels, and the 'non-academics'.[2] This division did not correspond neatly to the distinction between the achievers and reluctant stayers, who were chosen in consultation with staff on criteria other than simple examination entry. In effect, the reluctant stayers were chosen from that group of pupils who would have left school at fifteen had that still been possible.

It is important to stress that the two groups of pupils I worked with were exclusively male and white (as were their teachers on the days in question). These exclusions reflected the way the sexes and their teachers are streamed, and was a direct consequence of my own assumptions and the sexist and racist priorities of much sociological research (Griffin, 1985b). This had clear implications for the way in which I understood RSLA as an educational policy and as a school problem – around overt discipline and classroom control – and for the research programme I followed. In important ways my priorities marginalised and obscured the experience of young girls. Their active negotiation and resistance to the demands of compulsory schooling were frequently eclipsed in the eyes of male teachers (as well as of the male researcher) by the aggressive masculinity of the reluctant stayers and the general assertiveness of the boys. The exclusion of young black people was the result of an equally dangerous assumption about what constituted the 'typical' experience of RSLA. It was also a testimony to the stark racial divisions in many school catchment areas.

Educational objectives and classroom control

Newsoms projected a very public educational ideology constructed around its motto 'Learn to Live'. The objects of the school were clearly described in a booklet issued to the parents of first year pupils:

> We attach great significance to honesty and truthfulness, to respect for older persons (whether parents or teachers), good manners at all times, helpfulness where possible, and reasonable behaviour. Gradually we are trying to establish the atmosphere of a large family where every member is interested in and concerned about every other member and you, as parents, are invited to co-operate with us in this respect. The discipline is firm without being rigid and your child will have the opportunity of being responsible and independent.

This ideal face of the educational promise, the offer of equal treatment in an unequal world, was contradicted by the daily practices of the school which were subordinated to the hierarchies of the examination system. The streaming which took place was a continuous practice which commenced in the junior schools and by the end of the fifth year delivered a cohort of youngsters to different forms of educational outcomes. In Newsoms, there seemed to be very marginal movement between streams, tapering off so as to be almost non-existent by the end of the fourth year.

In their answers to the questionnaires the teachers laid greatest stress on helping pupils develop their individual personalities. They also emphasised the necessity to cover and transmit their subject, enabling pupils to do well in exams. They had a responsibility to employers, but there was little endorsement of the idea of providing pupils with job-specific skills.

For the teachers, RSLA posed no real question about the nature of streaming or selection. The public, social objective of moulding individual personalities was, in practice, transformed into the gritty realities of getting through the syllabus and the exam. In this competitive struggle the least able, inevitably, were deemed to be less competent. Their apparent lack of academic skills was often viewed as symptomatic of a general inadequacy, rather than a specific response – and possible challenge – to the legitimacy of the school.

By and large, the critical variable seen to exist in the educational relationship was that of control. If the overt or implicit objectives of the school were to be attained then the teacher needed classroom control. Without it, as one of the senior teachers expressed it, 'a teacher might as well pack up. Nothing will be learned and nothing achieved. A complete waste of pupils' time, ratepayers' money and any expenditure on materials'.

Getting that classroom control was not an easy process. Teachers themselves required their own period of apprenticeship. For the male Deputy Head who had been responsible for implementing RSLA, and who was most in contact with the reluctant stayers, this experience was vital:

> You have a settling in time, but you see, it's the way you walk into the classroom. It's just the way you speak, it's the way you handle a class that they just smell, because it is that, right away, they smell experience, they smell confidence, they smell, you know, a teacher who's in control. Whereas just like a dog, they can smell fear, a dog will snap at your heels as you walk past if he thinks that you are watching out of the side of your eye, he can always sense the fear. It's exactly the same with kids, when they get a probationary teacher or a young teacher who walks in, and he's obviously lacking in confidence, he's a little bit nervous, and may not even show it really to the outsider, but it's almost the kids can sense this, this lack of confidence. Again that is experience, you know, there is just no answer to it.

In discussion with teachers a constant theme emerged about the relationship between practical experience and the maintenance of good control. This referred to both a particular kind of behaviouristic power – where you stood, how you spoke, how you prepared lessons, and so on – and also to a particular kind of relationship you had with pupils. They had to be kept at a distance because, as the Deputy Head put it, 'you can never be one of them . . . If you try to be liked, if you seek to be liked, they, you know, that will be wrong. They will not respect that'.

Strategies for coping with RSLA

The implementation of RSLA had been viewed with some apprehension in educational circles, and within Newsoms the response to a higher leaving age reflected this wider concern. The Deputy Head recognised that imposing a rigid discipline, with all its intractable and time-consuming problems, would have been shortsighted and educationally bankrupt. The emphasis to emerge at Newsoms was on securing the consent of the reluctant stayers by giving them a new stake in the system:

> **DH:** I mean, you know, you can wield the big stick so far . . .
> But ultimately it's got to fail. Ultimately it can't be successful because there's more than you for a start off, they can always get back at you in the last resort if they want to. There's nowt you can honestly do about it. But once they've got back at you once, they will permanently get back at you after that . . .
> It's awfully easy to go into a toilet and write all over the toilet wall, isn't it? There's nothing you can do about that sort of thing. If you can catch them, yes, but you're most unlikely to catch them. And once they've done it once, every time you belt them from that point on, they'll go and do it again you see. So you've got to be more subtle, and you've got to get these kids wanting to come to school, and when they're in school, wanting to do the lessons, right. Because they are motivated. Then you will be more likely to have their cooperation. And then you are more likely to have a reduction in any sort of discipline problems.

Within the school a complex curriculum with academic, vocational and practical elements was created. Alongside conventional courses in traditional subjects, new curricular areas were opened up in social, leisure and vocational classes. Particular use was made of teacher-controlled Mode III CSEs, and the school's own assessment scheme. Various work-related schemes were also introduced – from intensive work experience for some of the reluctant stayers, which included two weeks with an employer in the Easter term, to 'Operation Exodus' for the mass of the fifth year where they would 'invade the world of local industry', visiting factories and workplaces in small groups so that 'pupils . . . find out more about certain jobs before they leave school'.

CSEs and the dual comprehensive curriculum

From the available evidence it does not seem that the response in Newsoms was particularly idiosyncratic. As early as 1972, in a 'Progress Report on RSLA', the DES was pointing to the development of similar strategies and promoting them as models of best practice:

A number of new courses have emerged some aimed at examinations and others designed to cater for the non-academic fourth and fifth year pupils. Many authorities recognise that new CSE courses – especially CSE Mode Three – can provide an incentive to pupils who would otherwise lack one (p. 3).

In the years after RSLA was implemented it became evident that the extended leaving age was resulting in a massive expansion of CSE rather than GCE entries. In all modes, CSE entries increased from 1.4 million in 1973 (involving 324,000 youngsters), to 2.3 million in 1975 (involving 553,000 youngsters). This compared with an increase in GCE 'O' level entries from 2.3 million to 2.5 million, including students in further education – a 10 per cent increase in GCE entries, against a 65 per cent increase in CSE entries (DES, 1979, p. 5). Within comprehensive schools, a dual curriculum and form of certification emerged. When questioned about the implications of this for the wider goals of comprehensivisation, senior staff in Newsoms seemed relatively unperturbed. They in fact interpreted the goals of comprehensivisation very narrowly, feeling that a limited amount of mixed ability teaching was about all that was possible.

The most significant innovation was the creation of the school assessment scheme specifically designed for the reluctant stayers and least academically able; consider this extract from a conversation between myself and Newsoms's Deputy Head:

DF: *From the children's point of view, do you think they can,* *they themselves, know the difference between something like a CSE and the school assessment scheme?*

DH: I'm sure they do. I'm sure they are much more motivated if they are taking an external examination. They're much happier because they are going to get a piece of paper at the end of it . . . But you see the school assessment is a similar sort of thing in the sense that it does give them something to work for . . . Each month out to the subject teachers go these assessment forms. There is no mark put on, no grade put on. Just a simple straightforward comment as to the child's performance during the last few weeks. So, and then that is returned to the child's tutor, and then the child's tutor has a session with them, you know, and talks to them about it, the assessment and various subjects . . .

So there is constant attention to these kids who normally wouldn't have any attention. There's personal contact between him and a member of staff. It gives the member of staff a basis to talk to them. And, I'm not going to say it will ever be 100 per cent successful because it never will, because you have there some of the weakest and probably some of the most reluctant members in the school. But if it only does a 30 or 40 per cent success rate, then that is success. If it just keeps them going, and gives them some sort of motivation, which they wouldn't otherwise have, well then I think it is successful.

These curriculum changes were part of a *managerial* strategy evolved in response to the problems created by RSLA. This response acknowledged the threat posed to conventional pedagogic models by these new and unwilling clients. Its central elements involved the introduction of new forms of schooling which would capture the motivation of the reluctant stayers and create situations which reduced the potential for direct conflict and resistance, largely outside the conventional classroom. For the Deputy Head, the managerial problem was to put the reluctant stayers:

in a situation where there is a non-conflict. Right. There is nothing that they can hit against. You know, in the module area when working, if they don't feel like working a particular day, well they can sit there and do nothing, providing that their behaviour is not anti-social.

The great problem is that it probably doesn't put enough demands on them . . . I don't know if they can have it both ways . . . I suppose the purists would say that educationally it's a little invalid, because they are here basically to learn. If they're sitting doing nothing then they're not learning. But then you could equally argue that if their resentment was so great, would they learn in any case. I don't know. And providing that they don't behave in an anti-social manner, then probably there is some advantage in the sense that they won't damage the rest of the pupils in the group.

Intentions and reality seldom correspond, however, and what the Deputy Head put forward as a coherent strategy in theory or in the staffroom had to be implemented within the realities of the classroom relationship between pupils and teachers, both of whom may have had different priorities and expectations of the extra year.

Implementing the RSLA strategy: non-conflict situations

The classroom teachers assessed the value of the new forms of educational work in a very different way. The criticisms they put forward – around the educational content of the new modules, their relationship to employers' needs and job requirements, and the comparability with other qualifications – echo in many ways contemporary arguments about provision for the young unemployed.

After the initial year and flurry of activity around RSLA, the new courses and innovations had become routinised and seemed very much subordinate to work with examination classes and the achievers. It appeared that as long as the reluctant stayers were contained, then that was about the best that could be achieved. For the Head of the English Department, however, these non-conflict situations could be exploited by the pupils involved – 'the less able, who are relatively less able; let's face it they're not stupid, can see we are trying to create a non-conflict situation'. In his view, the new educational exchange offered to the reluctant stayers was a sham:

In their case it is a fraud, and they have every right to despise us completely, because we are not prepared to come out into the open and say, 'There are certain things which we think are valid, which we are trying to teach you'. And they can have no respect for us surely if we in fact, are not prepared to stand by the validity of what we are putting in front of them, if we in effect, admit to it being a holding operation, baby minding operation, a non-conflict situation.

An equally important set of criticisms, voiced by some of the teachers, related to the value of the new qualifications. The creation of new, 'artificial certificates', especially Mode III CSE, seemed to devalue the bedrock of educational ideology, where examination success could be translated into value in the outside world. The new developments encouraged teachers to adapt certification to classroom control, instead of using it as a form of objective testing of pupils' abilities and capacities. This was particularly the case with Mode III, which was constructed in the school, not subject to the rigour of an externally imposed syllabus and not really comparable, it was claimed, with other examinations. The Head of Science conveyed the point anecdotally:

I am a bit, you know, concerned that everybody might start to do a Mode III, in other words, everybody does their own thing. Now once that starts, then I think that leaves it open to somebody doing a Mode III which will be of little or no use . . . Let me tell you about a true story. (Laughs.)
No names again . . . it was a verbal discussion.
I went to do an assessment and I said, you know, let's have a look at their work, let's have a look at the exam paper. 'It ain't any bloody good' he said, 'the head of the school said that every child in the school will take an exam of one sort or another. You know equality for everybody, alright'. He said, 'So these buggers' that was his expression that he referred to the kids, 'these buggers had better do something' he says, 'Well I know they couldn't do CSE Mode I, no chance of CSE General Science', he said, 'so I've given them this to do'. He

said, 'Put forward the syllabus, I've called it Mode III, it's been accepted by the board, and the buggers jump through the hoop'. Now then, educationally, is that sound? It was containing them. They certainly weren't going round vandalising everything. Some of them would have worked at it and got a certificate . . .

With a Mode III you write the syllabus, you set an exam paper, and obviously, be honest about it, it's geared to what you like. What you think the kids need and it's because of that very thing, it should be a lot easier.

The new public and internal certificates were criticised because little thought had been given to their reception in the outside world. In Newsoms, the Head of Science thought the new forms of assessment were 'a very nice way of cleaning and sweeping up all the kids who couldn't do anything else'.

The ultimate reservation was about whether the new certificates and forms of assessment would actually work in the classroom. The Head of Science doubted whether they would get the motivation of the reluctant stayers or substitute for the active role of the teacher:

I've never found, and this I suppose is experience, that I need a certificate at the end of the line, to motivate the kids, because I believe that motivating kids is between the teacher and the kid and the work being done. Never mind that certificate at the end of the line.

The 'onus is surely on the teachers to motivate children within the classroom'.

It was hardly surprising that in their questionnaire responses a large majority of the teachers were sceptical about the educational benefits of the new approaches. Of those who were positive about the impact of these developments – eleven – eight of them were male teachers in managerial positions. Over 80 per cent of Scale 1 and Scale 2 teachers were sceptical about the educational worth of the schemes.

The formal classroom

Implicit in many of these criticisms was an assumption about the quality of the relationships in the traditional setting of a formal classroom. It became apparent, however, that conventional lessons were hardly the paragons of educational transmission and practice which the critique of the new educational forms suggested. These formal settings were also subject to strategies of negotiation between pupils and teachers, and between teachers themselves. The hierarchies of teaching practice meant that the reluctant stayers were usually taught by younger and less experienced members of staff, and the examination streams were taken by Heads of Departments.

The early baptism of many young teachers in the formal classroom setting was a crucial aspect of the practical experience which most teachers emphasised when explaining their professional development. It was here, when negotiating the frontier of control, that both teachers and pupils learnt about each other's expectations, weaknesses and strengths; and where teachers became aware of the negative power that pupils had to block or subvert new initiatives or directions.

Overcoming a non-conflict situation, recreating something like an educational exchange, was no simple matter of imposing authority and discipline, as many advocates of traditional methods would assert. Any attempt to come down 'heavy' on the reluctant stayers would have been counterproductive and could have provoked an equally violent response. For the young maths teacher of the reluctant stayers:

> They don't like it. You'd have, with some of them I think you'd have a situation where teachers are getting punched, you know, if you try to put too much pressure on them. I mean, that's why I don't. They realise their limitations and there is no way in which I'm going to overcome their limitations by coming heavy handed with them.

The demands made on him in relation to the reluctant stayers were minimal, 'they're quite pleased that they . . . don't run riot'.

Unfortunately for the teacher, whose job is also about effective communication, this could prove to be a frustrating experience.

Despite various ploys and attempts to gain their interest and reintegrate them into a modified form of the educational exchange, the reluctant stayers remained decidedly uninterested in much of what was on offer. Getting negotiated control did not necessarily create an attentive audience: 'you've perhaps noticed, they will be quite for two or three minutes, but . . . how many people are actually listening, how many of them are actually interested?'

This passivity and lack of responsiveness was not peculiar to the reluctant stayers, and appeared in many classes across the ability levels. Even the achiever's commitment to exams would rarely go beyond a passive involvement in class. It was possible to get control across the ability levels, albeit in a variety of forms, but this did not necessarily mean that any learning was taking place; this comment was made by Newsoms's Head of English:

> Well, these days, I think in secondary comprehensive schools, the most difficult thing is to achieve the necessary measure of concentration on the part of the kids. That actual progress is being made. I know it's fashionable to say the most important thing is discipline, without the framework of discipline you can't teach anyway. But in actual fact, most people if they put their mind to it can achieve an apparently disciplined situation. Because to a great extent everybody expects them to, including the kids.
>
> But very often, if you're not careful in a comprehensive school, these days, an apparently disciplined or an apparently happy situation, I don't mean disciplined in the strict sense, but the sort of place you go in and say, 'Oh, there's a happy working atmosphere'. It is sometimes a bit of a fraud. The real difficulty these days to to make sure that there's some real solid progress being made, because everybody is inclined to settle for less.

Nowhere was this more apparent than in the final educational experience of those caught within the extra year. Whether in the new educational settings or in the conventional classroom, it seemed that teachers and pupils made minimal demands on each other. Although in part a response to the attitudes and activities of the young people themselves, it was also apparent that most of the teachers regarded the reluctant stayers as virtually ineducable in the fifth year and saw their task primarily as one of containment.

An exception? The remedial teacher and the reluctant stayers

In the day-to-day life of the school this general characterisation was qualified by some of the real human contact that took place between teachers and taught, and there was one exception in particular. This was the remedial teacher, who responded to the reluctant stayers in a more positive way and defined his role outside the conventional educational exchange. He was free from the constraints of examination classes and the aridity of certain subjects and it was clear that the reluctant stayers would work and to some degree accept the legitimacy of what he was offering. This relationship seemed to be the creation of a long struggle, where he refused to accept a 'truce':

> At the beginning of their time we used to talk . . . say, spend two periods in a week talking about various things, and we got round to the point of saying basically the reason that they hadn't done so well was because they hadn't done that amount of work. And now and again, when we had discussions, I sort of made a habit of a row, and it just broke down and we were all trying to talk at once and others not paying any attention. Well a couple of times I went really wild, and sort of said, you know, you've only got yourselves to blame, we're either going to work, you know, I'm prepared to put in a lot of, you know, give this big martyr story, I'm prepared to put a lot of time and energy on your behalf, to sort of give you the help that you so obviously need . . .
>
> I'd say it's just as easy for me to sit here on my backside doing next to nothing, not even bothering to control you. I get paid the same amount, I said, and you're the only person who's suffering. It's a lot easier for me to sit here and do nothing, than rather to prepare some work for you to keep you working. And they seem to accept that, I'd say without exception, they accepted that perhaps it was an opportunity that hadn't happened in past English.

The remedial teacher was less successful in communicating with the female reluctant stayers who found much less to relate to in his approach. Nevertheless, he seemed interested in the reluctant stayers as individuals, gave them a lot of informal help and advice, did not see them as special problems, and was concerned through his curricula materials to treat them as maturing adults:

> It's quite adult material. Either it's asking them their opinion in lots of cases, which I don't think they've been asked a lot. Before they've been told, that's right, that's wrong . . . I've always said to them what you say goes because it's your school and not mine, you know, and your opinions are more valid than mine because it's your education we are talking about and not mine and if I say one thing don't just take it as Gospel . . . If any other teacher says something it's not necessarily right. But I mean basically that is true but I don't think they are told that. Things are given to them on too simple a level and they sort of lay down the thinking as well, and that's taking away basically their personality . . . But it's difficult because a lot of them are not prepared to say what they think.

To some extent he seemed to have been able to create an individual exchange with most of the male reluctant stayers where they appeared willing to give him some investment of effort and self in return for the knowledge and rudimentary skills, especially concerning literacy, that he offered. He did not subordinate the youngsters' outside life to examples from an inert subject matter, but tried to make the educational experience relate to, illuminate, and extend what were obviously important and dramatic changes taking place in their lives outside school:

> They've got quite, although they tend to put it down, sort of quite an exciting life; some of the things they do . . . It's all moving pretty quickly, and I think it's important they, I always say that they've got to sort of understand themselves before they can go on and understand anything else, and that's basically what they think school's nothing to do with. They think school is learning how other people, that's what I think they've thought in the past, school's learning about other people and other things. They're not part of it, they're an outside part, and school's nothing to do with it. Their actual immediate life, whereas it's absolutely everything to do with it.

The reluctant stayers

Notwithstanding this glimmer of optimism, the reluctant stayers were themselves sceptical about the value of another year of compulsory schooling. The school assessment scheme, for example, was seen to be largely irrelevant and had little impact on either their immediate activity or on how they thought in terms of their post-school futures. Overall, the youngsters I talked to, for whom RSLA was supposed to deliver so much, were deeply suspicious of the motive underlying educational change. For them the educational exchange was largely an irrelevance. It offered them nothing other than a definition of themselves as failures, in contrast with the real social and cultural transitions they were experiencing in other areas of their lives. For Des 't'aint no use us sitting in the class and doing school work is it?' In school, the teachers 'are just like coppers to we [us] now'. As the end of their school life grew closer, their resentment of the teachers and antipathy to the school became increasingly pronounced:

> **Des:** They tek no notice [imitating teacher's voice] 'You gotta put up with things what you have'. That's right. Who can put up with that, this life eh.
>
> **Mart:** I've just about had enough of this lot. I mean . . .

There was a direct rejection of what the school overtly offered to all its pupils, based on a vague awareness of the inability of the school to fulfil the promise of social mobility for all but a few of its charges. In this context it was hardly surprising that they refused an educational definition of themselves which demanded conformity and passivity in return for their classification at the bottom of the credential pyramid. Instead they carried their own definitions and values into the school, and the school had, in the pursuit of control, to accommodate itself to those realities in many areas of the curriculum.

The small collectivities created in the anti-school subculture have been analysed from various perspectives; but all agree that it is within these groups that many young people construct their individual and collective identities, in opposition to the demands of the school, but in conformity with the wider rhythms of growing up working class. Paul Willis (1977) emphasised that it was this wider preparation for their future destinies which enabled the young people he talked with to interpret the value of the educational exchange and negotiate the demands of the school.

So what were the broader economic and social transitions the reluctant stayers were experiencing, and in what ways were they part of growing up working class?

I went on to ask the fifth formers in Newsoms about some of these broader changes in their lives. In particular, I wanted to establish the nature and extent of their involvement in domestic work and the hidden economy of child labour, and the changes that were taking place in their leisure activities and patterns of consumption. In a context of RSLA, I was also interested in finding out about the particular job choices they were making, and the changes they were anticipating when they made the transition to work.

Relationships with parents and friendship groups: leisure and consumption

One of the major transitions experienced by teenagers is the way in which the exercise of parental authority changes and – from the youngsters' responses – it seemed that many parents exercised less direct control than they had previously.

Perhaps the most obvious way in which parental authority was changing was in the control exercised over the social activities of the boys and girls. From the total dependence of childhood, most of the young people were now going out independently. Nevertheless, parental anxieties and constraints exercised an important influence on the length of time which they could stay out, and no doubt – though with less direct enforcement – on the places they could go to and the activities they could indulge in. Moreover, a pervasive fear of 'trouble' or of sexual or territorial violence clearly circumscribed where many of them, especially the girls, would go, who they would go with, and how long they would stay there.

The young people were now being given responsibilities and choices which emphasised the degree to which parental authority was increasingly tempered by their developing maturity. Less than a fifth said that their parents would interfere with their choice of friends. Most of the fifth formers were in possession of one of the basic freedoms of the market – within negotiated limits they could choose what to spend money on, they had the power of consumption. They all exercised degrees of choice over the style of clothes they purchased and, indeed, a substantial majority with either their own or their parents' money, went out and bought clothes on their own.

In terms of their tastes and preferences they were making the transition to more adult forms of consumption. Boys were spending more money on beer, pub and arcade machines, cigarettes, and so on; girls were spending more on clothes, make-up, and the other commodities needed to fashion a growing femininity. The importance of these commodities was not confined to their immediate use. The most 'spectacular' commodities – clothing, jewellery, make-up, music, tobacco and alcohol – were used by young people to mark their difference from the drab forms of the school. They were able to transform the rewards for an adult life of work and obedience into styles and forms of expression which questioned the ostensible rewards on offer in the educational exchange. These commodities may often be packaged in a way which exploits young people's quest for a different identity, but that should not obscure the creative and oppositional meanings they can be given by their users, especially within the school.

The young people were also making the transition into more gender-specific forms of adult consumption and leisure, and were starting to orient themselves to their future domestic roles. When going out, apart from specific hobbies and pastimes, the emphasis was on getting access to pubs, discos and dances when possible and when their finances permitted it. For the girls many activities were focused around the home and consumption, involving visiting each other's houses, babysitting, window shopping, etc. In contrast, many of the boys, especially the non-academics, reported activities which focused on the streets and open places, 'doing nothing' (Corrigan, 1979).

The constraints on their leisure time and forms of consumption were not merely social or parental. They were now involved in starting to make a living. The vast majority received pocket money from their parents but anything extra was rarely given without an exchange involving their time and effort. These parental contributions could be used to reinforce an orientation to the demands of school work, but more commonly, especially for girls, seemed to amount to a form of 'domestic sub-contracting' (McRobbie, 1978). Many of the youngsters had also become more involved in part-time work and this too imposed material constraints on their leisure activities.

Domestic labour and part-time work

The questionnaire I asked the fifth formers to complete was designed to obtain information on their social and economic activities as well as elicit their responses to a higher leaving age.

The results showed that many of them, especially the girls, were already involved in helping out in the home, and this domestic apprenticeship was giving them critical lessons in how they perceived men's and women's work. If adult men were expected to work for a full-time wage outside the home, and adult women were seen to be responsible for maintaining the home and caring for dependants, then it was hardly surprising that boys and girls were recruited differently in response to the demands of home life.

There were clear disparities in the frequency and types of work carried out in the home. Girls were almost exclusively involved in the tasks of washing and laundry work, cooking meals, cleaning the house, looking after other children, and sewing or mending clothes. Boys by contrast were more likely to be involved in manual tasks, odd jobs and washing up.

The amounts of pocket money they received ranged from 25 pence to £3 a week. On average the academic boys and girls were getting £1.20 and 90p respectively; the non-academic boys and girls were receiving £1.30 and 98p. To get access to more expensive, more adult forms of leisure and consumption, required a supplementary income. In the main, this was available only if they took paid part-time work.

At the time of the research over half of the fifth formers were involved in part-time jobs. Unfortunately, the way the questions were asked probably underestimated the numbers involved in the informal economy. They may have excluded, for example, those

Table 4.1 *Did their parents expect them to do work around the house, percentage?*

n = 152	Academic			Non-academic			All		
	M	F	Total	M	F	Total	M	F	Total
All the time, at least once a day	0	1	1	5	6	11	5	7	12
Regularly, several times a week	2	1	3	9	15	24	11	16	27
Occasionally, say once a week	5	5	10	19	12	31	24	17	41
Hardly ever, not every week	1	0	1	15	3	18	16	3	19
No answer	0	0	0	1	0	1	1	0	1
Totals	8	7	15	49	36	85	57	43	100

who had only held holiday jobs, or those who had previously held part-time work. The questions also discouraged girls who may have been paid for domestic work such as babysitting from defining that as paid work. Subsequently, when I allowed for these dimensions in a similar survey I carried out across four schools in another part of the West Midlands, the proportions of fifth years with some experience of the child labour market increased to 75 per cent (Finn, 1984b, p. 36).

Table 4.2 *Did they have a job outside school, percentage?*

n = 152	Academic			Non-academic			All		
	M	F	Total	M	F	Total	M	F	Total
Yes	5	4	9	25	17	42	30	21	51
No	3	3	6	24	18	42	27	21	48
No answer	0	0	0	0	1	1	0	1	1
Totals	8	7	15	49	36	85	57	43	100

In 1972, a national survey commissioned by the DHSS found that nearly half of 2,500 sixteen year old pupils were involved in some form of paid work (MacLennan, 1980, p. 16). In 1975 the DHSS estimated that a quarter to a third of all children between the ages of thirteen and sixteen were in employment regulated by law (MacLennan, 1980, p. 13). From the age of twelve or younger, an increasing proportion of school pupils become progressively involved in paid employment. By the end of the fifth year, it would appear that something like four out of five working class pupils are likely to have had some experience of the child labour market.

The pattern which emerged in Newsoms was similar to that identified by Spittles in 1973, where the paid employment done by school children prefigured their destinies in the sexual division of labour (Frith, 1978, p. 31). Although there is considerable overlap in the categories used in Table 4.3, girls were predominantly involved in casual, home-based tasks like babysitting or light shop work; the boys were involved in the more systematic work of milk and egg rounds, stacking and warehousing in shops, or on market stalls. There was also some multiple job holding, where the young people involved would commonly have a weekly paper round and a Saturday job.

Table 4.3   *Nature of jobs held, percentage*

| | | Academic | | | Non-academic | | | All | |
n = 79	M	F	Total	M	F	Total	M	F	Total
Babysitting, Child minding	0	3	3	0	9	9	0	12	12
Paper, Milk, Egg rounds	0	0	0	15	0	15	15	0	15
Shop assistant, Market work	5	3	8	17	18	35	22	21	43
Cleaning, Domestic work	0	0	0	3	1	4	3	1	4
Waitress work, Catering (including Bakery)	4	3	7	10	4	14	14	7	21
Miscellaneous (e.g. Groom, Painting, etc.)	1	0	1	3	1	4	4	1	5
Totals	10	9	19	48	33	81	58	42	100

In terms of their hours of work, which were additional to the time spent in school, over 60 per cent of the working fifth years were doing between five and ten hours a week, predominantly on Saturdays. 20 per cent, almost exclusively male, were working between twelve and sixteen hours a week, and six boys were working in excess of twenty hours per week. For their labours they were receiving between 15p and 75p per hour. On average the boys were getting just under 40p per hour, and the girls 33p per hour.

This part-time labour market represents the contradictory legacy left by compulsory schooling and the regulation of child labour at work. The employers involved were the small shopkeepers and large retail and distributive companies which dominate the child labour market. The work carried out was not simply that commonly defined as 'child's' work, such as newspaper rounds, but included jobs done by adult workers.

Notwithstanding the subsequent impact of youth unemployment, and the characterisation of school leavers as inadequately prepared for (and ignorant about) the world of work, evidence has consistently emerged about the durability and extent of the child labour market.[3] By 1985 the Low Pay Unit was estimating that some 2½ million school children had part-time jobs (MacLennan *et al.*, 1985).

School children are attractive workers because they can be paid low rates of pay, they do not incur any costs arising from employment legislation and they will work at times when adults are not available or are unwilling to work: at the weekend, in the evening or early in the morning. Although the work of children is subject to legal regulation they are particularly vulnerable to exploitation. Few enforcement agencies exist and their personnel – who often have difficulty in gaining evidence or access – are charged with implementing a complex set of regulations with minimal sanctions. The 1972 survey found that many employers using child labour were guilty of some kind of statutory infringement – covering areas such as hours of work, rest periods, age of employment and so on (MacLennan, 1980, p. 16). The Employment of Children Act 1973 did empower the government to issue national regulations to 'introduce standard conditions of employment throughout the country', but these have never seen the light of day.

For many of the young people in Newsoms part-time work was a positive experience: they became part of a more adult world, and it gave them access to the commodities which proved it. For some it would be a direct source of post-school employment. One employer, a hairdresser, employed one of the girls for eight hours each Saturday largely sweeping up, for the sum of £1.50. She had no complaints, however, because she had the promise of subsequent full-time work and training.

The primacy of the needs of some families and the demands of part-time labour could themselves make incursions into the formally regulated time of schooling. It is still accepted that girls have time off to help in the home, or that recalcitrant fifth year boys should be allowed to leave early to secure work with a prospective employer. Nevertheless, the attendance regulations were policed and blatant infractions prosecuted. In the Easter term, the parents of two Newsoms fifth year girls and a local shopkeeper were fined when the girls were caught working on school days in addition to their normal Saturday job.

The importance of drawing attention to all the hidden transitions these fifth formers were involved in is to emphasise that when they were making their judgements about the worth of qualifications and the costs of the educational exchange, they were not simply drawing on some ignorant 'mass culture'. However subterranean and hidden, their choices were made as a consequence of material experiences and some knowledge of what is possible for the young working class. They could in no way be described as mindless choices made in the vacuum of educational failure.

With respect to the child labour market, for example, not only does it give some direct access to jobs, but it gives others experience of the types of work which predominate in the unskilled sectors of the juvenile labour market. They learn about workplace discipline and about the routines and practices of the 'trade'. They cope and adapt to change. They also learn about informal job-finding networks, where contacts are made through relatives and friends, or where jobs are obtained by asking around and knocking on doors. Even though most of the youngsters rejected the option of doing their part-time jobs full time – either because they disliked the work, felt it was boring, or too hard, or paid too little – their involvement in paid employment represented a powerful learning experience.

Job choices and the prospects for work

By and large the job aspirations of the fifth years were related to their sex and academic grouping, and the majority were anticipating a transition to working class jobs. Nearly a quarter of the non-academic boys wanted labouring or manual work, and just under half wanted an apprenticeship. Over 40 per cent of the non-academic girls wanted shop or catering work, 16 per cent wanted office jobs, and 16 per cent wanted to do nursing, predominantly nursery nursing.

Overall, expectations of what work would offer were relatively straightforward. They placed most emphasis on obtaining work that was in some way interesting – either intrinsically or in terms of its physical or social context. Over half the fifth formers stressed this as the most important thing about any future job. One in five wanted work with some possibilities for promotion, and a similar proportion wanted to obtain 'good wages'. The stress on interesting work, with some variety, was part of a reaction to the often tedious experience of the final years of compulsory schooling and of part-time jobs.

Although their aspirations were modest, the fifth formers were aware that the labour market was becoming hostile. The vast majority, especially of the non-academics, felt that it would be difficult if not impossible to get work. They thought that too many school leavers would be looking for work at the same time, giving employers a free hand to pick and choose who they wanted. Others stressed the competition they might face for specific jobs or expressed a fear that they would not have the appropriate, or enough, qualifications.

Of those who thought they would have no problem, a significant minority of the non-academics (fifteen) had already arranged jobs at the time of the survey, primarily with their part-time employers. Some stressed the ability of parents or relatives to set them up with work. Many of the academics felt that because of their anticipated qualifications they would have no problems in obtaining the work they wanted. Finally, a small group, across the ability ranges, stressed the availability of work if you looked around hard enough and were not too choosey about what you did.

School leaving age and the transition to work

In spite of the fear of unemployment, and despite advice about staying on and getting better qualifications, less than 50 per cent of the academics, and only 4 per cent of the non-academics, had any intention of continuing full time in school or college. In fact, 22 per cent of the non-academic boys and 13 per cent of the girls were going to leave school at the first opportunity in Easter, 1976.

Table 4.4   *When would they be leaving school?*

n = 152	Academic			Non-academic			All		
	M	F	Total	M	F	Total	M	F	Total
Easter 1976	0	0	0	11	5	16	11	5	16
Summer 1976	3	6	9	36	29	65	39	35	74
Going to College/6th Form (if enough qualifications)	5	1	6	2	2	4	7	3	10
Totals	8	7	15	49	36	85	57	43	100

A majority of the fifth formers (63 per cent) were actually in favour of pupils being able to leave school when they were fifteen; 38 per cent of the non-academics (47 per cent of the boys and 26 per cent of the girls) would have left school earlier if they could. Only two of the academics would have left earlier.

The fifth formers were deeply critical about the relevance of what they were offered in school. Most felt that the content of the curriculum would be of little help when making the transition to work. Much of the criticism focused on the perceived irrelevance of academic subjects to the jobs they wanted. 40 per cent of the non-academic girls and 26 per cent of the non-academic boys were completely negative about what the curriculum offered.

Those who gave a positive response to some aspects of the curriculum tended to focus on the value of instrumental provision, either in the form of subjects such as woodwork or typing, which employers would look for, or in terms of more immediate 'job-hunting' advice, about writing applications and getting references. Only a small group of the academics endorsed the general value of the school curriculum and examinations, largely because they were required for future progress up the credential pyramid.

The major reason for wanting to leave, however, was the desire to make the transition to work and a more adult world. Even so, nearly one in six had mixed feelings about the prospect. They were reluctant to leave behind friends and experiences they had enjoyed. With another 13 per cent of the fifth formers, who were not looking forward to leaving, they were apprehensive about the prospects of finding work and the pressures and insecurities of getting a job.

Table 4.5 *Were they looking forward to leaving school?*

n = 152	Academic			Non-academic			All		
	M	F	Total	M	F	Total	M	F	Total
Yes	5	5	10	39	22	61	44	27	71
No	2	0	2	5	6	11	7	6	13
Mixed feelings	1	2	3	5	8	13	6	10	16
Totals	8	7	15	49	36	85	57	43	100

The fifth formers who positively wanted to leave stressed two things. Their dependent role at school had become oppressive and they expressed a dislike of the institution, and of the petty rules imposed. They were fed up of being 'treated like children'. Most, however, wanted the maturity and independence they would get from going to work and earning money; holding down a paid job would help them acquire a different status. Some of the answers also emphasised bringing money back into the family. Others stressed a desire to do new and interesting things.

Educational failure and jobs

Most of the fifth formers understood the relationship between qualifications and jobs, but this did not always result in an overwhelming desire to pass exams. Not only was there an appreciation that it was a competition which inevitably produced more losers than winners, but there was an awareness, particularly amongst the reluctant stayers, of the irrelevance of exams for many of the jobs they wanted:

> **DF:** *What sort of jobs do you think they'll get with their exams?*
> **Joe:** Bank Managers.
> **Des:** Clerks . . .
> **George:** Some on the dole though, some'll just go on the dole though.
> **DF:** *Do you think they've got a better chance, 'cos they've got exams?*
> **Des:** I think they've got a better chance than we [us].
> **George:** I don't think they've got a chance for hard work. Like, when a bloke just wants ya for being strong, carry bricks up on a building or summat. They ain't got no chance of getting that have they? They ain't no stronger, just 'cos they got exams.

Far from seing themselves as failures, condemned to a future of unskilled, intrinsically meaningless work, they asserted the worth of their judgements of the educational exchange by referring to their own knowledge of economic life. Even if exams offered some possibility for social mobility they would cost too much in terms of a loss of day-to-day independence and autonomy. They wanted to get into the so-called unskilled labour market because it offered the possibilities of a much better life where you got around and could have fun and 'a laff'.

> **DF:** *I mean, could you ever see yourselves living like that?*
> **Des:** They'm say, they'm say they working hard, they'm working hard at school, but when they'm still doing the exams and we'm working, we'm working harder than them . . . When they'm going on to the first stage on a good job . . . see it's worrying them, whether they'm gonna pass a CSE exam, I think it is . . . but they got . . . [mock teacher's voice] 'Take your exam you will get a better job than those nutters who are leaving at Easter'. That's right, ent it?
> **DF:** *Is that . . .*
> **Des:** I . . . I don't think, they're not gonna get a job a lot different from what we'm gonna get.

DF: *Is that . . .*

Mart: Abby's bright. He's got an 'O' level in English. He's a labourer on a building site.

DF: *So you can get that job without them?*

Mart: Ar [Yes], the only thing is if you'm got a criminal record they kick you out.

Des: When you'm go, they say, 'have you got any exams?' . . . you go 'no', 'well it don't matter, that's alright, you got the job'.

Mart: I think they'd say that.

DF: *So do you think, do you think it's a bit of a con?*

Mart: Ar [Yes] . . .

DF: *I mean, not the high fliers, but the kids who are only gonna get a few CSEs?*

Des: Ar [Yes], we can go far we can. We can go places we can.

Mart: I reckon I can have a better life than them.

Des: We can go places . . .

The social costs and disciplines imposed by the academic route, that the reluctant stayers associated with the lifestyles of the achievers – and, crucially, the teachers – were too high to pay. To adopt such a lifestyle would have contradicted a machismo which valued physical strength and denigrated mental work. Their contempt for the achievers' way of life could be unequivocal:

Des: They're a bunch of arseholes for the teachers, like get round 'em and that, for the jobs.

Mart: Let's face it, none of us lot are gonna get a banker's job am we? We'll be the labourers and that lot.

DF: *What, wouldn't you like that sort of life?*

Mart: No, I don't like that. I mean working in school, and then studying all night. I couldn't do that, stopping in and that.

These criticisms were extended to what they perceived to be their teachers' lifestyle. Careers advice and judgements, coming from such sources, could for that reason be regarded with scepticism:

Des: You say 'did you watch that thing on the telly last night sir?' 'Oh I ain't got a TV. I'm . . . I'm marking me books and work and that'.

Mart: Mr Grey, that is, no television. 'Do you ever go to the pub?' 'I never drink' – never drink!

Des: 'Smoke?' 'Oh no' he says . . .

Des: They tell we [us] about our future, right. They say 'you . . . you'll have a bad future in the finish you will. If you want to get married and that like, you'm going the wrong way about it and that lot, you'm playing up too much and that' . . . They doe [do] tell . . . I wonder what they're like, I bet when they get home at night and we'm in trouble, they got nothing to do, just watching the telly like . . .

The concepts of occupational progression and choice which formed the basis of their careers education seemed to be irrelevant. The reluctant stayers were unwilling to defer gratification for theoretical career paths. They were disposed towards a future of manual labour which, so long as it met informal criteria and provided the wage, could be almost anything. At the careers interview this tended to make for some meaningless encounters:

DF: *Do you know how to go about getting a job?*

Des: Yea, they explained to we, ar [yes].

DF: *So have they explained what sort of jobs you should go for in the [careers] interview?*

George: No . . .

Des: No, say you say . . . and they just write it down on a slip, you know, what jobs you like and you says 'you'm open for anything', anything, any job, so just give you the slip and that's it.

DF: *And that's all?*

(Laughter.)

Cos: Ar [Yes].

George: That's all.

Choosing unskilled manual labour

As the leaving date drew closer the reluctant stayers withdrew even further from the educational world and considered their prospects in the terms of more local experiences. Friends, neighbours, parents and relations became the source of 'useful' knowledge, and their advice, ideas and lessons were mulled over continuously:

> **George:** Mr Brown, like, this morning last week; and he come in science dayn't he and he asked us if we want to do exams and that, and half of them says no, there was only one or two. Garry Watts did and I think another one did . . . but about ten of us dayn't do it.
>
> **DF:** *What, you just don't want to do it?*
>
> **George:** No, tain't worth having 'em is it?
>
> **DF:** *What about having them for jobs?*
>
> **George:** No, cos . . .
>
> **Des:** Half our mates have got goods jobs, and they dayn't have no exams.
>
> **DF:** *What do they do?*
>
> **Des:** You know, tiling, like roofing and building and that . . .
>
> **DF:** *So you think you're just as well off without exams?*
>
> **Cos:** Ar [Yes].
>
> **George:** Say if you've got an exam if you wanna go on a building site, you don't need exams yea, so you've wasted your time then . . . That's about the best – building, bricklaying, tiling and that . . .
>
> **Des:** What I'd like, you know, say me and my old man get together in the boozer, you can have a good talk can't you. You can talk about what you wanna do like, and there's nobody there to stop you and that is there?
>
> **Cos:** That's what we do when we go down the pub of a night . . .
>
> **Des:** . . . that's what we do when we go down we have a talk doe [don't] we, about jobs and that.

What then were they most looking forward to when they started work?

> **Cos:** The money.
> **Joe:** The money.
> **DF:** *Nothing else?*
> **Cos:** Just the money.

There was an understanding here that for many working class youngsters the kinds of jobs on offer would provide little intrinsic satisfaction. They recognised the costs of the wage, the physical and temporal demands of unskilled work, but it was assumed that these would enhance the enjoyment of lunchtime, the evenings and weekend:

> **DF:** *How do you think work's gonna be different from being at school?*
> **George:** It's gonna be harder.
> **Eddie:** You'm get paid for it.
> **Cos:** Murder, you have to get up earlier.
> **Des:** You do get paid though, don't ya, you do pick up money at the end of the week, but . . . here at the end of the week, this, just a couple of bob.
> **Eddie:** You'm looking forward to Saturday and Sunday, and stop in the pub at lunchtime.
> **DF:** *One of the things you don't like about school is getting up, but when you work you'll have to start earlier than here?*
> **Eddie:** Ar [Yes], but you get paid for it, don't ya, you'm on a job.
> **George:** You'm looking forward to things.
> **Cos:** You'm looking forward to Friday then.
> **George:** You got nothing to look forward to when you'm here. Say you'm on a building site, you'm alright aren't you, 12 o'clock comes, great, go for a pint.

This did not mean that the kind of work was completely irrelevant. There may have been few career choices, but there were many jobs to choose from. They applied other kinds of criteria which highlighted the human and social relations of work. The jobs they wanted had to be ones where they could move about, or were in the open. They should offer the possibility of meeting people, 'skiving', making your own time or even, hopefully, 'work with wenches'.

There was a central masculine assumption about the dignity of labour. The particulars of the job were less important than the fact that if you worked hard for the wage you would be entitled to a new status as a 'working man':

> **DF:** *When you start work, how much do you think the gaffers will be like the teachers here?*
> **Joe:** They'll be stricter won't they?
> **Des:** They won't.
> **Joe:** They'll be stricter.
> **Cos:** No, they'll just treat you like working men.
> **Des:** They'll treat you like working men, they won't treat yer like school kids.
> **DF:** *But how do they treat working men, do they treat them any different?*
> **Des:** No, not really.
> **Cos:** Well, they don't say anything to them, unless they don't work . . . I mean they work, they work just to get the money doe [don't] they?
> **DF:** *Do you think at work then, you'll work hard?*
> **Cos:** We'll have to, if we want to get our money.
> **Des:** Ar [Yes].
> **DF:** *You won't skive at work then?*
> **Joe:** I fucking will.
> **Cos:** If I can . . .

It seemed to be that what appeared to be failure at school was in fact part of a successful, if subterranean, preparation for work.

The transition to work

This celebration of the transition to wage labour, the honeymoon phase which many young people experience when they first leave school and start work, can be a short-lived phenomenon. They could soon find themselves sweeping-up and making tea; subject again to arbitrary adult authority. They might confront a workplace reality of discipline and mundane labour. Some will become frequent job changers.

As they mature and acquire the responsibilities of homemaking and settling down they may, with luck, become the 'affluent' workers whose steadiness and instrumental commitment to the workplace and the wage is so highly valued by employers in the primary labour market (Blackburn and Mann, 1979). But many of these young men would have remained in casual, unskilled labour markets, getting older and more vulnerable to the vagaries of economic forces.

Most of the girls who were leaving school as early as possible were making their job choices from an even more limited range of options. They stood little chance of getting a job with long-term training prospects that might at some point pay a living wage which would allow them to live independently.

For the young people in Newsoms the attractions of wage labour included the possibility of earning money, of having greater independence, of being subject to less petty discipline, and of acquiring what was perceived to be an adult status. You could pay your own way, no longer dependent on your parents; you could bring money into the home, even stand on your own two feet. Many looked forward to the variety and interest they expected from work.

These attractions may soon have dulled under the impact of authoritarian relationships within the labour market, but they were eagerly anticipated at school. Obtaining the wage would signal in the most visible and material way the social and cultural transitions they were experiencing, and would provide the wherewithal for their future development.

This process was disrupted by raising the leaving age, and has subsequently been threatened by the rise of mass youth unemployment. An extra year of schooling extended all the transitions that were taking place in this stage of life – it prolonged dependence on the family and school, and it denied the wage and economic maturity. The response from the school was to attempt to create a new artificial process of transition through the introduction of new curricula and approaches to teaching.

Teachers' views of RSLA and comprehensive education

The school's internal adaptation to RSLA defused the threat posed by the reluctant stayers but in no way integrated them fully into the promise of the educational exchange. The strategy became one of containment. It offered some inducement in the new forms of certification but it created the possibility for negotiated 'non-conflict' situations. Within these parameters, the reluctant stayers were given – or at least exercised – considerable freedom.

Yet, in developing and elaborating new types of learning and new forms of pastoral care the school had begun to create a curriculum more responsive to the youngsters caught within it for an extra year. This was not yet a response to the directly perceived needs of the labour market. Rob Moore (1984) has made the point that the changes in educational practice associated with RSLA cannot be equated with changing requirements in the occupational structure. What was witnessed in Newsoms, as in other parts of the country, were practical responses to the control and curricula problems generated as a result of important changes in the social composition of the school's intake.

Despite considerable scepticism, most of the teachers were not in favour of abandoning RSLA, even though seventeen out of twenty-eight thought it had created extra problems for the school. Many had reservations about the schemes and certificates which had been introduced, and complained about the problems caused by a lack of resources and development work. They saw themselves as doing their best in a difficult job, with inadequate resources and difficult pupils. Only five wanted to return to a leaving age of fifteen, but overwhelmingly they wanted to maintain the safety valve of an Easter leaving date.

Their lukewarm endorsement of a reform which had been promoted as the final element of secondary education for all should be seen in a context where even the benefits of comprehensivisation were viewed sceptically. *Less than half* of them felt that the education of even the majority of young people had improved in comprehensive schools. These teachers reacted to comprehensive reorganisation and RSLA pragmatically. It was something imposed from the outside, to which they could only adjust. Within the school, the terms of this adjustment were engineered by a new managerial elite which emerged through the experience of reorganisation, larger schools and expenditure cuts. For the Deputy Head who had implemented RSLA:

> I'm not a critic of comprehensives, but I'm not committed, convinced. Although I'm a Deputy Head and probably one day, maybe tomorrow, might be a Head of one. Not totally convinced that they were the right answer. We've got them, and we've got to live with it. You know. There are a lot of things in society that we have, that we have to live with and make the best of. I'm not sure that it was the right move . . .
> Teachers now, in my position and the Head's position, have to be managers. Very much so, managers. And these skills, you know, really put you on a par with people in industry who are doing a similar sort of job, and gradually these people in industry are beginning to see this, and recognise this. That running a large comprehensive is as important as running a large factory.

The pupils' response

In 1968 a Schools Council Enquiry into the attitudes and aspirations of young school leavers warned of the dangers that would follow if the reluctant stayers were not integrated into the educational exchange:

> The success or failure of raising the school leaving age will hinge on the success of the attempt to engage pupils more closely throughout their new five year course. Put at its lowest, the raising of the age could mean little more than the extension of a struggle between pupils who feel that school has little to offer them and teachers who feel that they meet little other than boredom and resistance (Schools Council, 1968, p. iii).

The research in Newsoms confirmed this pessimistic prognosis. Most of the fifth year pupils were in favour of an earlier leaving age, and many of the non-academics would have left at fifteen. Their response was not a simple reaction to inadequate provision or poorly-trained teachers. The reluctant stayers made a realistic assessment of what was on offer to them in the educational promise of an extra year. Even the fifth formers who had a stake in the system, who were voluntarily staying on to obtain qualifications, had considerable reservations about education and were equally reluctant to subordinate their personalities to the demands of the school.

In contradiction to much that is suggested in educational sociology and psychology these young people were more perceptive than they are usually given credit for. The fifth formers were working the system with subtlety and evaluating what it offered, how much it offered and how much they wanted to give. Educational outcomes were, for many, the result of what they were willing and prepared to do; they were not an absolute testament of what they could or could not do. The remedial teacher recognised this, but was at a loss to explain it:

Oh yes, why they go that way I don't fully, fully know. Like that kid there [one of the reluctant stayers]. He's as bright as a sort of brass button. He can't possibly be dumb, it's one of those things he does, they're ever so, they're so funny that they've got to be clever to be that funny. Then why they've gone one way or the other, I don't know, I almost think sometimes that they've thought they've really thought about it. Obviously, they haven't but they've really thought . . . , well, this is a . . . I'm enjoying myself and why should they do otherwise. But a lot of them have got potential, but I think they've been, maybe junior school, early secondary school, they've been totally rubbed up the wrong way by, well, it can only be teachers or even at home things have, they've gone wrong, which has sort of switched part of them off.

The alienation between many young people, their parents and the schools, was the product of an education system which defined them as failures, 'pushed them around', and marginalised many of the skills and abilities they possessed. Even where an instrumental commitment to qualifications existed the school was still experienced as a bureaucratic institution. It could, for its own incomprehensible reasons, undermine your expectations through streaming and its control of examination entry. At the end of it all there was the lottery of the examination itself which could easily crush the most modest of ambitions.

These experiences were hardly the stuff from which a strong commitment to education could be created. So who in a developing context of expenditure cuts was likely to defend the schools and the benefits of social democratic expansion?

Cuts and the defence of education

It was during the mid-1970s that the first rounds of expenditure cuts were starting to nibble at the education budgets of local authorities. These cuts clearly signalled the movement from expansion and consensus to contraction and the ideological storms which were to characterise the debate about education in the late 1970s.

These developments exposed important tensions in the teachers' relationship with parents, and the contradiction between the parents' concern with the process of education and teachers' professional interests. Parents could be asked to support the work of the school directly in terms of money and resources, or even asked to support teacher-defined resistance to cuts and economies, but this always had to take place at arm's length. It could not be allowed to spill over into areas that were seen as falling within the purview of the teachers' professional skills and classroom autonomy.

The teachers were now faced with calls to economise and were using, in their view, much dilapidated and substandard equipment. However, it was only around the issue of the pupil–teacher ratio that union action, with national backing, was to be initiated. In Crowtherville, a period of no-cover sanctions repulsed an attempt to increase the pupil–teacher ratio, but it did not prevent a proposed cutback in capitation and capital spending on schools.

The teaching unions described the campaign as one of the defence of education for the children of Newsoms, but it was evident that the central objective was the protection of teachers' jobs. Presented with a rhetoric of educational concern, the clear priority was the defence of the profession, and while they were linked there was no simple identity between the interests of pupils, parents and teachers. It may have just been credible to suggest that the proposed cuts might affect some of the academics' chances of obtaining qualifications. It was completely mysterious as to what the reluctant stayers and their parents were being asked to defend.

Moreover, the exclusion of young people from struggles and arguments about the nature and conditions of their schooling left little space for anything other than an instrumental commitment. When politics, power and conflict appeared in the curriculum it really was, as Mark, an academic, expressed it: 'like a dog doing a trick . . . get a biscuit if you get it right'. Many of the reluctant stayers saw little to defend in a system which labelled them failures, compelled them to say, and infantalised them.

Small wonder that the exponents of social democratic education and organised teachers became politically isolated. Their initial struggles against the cuts, which were justified as a defence of 'our children's education', could for a time succeed, as in schools like Newsoms. But when confronted with the full demands of monetarism their inability to defend schooling, to construct new political alliances, was cruelly exposed (Education Group, 1981, pp. 202–5). The many contradictions in their own ranks created problems for mounting effective campaigns. A teaching body that was itself unconvinced of the merits of comprehensivisation, that was itself confused and divided about what it was providing, that was rightly sceptical about what it could offer to many young-sters, was hardly in a position to defend the advances of the 1960s.

Subsequently, when questions were raised about the assumed benefits of comprehensive reorganisation, when thousands of sixteen year olds were leaving school to face unemployment *despite* an extended education, there was to be little effective resistance to the creation of a new 'common sense' about schooling which was to be given its most public expression in the Great Debate on education, launched in 1976.

5

The Great Debate on Education, Youth Unemployment and the MSC

As a new generation of working class youth became acclimatised to an extended period of compulsory schooling, the educational consensus out of which RSLA had been created was disintegrating. Rather than opportunities for social mobility, an increasing number of minimum age school leavers were confronted with more or less extended periods of unemployment. It seemed that young people had become less acceptable to employers and their exclusion from the labour market was to generate problems of social control and political legitimacy.

The 1970–4 Conservative government had implemented RSLA, presided over large schemes of comprehensive reorganisation and in its first White Paper in 1972 declared its commitment to 'A Framework for Expansion'. The Conservatives accepted many of the terms of the social democratic consensus. However, the assumptions of that period were now under attack from a wide variety of groups from across the political spectrum (Education Group, 1981, Chapter 9).

Crucially, economic decline undermined the claim that an expanding education system contributed to economic growth and efficiency. An aggressive new school of economics began to assert that educational expenditure, as part of an ever growing public sector, was actually precipitating the decline of British capitalism. The New Right in and around the Conservative Party identified school reform and progressive teaching methods as important causes of the moral and political malaise of the period.

The most important pressure group in this new politics was the alliance created through the pages of the Black Papers on Education, whose first report in 1969 had been laughingly dismissed by the educational establishment. By 1975, it had helped to discredit the achievements, purposes and resource arguments of the educational world as they had been expressed in the 1960s. It was campaigning for new controls to be imposed on schools and in the process was changing the terms of reference of the debate about educational means and ends.

In the 1975 edition, which was marked by the emergence of Dr Rhodes Boyson as co-editor, the analysis of schooling's failure was given a political dimension. A more populist argument emerged; parental involvement in the work of the schools became a basic element of the programme. This contrasted the concerns and anxieties of parents with the anonymity of the state and insularity of the professionals who worked for it. It exploited the fears of parents who were apprehensive about their children's futures and harnessed the dissatisfaction that was felt by many who saw that schools were unable to develop the abilities and talents their children possessed.

Populist definitions of the purposes of education, and of the most appropriate teaching methods, were invoked against the alleged orthodoxy of progressivism as practised by 'trendy' teachers owing responsibility to no-one outside the school. The demand was for higher standards, to be secured by making teachers more accountable. The central challenge to the legitimacy of schooling – for both school leavers and their parents – was the changing relationship between qualifications and jobs. With rising unemployment it became more difficult to sustain the argument that if they attended, behaved well and worked hard in school, then young people would get access to better job opportunities. This not only affected those incarcerated by the extra year but increasingly blighted the prospects of the achievers, whose qualifications seemed to have less and less value on the labour market.

Under the 1974–9 Labour government this crisis of education resulted in a major attempt to redefine the nature and purposes of schooling. In attempting to explain this transformation, I want to concentrate on the way in which schools were held responsible for the growth of youth unemployment and how this argument created the political space which allowed for a rapid expansion of special unemployment measures organised by the MSC. These were to be rationalised in 1978, to produce the Youth

Opportunities Programme (YOP), which was intended to remedy the faults of the young working class and provide them with a route into jobs.

New definitions of the relationship between education and work-based training were to be explored through the concept of *vocational preparation*. In place of day release for purposes of general education the objective of reform became preoccupied with making young workers more acceptable to employers. Early in 1979, proposals were put forward (DES/DE, 1979) for creating a national system of traineeships which would be extended to all those young workers who received no further education or training at work.

The Great Debate: education and working life

The Great Debate on education, initiated by James Callaghan at Ruskin College in October 1976, marked at the highest political level the end of the phase of educational expansion which had been largely promoted by his own party, and signalled a public redefinition of educational objectives. As the Tories took up the arguments popularised by the Black Paper writers, Callaghan was to 'steal their clothes' and undermine the polemical force of their critique of Labour's educational past. The debate was also a response to more immediate events – the acute economic crisis, escalating unemployment, cuts in public expenditure, and the anticipated fall in pupils as the number of infants started to decline.

This intervention by the Prime Minister represented an attempt to win political support and secure a new educational consensus. It marked a clear shift on the part of the Labour leadership towards policies which would facilitate greater government control of the education system. This was required because it was now assumed that the quality of the labour force was a major problem encountered by industry in the economic crisis. The new educational consensus was to be constructed around a more direct subordination of education to what were perceived to be the needs of the economy. As the subsequent Green Paper made the point:

It is vital to Britain's economic recovery and standard of living that the performance of manufacturing industry is improved and that the whole range of government policies, including education, contribute as much as possible to improving industrial performance and thereby increasing the national wealth (DES, 1977, para. 1.16).

The core theme of education's relationship to economic performance did not attain its prominent position on the agenda of the Great Debate as the result of some natural process. It was defined as a central issue within a wider debate about Britain's economic and social problems. Constructed over a number of years, and articulated in various reports and media, consistent complaints about falling standards, progressive teachers and education's lack of relevance to working life were transformed into a wide-ranging critique of the 1960s developments.

The relationship between reforms in secondary schooling, the characteristics of young workers, and the nature of work discipline were highlighted by the growth in youth unemployment and by the complaints of employers. It was argued that because of developments within schooling, the pattern of educational control and the habits and characteristics it created were actually developing in opposition to the patterns of behaviour required at work. In an early paper, which first outlined the objectives of vocational preparation, the MSC underlined the extent of these changes:

In recent years the social environment in a number of schools, with more emphasis on personal development and less on formal instruction, has been diverging from that still encountered in most work situations, where the need to achieve results in conformity with defined standards and to do so within fixed time limits call for different patterns of behaviour. The contrast is more marked where changes in industrial processes have reduced the scope for individual action and initiative (MSC/TSA, 1975, p. 15).

Accumulating evidence suggested that this contradiction between the demands of employers and the characteristics of young workers was getting worse.

A major survey of employers' reactions to young workers was carried out by the National Youth Employment Council (NYEC) in 1974. Drawing on evidence from a wide variety of bodies, including the CBI and the Institute of Careers Officers, the report concluded that employers were placing increasing emphasis on 'motivation': 'coupled with the fact that a large minority of unemployed young people seem to have attitudes which, whatever their cause or justification, are not acceptable to employers and act as a hindrance to young people in securing jobs' (NYEC, 1974, p. 29). Most employers complained of a change of attitude in young people who were now 'more questioning', 'less likely to respect authority', and 'tend to resent guidance about their appearance' (p. 74).

These perceived changes in the characteristics of young workers, and the implicit criticisms of the education system, were dramatically expressed in the period immediately preceding the Great Debate. In a marked break from postwar tradition, some of the major contributions to this critique of the schools came from representatives of industrial capital. Given prominence in the media, the criticisms of Sir Arnold Weinstock (Managing Director, GEC), Sir John Methven (Director General of the CBI), Sir Arthur Bryant (Head of Wedgwood Pottery), and others, portrayed unaccountable teachers, teaching an irrelevant curriculum to young workers who were poorly motivated, illiterate and innumerate.

By the time of Callaghan's speech, rather than there being an assumed loose fit between school and work, it had become commonly asserted that there was a mismatch. The Prime Minister was concerned that some schools 'may have over-emphasised the importance of preparing boys and girls for their roles in society compared with the need to prepare them for their economic roles'. Teachers were ignorant about the world of work; they were directing their pupils into the wrong subject areas (too much arts and humanities) and prejudicing them against industrial employment. More fundamentally, he echoed complaints from industrialists that young people left school without 'the basic tools to do the job'. He concluded that there was 'no virtue in producing socially well adjusted members of society who are unemployed because they do not have the skills' (quoted in *TES*, 22 October 1976).

The Great Debate had a dual purpose. Not only were the aims and objects of education redefined but, at the same time, the *actual processes* of the education system were being restructured both to achieve those new goals and to fit the new patterns of reduced state expenditure. However, this restructuring of the social relations of schooling was necessarily a long-term process – with contradictions and potential resistances. In the meantime, increasing youth unemployment meant that the need to ensure a disciplined, productive and malleable labour force, or as the MSC's Holland Report (1977) put it, 'building a workforce better adapted to the needs of the 1980s', was too important to be left to the vagaries of the labour market and the streets, or in the hands of an unreformed and now suspect educational apparatus.

There's work to be done? The rise of the MSC and special measures for the unemployed

The MSC was created by the Employment and Training Act 1973, which gave it power to make arrangements for 'assisting people to select, train for, obtain and retain employment, and for assisting employers to obtain suitable employees' (HMSO, 1973, p. 2). It was given two executive arms, the Employment Services Agency (ESA) and the Training Services Agency (TSA), through which it would modernise and rationalise existing provision.

The Commission was given control over its own budget, considerable administrative powers and a broad remit. It became responsible for a wide range of services and insitutions ranging from the ITBs and Skill Centres, through to the Job Centres. It was required to organise any training activities of 'key importance to industries or the national economy'. The actual Commission was made up of an equal number of TUC and employer representatives. These were not delegates, and the individuals involved were expected 'to take decisions without continual reference back' (HMSO, 1973, p. 1).

The apparent powers of the MSC were subordinate to those of the Secretary of State for Employment who set the Commission its targets but was under no obligation to accept any recommendations it might come back with. The Secretary of State was given power to 'direct' the Commission and even 'modify' its functions: the possible duties that the Commission could be asked to perform were openended and allowed space to take up any new 'directions' that the Secretary of State thought suitable. Through the Commission, the government could now effectively – if indirectly – control training and any unemployment measures it chose to introduce.

At the same time that the 1973 Act created greater centralised control, it also weakened the previously autonomous, more directly interventionist, industry-based training agencies. In responding to the pressure of the small firms lobby, the Conservative government replaced the levy grant system by which ITBs raised their funds with a levy-grant exemption system which had the effect of making the Boards far more dependent on direct exchequer support, and less able to intervene in individual employers' training practices.[1]

As unemployment began to creep upwards the MSC (which was formally launched on 1 January 1974) commissioned, as one of its first acts, a study from the Cambridge economist Santosh Mukherjee in order 'to prepare contingency plans against the possibility of unemployment rising to a higher level and for a longer period than we have had since the war' (1974, p. 3). The report's ironic title, 'There's Work to be Done', suggested that even in a context of escalating unemployment there were plenty of tasks waiting to be done.

As Britain's industrial decline accelerated in the mid-1970s, the Conservative, then Labour governments had attempted to alleviate its effects on employment by introducing a series of direct financial subsidies and inducements to employers to salvage and preserve existing jobs. Mukherjee and the MSC now proposed a new kind of programme where the waste of resources represented by the unemployed could be transformed into 'an opportunity' to fulfill otherwise unmet social needs. The ensuing Job Creation Programme (JCP) was introduced in October 1975, with an initial budget of £30 million to create some 15,000 temporary jobs. Special emphasis was given to recruiting the two age groups hardest hit by unemployment – those under twenty and those over fifty.

At the same time, the Department of Employment introduced a Recruitment Subsidy for School Leavers (RSSL), which offered employers £5 a week for six months for recruiting an unemployed school leaver. It was to have mixed effects. It displaced unemployment on to other groups, it failed to benefit those school leavers most affected by unemployment, and it created very few extra jobs (Casson, 1979, p. 111). As a result, it was replaced in October 1976 by a Youth Employment Subsidy (YES), paying £10 a week for *any* young person under twenty who had been unemployed for more than six months. This also encountered problems and the evidence 'suggests that it was no more successful than the RSSL in increasing net employment' (Casson, 1979, p. 111).

There was considerable criticism of the JCP for not reaching the groups most at risk from prolonged unemployment. Contrary to expectations, for example, it ended up employing a high number of unemployed graduates, and not enough of the young long-term unemployed. In September 1976, JCP was supplemented by the creation of a Work Experience Programme (WEP). This scheme provided work experience places for six months for unemployed young people under the age of nineteen, who received an allowance of £16 a week. It was envisaged that the programme would cost £19 million and provide places for 30,000 young people. Early evidence indicated that few WEP schemes had been fully subscribed and, as with JCP, about half the participants left during the course of the programme.

As unemployment stubbornly refused to fall in line with government policy it became evident that these *ad hoc* responses would need to be rationalised. It also seemed that employers were ignoring the exhortations of government to recruit more of the young unemployed. An MSC survey of 13,000 employers found that most of them 'were not prepared to support' government-aided schemes for reducing youth unemployment. Seventy-eight per cent of the employers interviewed said they would not increase their recruitment of young workers. Even if their businesses expanded by 10 per cent they would rely on getting more out of their existing workforce. If they had to increase recruitment most put youth at the bottom of their list of potential recruits (*Observer*, 12 June 1977).

At the same time that Mr Callaghan launched the Great Debate, the MSC published 'Towards a Comprehensive Manpower Policy', its first major policy statement. This spelled out what the Commission understood as its primary objectives. It described what already existed, set out future projections, and made many administrative and programmatic recommendations. It also emphasised that there was an ideological dimension to its activities:

> It is the Commission's task to define and articulate . . . a comprehensive manpower policy . . . It would however be wrong to suppose that there is some magic list of extra manpower measures . . . *The task is rather to create a new attitude to manpower* (1976a, p. 6, my emphasis).

Within its proposals for the future, the MSC identified the vocational preparation of young workers as an issue of particular concern, which had been accentuated by youth unemployment. The policy statement outlined the various youth initiatives it was involved in, including those which it now ran directly for the Department of Employment. The JCP and WEP would come to an end in 1977, and would need to be replaced. It proposed 'ambitiously', that it should have the objective of ensuring: 'that all young people of 16 to 18 years of age who have no job or who are not engaged in further or higher full time education should have the opportunity of training, of participation in a job creation programme or of work experience' (1976, p. 22). A working party was set up in October 1976, chaired by Geoffrey Holland, which reported in May 1977. The proposals were accepted by the Secretary of State for Employment in June, who wanted them to come into effect by April 1978.

The Youth Opportunities Programme (YOP) replaced the older schemes with courses designed to: 'prepare young people for work and different kinds of work experience'. It aimed to provide 130,000 places, to accommodate 234,000 youngsters a year by 1978. The adult unemployed were given their own Special Temporary Employment Programme (STEP),[2] and YOP was restricted to sixteen–eighteen year olds who were to receive an allowance of £18 a week. The programme consisted of Work Preparation courses – from employment induction (two weeks) to Short Training courses (three months); and Work Experience – from six months on employers' premises, to one year in training workshops or community service. It was intended, given the emphasis on placing youngsters in conventional jobs, that work experience with employers would constitute the dominant element of the programme.

What started out as contingency plans were assuming increasing importance in the MSC and transforming its objectives and structure. A further 'Special Programmes' division was added to the already existing Employment Services and Training Divisions. New mechanisms for local delivery were to be created, and the scheme had to be marketed to an ever-growing number of sponsors and potential trainees.

The DES and the MSC

This rapid expansion of MSC programmes soon had a direct impact on the most work-related element of the education sector, the colleges of further education. As apprentices disappeared, they were gradually replaced by a new client group. In evidence to a House of Commons Select Committee in 1976, the Commission emphasised that its leading role in responding to youth unemployment was inevitably changing the nature of what took place in colleges: 'it is a fact that we have been expanding our training activities . . . much more rapidly than education activity has been expanding', and 'much of the initiative in terms of new plans and progress has come from our side of the fence rather than theirs' (HMSO, 1976, p. 400). NATFHE, the college lecturers' union, argued in their evidence that the MSC was now posing 'fundamental issues of educational principle' (p. 238). The Commission was both offering its own solution to the problem of young people and work, and it was bypassing the political relationship between central government and local authorities through which educational change had previously been negotiated.

During the proceedings of the Select Committee it became clear that far from dictating educational policy central government was significantly hamstrung in its activities. Policies had to be translated into practice via the financial and political autonomy of LEAs. This barrier posed acute problems for any national policies. This was especially the case in trying to evolve a coherent and unified response to the education, training and employment provision of the sixteen–eighteen year age group. There was also intense competition between government departments.

The Select Committee concluded that the 'DES and the Department of Employment are in a sense competing for resources and liable to be judged one against the other by result'. The DES was thought to be 'less nimble in a situation where objectives themselves are changing' than in more routine matters, and that the MSC 'has moved at a tempo which DES could not (and indeed should not try to) emulate'. The Committee welcomed the 'enthusiasm displayed by the MSC' (p. xxviii).

It is in this context that we have to see the rise to power of what was called 'manpower-servicedom'. Unfettered by the political and financial constraints on the education sector, and more ideologically in tune with the then government's industrial strategy, the MSC was able to win control over this whole area of institutional expansion.

Despite this success, there was a central ambiguity in the MSC's approach to young people. On the one hand, it was attempting to reform work-based training and extend it to all minimum age school leavers. On the other hand, it was expanding provision for the young unemployed. This distinction made sense only if the assumption that youth unemployment was a cyclical phenomenon could be sustained, and YOP was originally designed as a temporary programme with a five-year life span. However, as youth unemployment continued to grow, it became apparent that it was not merely caused by the recession or poor quality of school leavers but was part of a more fundamental shift in employment patterns. The conclusion increasingly drawn was that the nature of the relationship between minimum age school leavers and the labour market required a permanent change.

Cyclical and structural youth unemployment

During the 1950s and 1960s the average rate of recorded unemployment was 1.5 per cent; between 1971 and 1975 this rose to 3.5 per cent, and this continued to increase under the Labour government until 1977 when unemployment exceeded 1.3 million. There was a slow decline thereafter, but at its lowest point in September 1979 it still exceeded 1.2 million, or 5.1 per cent of the labour force. Job prospects for young people changed dramatically. In the early 1960s the youth unemployment rate was not dissimilar to that of adults, but afterwards the relative position of young workers grew steadily worse (MSC, 1974, p. 28). Between January 1972 and January 1977, for example, overall unemployment increased by 45 per cent, but for those under twenty it had risen by 120 per cent.

Evidence showed that young people were being disproportionately affected by *cyclical* unemployment – due to the recession and other short-term factors, such as young people's propensity to change jobs rapidly; trade union insistence on 'last in first out' and no recruitment policies; and employers' reluctance to take on marginal workers in response to demand because they would be covered by employment protection. Research carried out for the Department of Employment, which reviewed the evidence up to 1976, concluded that 'changes in youth unemployment are closely associated with changes in overall unemployment, but move with a greater amplitude' (Makeham, 1980, p. 235). There were other factors, but it was overall levels of unemployment and the general condition of the local economy which provided 'the major explanation of variations in youth unemployment' (p. 236). The policy implication was that if significant changes in youth unemployment were to be effected, then there needed to be an improvement in the economy as a whole.

However, there were aspects to youth unemployment which could not be explained by cyclical factors (Casson, 1980). There were significant structural causes of youth unemployment. The most obvious was the growth in the number of young people coming on to the labour market; this was expected to increase every year until 1981, when it would total 50,000 more than in 1976. With an anticipated increase in the number of women looking for work, the total labour supply was expected to increase from 25.75 million in 1976 to 26.5 million in 1981. Even if unemployment stabilised, 150,000 *extra* jobs per year would have been required merely to stop it getting worse.

The general decline in the manufacturing sector and the reduction in jobs for unskilled manual workers also undermined the demand for young people, especially those without qualifications. In evidence submitted to the National Youth Employment Council attention was drawn to the closure of large establishments, especially in the traditional industries of coalmining, shipbuilding, steel and railways. The apprenticeship system was collapsing. In engineering and shipbuilding, the number of apprentices almost halved between 1964 and 1974, falling from 140,000 to less than 80,000. In construction, apprenticeships fell from over 129,000 to just over 93,000 (NYEC, 1974, p. 20).

The point was made that the newer industries established were often capital-intensive, or preferred employing older women as part-timers. Revealing their preoccupation with the threat posed by male unemployment this report concluded that 'all over the country firms were improving productivity, and the tea boy, van boy, the messenger boy and the office boy had been weeded out in the process' (NYEC, 1974, pp. 56–7).

A 1976 Department of Employment study, a 'View of Occupational Employment in 1981', showed that whereas up to that point changes in the relative sizes of different industries were the key to changing occupational patterns, it was now technical changes *within* industries which were of increasing significance. Manual workers were subject to two important economic changes. They suffered from *displacement*, where jobs were lost without any prospect of new investment or job creation; but they also lost out from the *creation* of new plants, processes and jobs, which tended to be more capital-intensive and used less manual labour (examples quoted were the docks, railways, gas and telecommunications). For the British Youth Council, 'all of these factors . . . make the plight of the young worker . . . even more severe' (BYC, 1977).

Beyond this absolute decline in the number of jobs available for young people, the 1970s were to witness a change in employers' perceptions of the kind of young workers they were interested in. Traditionally, many young workers had been typified as irresponsible, poorly motivated and quick to change jobs. They found work in casual, blind alley trades, where they were controlled by direct discipline and supervision; they learnt their skills on the job, 'sitting by Nellie'. However, as unemployment increased, and more steady adult workers became available, the balance of costs tilted towards them. The return of married women to the labour market, which had been increased by the recession and by other changes in women's roles, also gave employers access to a supply of stable workers, many of whom were willing to accept part-time work. It seemed that young people and older female workers were competing for similar types of jobs: unskilled light manual or clerical work, predominantly in service industries (Casson, 1980).

Reviewing evidence on employers' recruitment practices in Coventry, Simon Frith concluded in 1977 that:

> Young workers today enter a labour market in which there are fewer and fewer openings for either skilled craftsmen or for unskilled casual labourers. The dominant demand is for generalised, semi skilled labour power. The shifting employment opportunities resulting from the rise of service occupations, technological changes in production, the decline of small firms means, too, shifting modes of labour control. It is in this context that the young compete unequally with experienced adults. They lack commitment and discipline and 'realism'. These are the qualities which schools have 'failed' to instil. These are the qualities which have to be instilled by the State, as it takes on responsibilities for the now lengthy period of transition from school to work (1977b, p. 4).

The political crisis of youth unemployment

The government's response to youth unemployment reflected more than a concern with their numbers. The extent and speed of state intervention was a product of the fears then expressed about the social and political unrest which might follow prolonged unemployment. At a Summit meeting held in London in 1977 the Heads of Western Governments declared their concern about the consequences and promised action. In Britain this apprehension was increased following the Carnival Riots in Notting Hill which in August 1976 were to open up a decade of riot and urban revolt by black British youth.

Attention was drawn to the emergence of black and white youth subcultures which were making sense of life without work, and to the alienation and despair of other young people excluded from the labour market. Youth unemployment itself reflected and recreated broader social inequalities. If you were black, a minimum age unqualified school leaver, or if you lived in certain towns or regions, your chances of obtaining work were more severely curtailed. The British Youth Council reported that between February 1975 and 1976, youth unemployment amongst ethnic minority groups increased by 110 per cent for males and 275 per cent for females: unemployment amongst West Indian youth was twice the national average (BYC, 1977, p. ix).

The MSC 'declared its fear' that the failure of young people to get a job could 'permanently alienate them from the world of work and from society'. Not only did this 'bode ill for the future productivity of the country's potential labour force, but it is also likely to cause high levels of crime and social unrest' (BYC, 1977).

The special employment measures introduced in the mid-1970s depended on more than administrative, financial or logistical considerations. They required a political and ideological realignment of the purposes and defined function of education and training; an amplification of causes and promotion of explanations of the crisis rather than a simple accommodation of its effects. If there was work to be done, that work lay as firmly in the political and ideological terrain as it did in the application of technocratic procedures to the operations of the labour market.

In this sense, a key feature of unemployment amongst the young was that theirs was not politically or ideologically equivalent to unemployment as it affected older groups in the labour market. Their predicament was not susceptible to the same explanations nor vulnerable to the same political critique. Novel explanations of their situation were required. The pursuit of such an explanation saw attention move away from employment towards the changing nature of young people as they emerged on to the labour market. The political crisis of youth unemployment was transformed into an *educational* crisis.

The crisis in education

In the crisis of education of the late 1970s I have emphasised the significance of two key policy developments – the growing involvement of the state in training, epitomised by the creation of the MSC, and the increasing pressure on schools to be responsive to the needs of industry. Both these policies were attempts to grapple with the effects of recession and the collapse of youth employment.

For the government, the most dramatic problem posed by the young workless was that of social and political unrest. The educational problem, however, was employability. The state had to ensure that the young unemployed would be good workers when they did eventually get jobs.

The immediate consequence of youth unemployment was that the transition from school to work now lasted a long time. School leavers no longer got immediate work experience and so schools and training programmes had to become the source of something like the work ethic; the state was to be held responsible for the processes of work socialisation that used to be a normal part of leaving school and getting a job. Some of this new responsibility was to be taken up by the MSC, but schools were also expected to put a new emphasis on vocational preparation.

Substantial changes were to be promoted in schools, designed to create a new relationship between education and work. Two national curriculum projects were set up, one by the CBI, the other by the Schools Council. A host of local developments were initiated including opportunities for teacher secondment to industry and school–industry twinning schemes, where teachers and employers discussed the curriculum and the expansion of work experience. Unconnected with any established academic discipline, and given official blessing by the Great Debate, this growing curricular input was able to bypass the traditional gatekeepers of school knowledge, especially the examination boards (Bates, 1984). The central preoccupation was with inculcating positive social attitudes to industry and the 'wealth-making' process. Indeed, the Schools Council Careers Education and Guidance Project was directly censored; they were told that industry should be presented in a more 'positive' light and that their materials placed too much emphasis on the 'exploitation of young people': the materials were subsequently modifed (Bates, 1984, p. 202).

At issue in all these developments was not the school's usual role in the classification and qualifying of young workers, but a concept of education as a direct preparation for work. Schooling for unemployment was to involve, paradoxically, more efficient education for employment; teachers were expected to instil the work ethic deeply enough for it to survive lengthy periods of non-work. The stress was on a particular kind of realism. Work experience schemes became as important as lessons in Maths and English. All teachers were expected to become employment-conscious, assessing their subjects and their pupils with reference to local job opportunities.

The impact this new orientation had on actual classroom practice is hard to assess. However, the analysis itself had considerable potency, not only in explaining youth unemployment but also in explaining the dissaffection of a large number of school leavers. It suggested that the reluctant stayers should be given a more work-related curriculum in a new exchange, which would both meet their expressed interests and make them more acceptable to employers. For the achievers it suggested that they should be taking courses which were more directly relevant to their future employment rather than dominated by the academic preoccupations of the examination boards. Schools were to become more directly involved in preparing young people for work. The conventional distinction between education and training had been blurred, and was in the process of being redefined.

Before evaluating that process of redefinition, which was to be expressed in the concept of vocational preparation, it is worth exploring in some detail why employers were dissatisfied with young people. What were these needs and requirements they had which schools and young people were failing to meet?

Employers' needs and young workers' attitudes

On examination, it turned out that employers' educational needs were extremely ambiguous. They could in fact be contradictory, confused or simply unknown. Even though it carried out its review of education, training and industrial performance from a single point of view – from 'the "needs" of the world of work' – a 1980 Think Tank report had to conclude that:

> There are quite serious difficulties about interpreting what the needs of industry are . . . These [needs] are far from uniform; there are inconsistencies between what employers say they

want and the values implicit in their selection process; their conception of their needs, present and future, is frequently not explicit and clearly formulated (CPRS, 1980, p. 7).

There are also significant differences between industrial interests and the interests of other employment sectors. The issue is not so much a question of the needs of employers as the logics of capitals. A very different educational logic will attach to businesses with a high ratio of technically or commercially skilled labour – say the banking or telecommunications industries – to businesses which have found a way of exploiting casual labour by for example, a reversion to domestic outwork. The former represents educational requirements at their most advanced, the second an extension of nineteenth-century modes of exploitation which were crudely anti-educational in their effects. Yet both forms coexist in one society and under the same state.

Employers may require certain technical and scientific skills in their labour force at any given time, but the range and pace of innovation in modern industrial processes soon makes specific skills redundant. Employers have an interest in minimising training costs and gearing it to their immediate requirements. For them training needs to be as brief as possible for jobs which are likely to change or disappear in a short space of time. Yet time-serving methods of apprenticeship training preserved trade union organisation and recreated a now unwanted division of labour. As they adapted to international competition and new technologies manufacturing companies were abandoning their traditional ways of recruiting young workers.

Employers now required skilled workers with the flexibility, adaptability and disciplines which would enable them to be quickly trained (and retrained) for specific jobs over relatively short periods of time. There is a real sense in which employers cannot know what *particular* skills they require from their workers' general education and training. Moreover, the actual evidence on the skill requirements of many working class jobs shows that their educational demands are very limited. Blackburn and Mann (1979) in their study of the working class labour market in Peterborough, estimated that 85 per cent of the workers could do 95 per cent of the jobs surveyed. They pointed out that most workers exercised more skill in driving or getting to work than they actually used while there. The experience of women during the world wars, where they were involved in taking over areas of production from men, also demonstrated the ease with which apparently untrained, unprepared or 'weaker' groups can function in the production process without great problems. In reality the skills required across a very wide sector of the labour market are relatively easy to acquire, and are well within the grasp of most workers.

What are articulated as the needs of employers are never a straightforward or unproblematic expression of the needs of the labour process. Individual employers have specific requirements of their workforce, but the translation of these needs into a coherent set of demands on the state, and their resolution in certain policies, is a political process and involves far wider issues than the simple representation of objective problems encountered in workplaces.

Ignorance or knowledge?

On closer examination it turned out that the comments on falling educational standards were inextricably entwined with an argument about attitudes. Not only were school leavers barely literate or numerate, but they also 'don't know what working life is about'. The Holland Report linked employers' complaints about literacy and numeracy with simultaneous comments about poor motivation (MSC, 1977, p. 17). Most employers, it seemed, were looking 'for a greater willingness and a better attitude to work from young people' (MSC, 1977, p. 17). The criticism of schools for producing ignorant workers was simultaneously a criticism of school for producing unwilling workers.

What was at issue here, as Simon Frith (1977) pointed out at the time, was not ignorance but knowledge: what was worrying employers was that their young recruits knew all too well what work was about. Theresa Keil, for example, in her 1976 study of the transition from school to work in Leicestershire, found that 'young people have a wide range of knowledge about their work situations' (p. 49), acquired before starting their jobs from friends, relatives and neighbours. Their biggest area of ignorance was actually about the role of trade unions.

A study of 200 young workers at GEC in Rugby in 1977 found that 'the expectations of many young people that industrial work is boring and repetitive are broadly realistic' (Simon, 1977, p. 64). The research exposed a key contradiction faced in the management of young workers in that if young people had high expectations of their jobs they tended to become disillusioned and dissatisfied with the reality they went on to experience, whereas if they had lower, more realistic expectations they showed little interest in the job at all (Simon, 1977, p. 5).

A comprehensive review of evidence about 'Young People and their Working Environment' was published by the International Labour Organisation (ILO) in 1977. It provided evidence about the conditions which confronted many young people in industry. It drew attention to the lack of congruence between education and work, but emphasised that 'many of the jobs now available in industry are unsuited to most workers' standard of education' (p. 2). The report pointed out that despite their education or training many school leavers found themselves in semi-skilled jobs, usually in a secondary labour market. Their jobs had a catalogue of disadvantages going with them, ranging from low wages and poor career prospects through to their greater exposure to accidents and experience of monotonous or menial jobs. Wage discrimination against young people was common to all countries, especially in industry. Young people were often required to accept the same working conditions and obligations as adults, but were frequently lower paid. As a result 'young people's lives are fraught with insecurity', especially in the case of those who had left home.

Young workers had a catalogue of complaints. What they most disliked about their working environments were 'cold, heat, noise, dirt, incorrect posture, carrying heavy loads, the loneliness and monotony which came from job fragmentation and repetitive tasks, and the lack of independence and responsibility' (p. 9). Poignantly, they found the wish for freedom, interesting work and comfort, was commonest in the youngest workers of all, who had not had time to realise what working life actually involved; 'older workers expect no more than they know they are likely to get' (p. 20).

Not surprisingly they found the swift emergence of an instrumental orientation to the working situation, 'young people are first and foremost realists' and 'model their ambitions . . . on the opportunities given them' (p. 19). In response to work which was devoid of interest, and where their future was uncertain, they tended to concentrate their interests on life outside the workplace. They were interested in work only insofar as it gave them the wage which they valued because it was 'the only means of getting the things that seem to them essential in a consumer society' (p. 19). Although their attitudes to industrial work varied greatly, 'it can safely be said that in almost every country they are predominantly negative' (p. 18).

At the heart of the problem was young people's attitudes to work. In the UK, however, these characteristics were not viewed as a realistic assessment by the young of the possibilities which awaited them, instead they were now defined as a pathology. The young unemployed were ignorant, their attitudes were wrong, they lacked even basic skills, and these characteristics explained why they were unemployed. By 1976, it was to be axiomatic for Sir Richard O'Brien, then chairman of the MSC, to announce that 'the expectations, aptitudes and attitudes of young people are often out of balance with those of employers and the world of work'. This was by now an established fact which all should deplore. Reforming the priorities and practices of schooling was only part of the solution. There was also the problem of what happened to school leavers when they started work.

Day release education and vocational preparation

The absence of systematic training for most young workers had been criticised by the OECD, and had been commented upon unfavourably in many other international comparisons. The National Training Survey in 1975 showed that 30 per cent of those under twenty-five had never received any work-based training. Part-time courses, usually on day release from work, were the most common form of contact with the formal education system, but in 1975–6 only one in five boys in work and one in eighteen girls under nineteen years of age were attending such courses (*Department of Employment Gazette*, November 1980).

The younger the school leaver, the more likely he or she was to enter employment which did not provide significant training.

Although vocational training was concentrated on young people, about a third of all training received by those questioned by the National Training Survey had lasted less than one month, and a further quarter for one month to a year. Young people with no educational qualifications were more likely to receive basic or initial training than further training, to be trained on the job rather than off the job, and to have a shorter duration of training.

Following the achievement of RSLA, many educational groups and the broader labour movement were to renew their demands for better provision for young unskilled workers, but they still stressed educational rather than training provision. In the 1960s it had been anticipated that the ITBs would have been able to extend day release provision to all young workers, but such illusions were shortlived.

The basic problem concerned employers' reluctance to make any provision for the young unskilled. At the same time that the apprenticeship system was contracting it was hardly surprising that employers were less than convinced of the benefits of giving day release to all their young workers. In 1972, the Engineering ITB commented on the naive optimism of the education service in assuming that the Industrial Training Act would result in an expansion of day release. It argued that although day release education may have been a desirable objective, the costs of what was essentially a social programme should be met by government, not by employers (FECDRU, 1980, p. 24). In 1972 the Director of Education and Training at the CBI specifically rejected the accusation that they were failing to create universal day release education:

> it seems fair to ask whether this criticism is directed to the right Act. There is no doubt that the resentment caused in industry by a tendency to seek the achievement of purely educational objectives through the Industrial Training Act and also to use it to seek to shift costs from the educational system to industry, has done a great deal of damage (FECDRU, 1980, p. 24).

It was to transform those educational objectives into terms acceptable to employers that the MSC began to construct the concept of vocational preparation. In its original 1975 discussion document it sketched out the elements of a new relationship between education and training. In deference to employers' priorities it replaced the historical emphasis on general education with a concern about how to make young people more effective and productive workers:

> it seems certain that properly conceived vocational preparation would raise substantially the ability of many of these young workers. More important still, the experience of 'learning to learn' things relevant to work would help them to adapt to change more readily and therefore work more effectively throughout their lives. Proper training for young people would in fact raise the whole potential of the workforce (MSC/TSA, 1975, p. 19).

Proposals were made to modernise apprenticeship training in ways which would prevent skill shortages occurring in the future. The report called for the introduction of development projects aimed at creating new forms of vocational preparation for the unskilled and semi-skilled; and short industrial courses to be provided by ITBs for the young unemployed.

The report echoed many of the themes feeding into the Great Debate. It suggested that those aspects of general school education which had vocational relevance should be extended and, without suggesting actual job training in schools, asked whether 'a directly vocational element should be included in the curriculum' (p. 21). The authors called for an extension of work experience and observation at school, and for a careful examination of 'where the balance should be struck between the responsibilities of secondary education and the role of industrial training' (p. 21).

These arguments provoked a sharp response from the TUC, which was unhappy about the dominance of the employers' perspective which pervaded the discussion document. The General Council rejected the assertion that schools should prepare for work. Young people should be encouraged to have a critical awareness of life at work, but schools must 'give overriding consideration to the personal development of their pupils and must create learning situations that reflect *the varied needs of their pupils not those of industry*' (TUC, 1975c, p. 2, my emphasis).

At a delegate conference, held in November 1975, the TUC

agreed that 'the introduction of day release education for all young workers was perhaps the single greatest priority for the trade union movement in this area' (TUC, 1975a, p. 2). They argued that a single Department of Education *and* Training was necessary to co-ordinate this policy. In their own discussion document on day release the TUC argued that the voluntary route of persuading employers had 'manifestly failed' and it would be 'futile' to pursue it further. They called for legislation to place a statutory requirement on employers to release all their young employees so that they could 'attend courses of their choice according to their individual needs' (1975b, p. 5). They consistently rejected 'vocationalism' in favour of a broad education related to the individual young person's needs:

General education at this stage will necessarily have to have some reference to the occupations and employments in which young workers find themselves, but will be concerned with the personal rather than the vocational development of individual young people. Young workers requiring specifically vocational education to complement sustained occupational training should receive additional release for that purpose (TUC, 1975b, p. 1).

The DES, which could have resisted the pervasive vocationalism of the MSC, was by this time trying to outdo it. Having lost the ideological initiative in the Great Debate and the practical initiative when the Commission had been given the resources to develop programmes for the unemployed, the DES was by now advertising its support for the government's industrial strategy. In its 1978 Annual Report, for example, the DES stressed how in 'its efforts to expand educational opportunity and participation the Department concentrated on the 16 to 18 year old age group, with the aim of producing a much more coherent approach to the central question of giving young people a better start in working life' – a set of objectives directly rivalling the broader objectives of the MSC (quoted by Tapper and Salter, 1981, p. 218).

The pilot programme of unified vocational preparation (UVP) which was introduced in 1976–7 represented a compromise. The programme was jointly administered by the DES and MSC. A constant theme in the government's initial statement on UVP was on the necessity to achieve a 'careful blend', a 'real synthesis of education and training'. By 1979, when the Labour government was proposing a national system of traineeships, the concept of vocational preparation replaced older definitions of education and training:

> The terms 'training' and 'education' have been commonly used as a rough and ready means of distinguishing between learning to perform specific vocational tasks (training) and the general development of knowledge, moral values and understanding required in all walks of life (education). But such definitions have obvious shortcomings . . . The concept of vocational preparation treats the entire process of learning, on and off the job, as a single entity, combining elements of training and education to be conceived and planned as a whole (DES/DE, 1979, p. 10).

While it was possible to create a new perspective which ideologically resolved the tension between education and training, translating that perspective into an employment reality was a different proposition. Employers had already demonstrated their reluctance to take on what they considered to be the social objectives of day release education and the government's original statement on UVP acknowledged that the case was 'still not recognised'. The government conceded that 'the economic gain from improved vocational preparation is not precisely quantifiable', but they appealed to employers' enlightened self-interest and assured them that there was 'no doubt' that vocational preparation would improve young people's attitudes and productivity (DES, 1976, p. 5). The government hoped that a series of pilot programmes would convince employers.

Few employers, however, made efforts to increase provision for their young workers. The MSC's 1978–9 Annual Report records just over 100 schemes with about 3,000 trainees; a year later it records some 250 schemes involving 3,500 trainees. Most of these experiments were sponsored by employers involved with the Distributive and Rubber and Plastics ITBs.

A national system of traineeships

1978 witnessed the emergence of YOP, of pilot UVP schemes, of reforms to the apprenticeship system, and experiments with grants for young people staying on at school. This chaotic pattern of provision was criticised by many organisations because it was leading 'to a plethora of dead-ends' and was characterised by a complete absence of 'common objectives' (RPPITB, 1978, p. 5).

The TUC put considerable pressure on the government. In February 1978, it called for a commission of enquiry to examine provision for the age group and to come back, as a matter of urgency, with comprehensive proposals. It demanded a mandatory system of educational maintenance allowances for all those staying on at schools or colleges, and for the government to commit itself to introducing vocational preparation for all young workers. As an indication of the developing consensus the contrast between vocational preparation and general education disappeared from the TUC's concerns, and it even considered that YOP 'might well provide the foundations of a permanent scheme of work preparation for young people' (*Guardian*, 2 February 1978).

The pressure for some kind of overall policy statement resulted in the publication of a consultative paper just before the 1979 General Election. This outlined proposals for a comprehensive system of traineeships for all sixteen–eighteen year olds starting work. These traineeships would be aimed at the 250,000 or so young people who were entering jobs with no further education or training.

Like apprenticeships, the traineeships would be work-based, but would be shorter, lasting from three–twelve months. They would offer 'an integrated programme of education and training both on and off the job'. Trainees would be given an induction to the job and to industry and working life generally, and taught both job skills and social skills. A certificate recording the content and coverage of the programme would be issued at the completion of the traineeship (DES/DE, 1979).

The scheme was to start on a voluntary basis, with employers being encouraged to participate with training grants. By the time the scheme was in full operation – covering about a third of the target group – the cost would be between £35 and £50 million a year, though this would be 'pump-priming' finance. It was anticipated that eventually the programme would become self-financing with employers meeting the costs themselves.

The period which had been initiated by the Great Debate and which ended with the fall of the Labour government was marked by a transformation of the debate about educational means and ends. As youth unemployment multiplied, and employers complained about the quality of young people, schools were blamed for not preparing their pupils adequately for the world of work. The MSC was able to colonise this area of institutional expansion because of its sensitivity to employers' needs and because it was directly controlled by central government. It evolved a special programme for the young unemployed which was described (by Albert Booth, Labour's Employment Secretary) as a new deal, and was intended to act as a testbed for new forms of work preparation.

By 1979, the Labour government was proposing to introduce a new comprehensive form of provision, its new synthesis of vocational preparation. This would realise the Labour movement's historical demand for day release provision for all young workers and meet employers' complaints about the attitude and willingness of their young recruits. Before these proposals were put into practice, however, they were to be swept aside in the public expenditure cuts initiated by the Conservative Party after their victory in 1979. It seemed that the monetarists in the new government were hostile to the MSC and were against this experiment in social engineering and the expansion in the role of the state it involved.

6

Mrs Thatcher's U-turn? From Youth Opportunities to Youth Training

The election of the first Thatcher government in 1979 marked an abrupt change in British political and economic life. Her political philosophy involved an explicit rejection of the consensus approach of her postwar predecessors. Trade unions were to be put in their place; public expenditure was to be cut by rolling-back the 'nanny' welfare state; and the British economy was to be purged of feather-bedding by a 'short, sharp shock'. Fundamentally, the introduction of monetarist fiscal policies provided the technical rationale for redefining the nature of social and economic priorities – away from maintaining levels of employment towards 'shake outs' of restrictive labour practices and control of the money supply.

Two basic assumptions of MSC practice and ideology disappeared. Its corporate approach and close relationship with the TUC were key features of the quangos which the new government wished to sweep away, and its interventionist strategy contradicted the monetarists' emphasis on freeing market forces. More significantly, under Labour the MSC's unemployment programmes had always been understood as 'special measures', required only until the success of the government's industrial strategy recreated full employment. But now the MSC had to come to terms with a different economic strategy.

In its first eighteen months of office, the new administration presided over what rapidly became described as the deindustrialisation of Britain. The number of people employed in manufacturing industry fell by nearly a million, and for the first time since the war the number of people employed in the service industries declined, by almost a quarter of a million people

131

(Aaronovitch, 1981, p. 7). Between March 1980 and 1981, unemployment increased from 1.41 to 2.38 million and total output fell by 10 per cent. In the first six months of 1980, registered unemployment increased by 40,000 a month, accelerating to over 100,000 a month by the end of the year.

The Conservative government's initial reaction to the MSC was hostile. The Commission was part of a bloated public sector which was seen as strangling the wealth-creating element of the economy. Training was to be returned to market forces, and unemployment would be diminished by tackling the 'why work' syndrome and weeding out the 'scroungers' who were living off state benefits. The immediate response to unemployment was to rationalise the procedures of the Department of Employment, and create a more stringent regime in relation to services for claimants. The 'Rayner' scrutiny of early 1981 was a costcutting exercise, which also introduced fortnightly signing-on and a narrower 'availability for work' test (DE/DHSS, 1981). New fraud squads were created to separate the deserving from the undeserving poor, and cuts in unemployment benefit had the result that most claimants would have to submit to a 'means test' to obtain supplementary benefit (Unemployment Unit, 1982).

The costcutting perspective also dominated early Conservative educational policies. In June 1979, the new administration cut 3.5 per cent off the education budget, severely affecting the school meals service and resulting in an estimated loss of 100,000 teaching, clerical and administrative jobs (*The Teacher*, 6 July 1979). They repealed the Education Act 1976, which had compelled recalcitrant local authorities to produce plans for comprehensive reorganisation. The government, however, remained wary of a direct assault on existing comprehensive schools.

Having satisfied those parents who aspired to place their children in the private sector by introducing an Assisted Places Scheme,[1] the main focus of Conservative policy moved towards increasing differentiation *within* schools and centralising control of the curriculum. The Thatcher administration continued work on defining a core curriculum, and announced its intention of setting national standards which would be monitored and assessed. Schools were to be compelled to publish their results and parents would be given new 'consumer' rights to shop around. Mixed ability teaching would be discouraged and for the 'least able', increasingly defined as 'the bottom 40 per cent', Mark Carlisle, the new Education Secretary, advised that:

> schools should concentrate more closely on relating the last years at school to the world of work to retain the interest of those who find the school atmosphere stifling (*Education*, 20 April 1979).

Traditional academic sixth forms were to be retained, and one of the first casualties of the expenditure cuts was Labour's experimental scheme of educational maintenance allowances for sixteen year olds in full-time education.

These changes had little impact on school leavers' job prospects and as employment levels collapsed, youth unemployment soared. Unemployment amonst under-eighteens reached nearly 20 per cent in January 1981, and amonst eighteen–twenty-five year olds topped 17 per cent. In the face of widespread anxiety from its own supporters the government was to revise its simple faith in the power of market forces. After some initial expenditure cuts there occurred the paradox of an overtly monetarist government devoting more resources to the MSC's special programmes. Indeed, by December 1981 a White Paper was proposing to spend £1 billion on a new Youth Training Scheme (YTS) for all minimum age school leavers. This apparent 'U-turn' was one of the most remarkable features of the employment policies of the first Thatcher government.

The government's apprehension about the political consequences of high unemployment is not enough to explain their conversion. It is vital to understand how the monetarists' perceptions of employment and training priorities were transformed. They shifted from viewing the MSC as an impediment on market forces to using it as a strategic policy instrument for getting changes which under other circumstances would have been vigorously opposed. Throughout its existence, YOP was understood not only as an immediate palliative but also a guide to the future; the controversy and criticism it experienced were to mould the direction in which government and MSC policy moved. In evaluating the transition from YOP to YTS we must assess the impact these schemes had on the experiences of the young unemployed, and understand why they enjoyed the support of the TUC.

From expenditure cuts to the New Training Initiative

In June 1979, the projected budget of the MSC and other special measures for the unemployed was cut by £172 million. In December there was another round of expenditure cuts and the MSC's 1980–1 budget of £850 million was reduced by £150 million. Yet another instalment of expenditure cuts was proposed in February 1980, reducing the MSC's budget to £670 million; it was to remain at that level for the following three years.

In the first revision of the expenditure cuts in 1980, it was decided that in response to an anticipated increase in school leaver unemployment YOP would be increased to cater for 250–260,000 young people. This just about restored the cuts to YOP imposed only seven months earlier. However, every other MSC programme was now threatened and the Commission, with the support of the CBI and the TUC, began publicly to voice its dissent. It argued that at the very time that the need for its services was increasing it was being subjected to severe cutbacks. This developing friction between the Commission and the government was avidly reported in the press. By 1980 the MSC was openly contradicting the government by pointing out that unemployment was likely to reach 2 million by the end of 1981, rather than the 1.65 million which the Treasury had been forecasting. The Commission warned Mr Prior, then Employment Secretary, that they would resist any further cuts in staffing.

Broader political pressures were also building up as the popularity of the government's policies waned. Unemployment amongst under-nineteens was expected to increase from the 254,000 it had reached in January 1979 to over 478,000 by January 1981. In November 1980, in the first indication of a shift in emphasis, the government adjusted its position and proposed a £250 million expansion of the special measures. A new adult scheme – the Community Enterprise Programme (CEP) – was introduced, with 25,000 places, and YOP was to be doubled to accommodate 440,000 young people. The measures were intended, according to Jim Prior, to 'kill the view that this government does not care about unemployment'.

In place of an uncertain future, school leavers were now guaranteed the offer of a YOP place if still unemployed by the Christmas of the year in which they left school. The Employment Secretary also committed the government to working towards the creation of a comprehensive education and training programme:

> We are trying, as resources permit, to work towards the point where every 16 and 17 year old not in education or a job will be assured of vocational preparation lasting as necessary up to his or her 18th birthday.
>
> This is an extremely ambitious programme. It is nothing less than a new deal for the young unemployed (21 November 1980).

As well as expanding YOP, vocational preparation schemes were to be accelerated to cover 20,000 young workers by the end of 1983 – some 10 per cent of the anticipated target group.

The impact that these cuts and expansions had on MSC programmes was substantially to shift its internal priorities. In effect, the expenditure cuts were to fall on the MSC's traditional training and employment services: spending on these was projected to fall by 18 per cent between 1979 and 1984, with a 19 per cent reduction in staff. Special programmes accounted for 29 per cent of the MSC's budget in 1979; by 1981 they amounted to 44 per cent.

The Conservative government had been particularly hostile towards the ITBs, and apart from cutting their expenditure in 1979, the MSC was also asked to conduct major reviews of their activities. The two reviews it produced in 1980 and 1981 found in favour of retaining the ITB network. This was unacceptable and in November 1981 the government announced that it intended to abolish 16 ITBs, that the scope of two more would be reduced, and that ITB operating costs would not be met by the government beyond March 1982. The new Employment and Training Act effectively removed trade unions from any influence by stipulating that even in those sectors which retained ITBs, decisions about the levy on employers to cover costs were to be taken by a majority of employers alone. Something like 100 employer-based voluntary organisations were created in the newly 'liberated' sectors (GLC, 1984).

Conservative policy did not consist of a simple expansion of provision to meet the growing numbers of the young unemployed. It involved an active restructuring of the various institutions and agencies which controlled training provision. Out of cuts and expansions, and the day-to-day pragmatics of political policy-making, coherent strategies were beginning to emerge. Throughout 1980 and 1981 a considerable change took place in the way that the government viewed MSC programmes, and in the way the MSC was establishing its priorities for the future. By May 1981, the MSC was to launch a consultative paper outlining what it described as its New Training Initiative (NTI).

The New Training Initiative

This document described the MSC's interpretation of the training problems which needed to be confronted (1981a). The labour market was in a period of transition. Unskilled manual jobs were declining whereas employment growth was concentrated in the service sector in white collar jobs at technician level and above. This trend was likely to be accelerated as new technologies were introduced across a whole range of service industries. Despite this, training was not regarded by employers as a priority, and was often viewed as a disposable overhead rather than an investment for the future.

Coupled with an inflexible apprenticeship system, which was restricted by age and passed on skills which were likely to be of less relevance in the future, it seemed as if Britain would again lose out to international competition because of the inadequate training and productivity of the workforce.[2] The paper called for a new consensus and national effort. It wanted government, employers, trade unions and the education service to combine forces to combat this deteriorating situation. It set out three objectives for the future:

1. The development of skill training, including apprenticeship, in such a way as to enable young people entering at different

ages and with different educational attainments to acquire agreed standards of skill appropriate to the jobs available and to provide them with a basis for progression through further learning.

2. Movement towards a position where all young people under the age of eighteen have the opportunity either of continuing in full-time education or of entering training or a period of planned work experience combining work related training and education.

3. Opening up widespread opportunities for adults, whether employed, unemployed or returning to work, to acquire, increase or update their skills and knowledge during the course of their working lives.

These admirable objectives have since been reiterated in the first pages of any significant training documents. The level of abstraction and of good intention is designed to invoke consensus – who after all could disagree? It was anticipated that after a consultative process, involving as broad a spectrum of opinion as possible, the Commission would formulate proposals which could be put to the Secretary of State for Employment. What remained ambiguous was the position of the government. How was it that they could be exploring these proposals with such public interest at the same time that they were dismantling the ITBs?

Clues to the thinking that lay behind this apparent change can be found in two Think Tank reports prepared for the Cabinet in 1980 and 1981 – one published, the other confidential. They illuminate the change in perspective that was taking place. It appeared that MSC programmes not only offered a means for being seen to be doing something about unemployment, but could also be used to facilitate other important changes in the expectations and attitudes of young workers.

The Think Tank reports: the hidden agenda

The Central Policy Review Staff (CPRS), nicknamed the 'Think Tank', was made up of a group of experts and policy-makers whose task was to give advice to government about impending policy decisions. By identifying contradictory and uncoordinated policies, and pointing to their consequences, it was expected to improve Cabinet decision-making which was normally dominated by individual departmental perspectives. As their reports often provide a unique insight into the arguments underlying particular government programmes, by examining the two on training it is possible to glimpse the analysis behind many of the changes taking place in MSC activities.

The first, which was published in 1980, discussed the relationship between education, training and industrial performance. The 1981 report, which became publicly available only after it was 'leaked' in the 1983 election campaign, suggested a strategy the state should adopt in responding to mass youth unemployment.

The 1980 report outlined a one-sided critique of traditional definitions of skill and apprenticeship training which the CPRS regarded as 'rigid, conservative and slow to respond to new requirements'. These archaic methods, it pointed out, amounted to 'restrictive' practices, which has as 'much to do with collective bargaining . . . as with . . . intrinsic training needs' (p. 7). The report called for the notion of 'skill' to be replaced by the more appropriate concept of 'competence', as determined by employers in relation to the narrow requirements of the jobs for which they wanted to employ workers. Time-serving should be replaced with training to standards, and the CPRS suggested that the 'modular system' of training, 'where skills and knowledge would be broken down into self-contained units', should be expanded as the model for the future.

UVP experiments were described favourably. The employers involved had found that young people's 'attitudes and adaptability improved' (p. 20). The report argued for 'greater integration between YOP and UVP', and noted that within a context of expenditure cuts 'if activities relevant to economic and industrial needs are to be expanded', then 'some desirable aspects of education and training must be cut back' (p. 4). The Think Tank recommended 'shifting the balance of resources from initial craft apprenticeships towards retraining and the vocational preparation of young people'.

The report also called for the expansion of work experience schemes within schools and, in a significant paragraph, set the agenda for subsequent curricula initiatives for those previously defined as the 'reluctant stayers'. In place of the developmental and social priorities which had dominated the debate around RSLA, the CPRS report was now asking what new educational exchange could be created for working class pupils which would make them more acceptable to employers:

> What appears to have been lacking so far is an attempt to identify what range of skills and knowledge the bottom 40 per cent, say, of the ability range ought to have acquired by the end of their compulsory school education; and what method of assessment is most cost effective in motivating such pupils, testing their achievements, and measuring what employers want to know (CPRS, 1980, p. 50).

It was with respect to unemployed school leavers that the other set of confidential Think Tank papers had been circulated in February 1981, with comments from the No 10 Policy Unit. It appeared that while the government had been publicly playing down the impact of rising unemployment, it was in private anticipating the consequences.

The CPRS report predicted that unemployment would exceed 3 million by 1983 and that 'the prospects for young school leavers are bleak. By the end of 1983 between 50 per cent and 70 per cent of the labour force under 18 might never have had a proper job. The effect in terms of future training, skills, attitudes to work and opportunities for crime and other forms of social disruption is undoubtedly a matter for justifiable concern'.

The proposals outlined contained the genesis of the government's subsequent initiatives. The No 10 Policy Unit agreed with the Think Tank's findings, concluding that 'we must show that we have some political imagination; that we are willing to salvage something – albeit second best – from the sheer waste involved'. The proposals were, however, not to be acknowledged as 'second best', but would have to be 'aggressively marketed', using national TV advertising and the full array of public relations techniques.

The motive for introducing what was then called a 'Training Year' was a long way from the egalitarian rhetoric of the MSC, which promoted its version of a training year as an extension of individual rights. Instead, the 'essence of the proposal is to reduce the size of the labour force by raising to 17 the age of entry to the normal labour market. We estimate that the Training Year would reduce the level of registered unemployment by about 200,000 above the 130,000 reduction resulting from YOP'.

A second advantage of the Training Year would be its impact on youth wages. A £15 a week allowance was suggested which, in time, would make it possible 'to prescribe a lower training wage for those being trained by their employer (including apprentices). This would be a means of achieving a particularly desirable objective – the lowering of the training wage, which is unlikely to be achieved voluntarily'.

The report contained a whole section on 'Action to widen wage differentials between young people and adults'; and proposed radical action – reductions in the level of benefits, removing young people from the jurisdiction of Wages Councils, and a campaign to persuade employers of the virtues of low pay. It outlined proposals for a Young Workers Scheme (YWS), which was advocated by Professor Alan Walters, one of the Prime Minister's chief monetarist advisers. This would involve paying subsidies to employers who paid below certain rates of pay. In the end, the Think Tank rejected the YWS on the grounds that 'youth employment is promoted at the expense of the Government, rather than that of the young people themselves'.

A final suggestion, under 'More Community Work', was aimed at the adult unemployed who, it was suggested, should undertake work for the community for which they would receive a 'small' addition to their unemployment benefit. This proposal was followed by the creation of an Opportunites for Volunteering Scheme (OFV), introduced by the DHSS in 1982 (DHSS, 1981), and by a Voluntary Projects Programme (VPP) organised by the MSC. These relatively small-scale interventions were, however, eclipsed by a bitter argument which followed a proposal outlined in the 1982 Budget to extend the 'voluntary' principle to all MSC provision for the adult long-term unemployed. The voluntary sector and trade union movement regarded this development as unacceptable, but in agreeing to a compromise expansion of provision they accepted the introduction of an explicit low-wage mechanism. The Community Programme, which was to provide 130,000 places, was subsequently restricted on any scheme to a rigid mixture of part-time and full-time jobs which would not produce an average wage in excess of £60 a week.[3]

In the pages of these two 'Think Tank' reports, we can see the emergence of a coherent strategy about restructuring the relationship between the young working class and the labour market. By July, Jim Prior was arguing with the Cabinet for a £1 billion scheme which would provide training for all 16 year old school leavers, remove them from the labour market and withdraw their entitlement to supplementary benefit. It was not at all clear, however, that Mrs Thatcher agreed.

Mrs Thatcher's U-Turn

Early in July, the Chancellor of the Exchequer rebuffed the Prior proposals as too ambitious and costly, requiring large-scale public spending commitments. Mrs Thatcher was also reported as having reservations about the likely impact they would have on broader perceptions of the government's sense of purpose. However, in that week a series of riots, which had been signalled by disturbances in Bristol the previous year, erupted in the inner areas of many of England's major cities. There were complex causes for each incident, but there were nine consecutive nights of rioting, looting and arson in more than 30 towns and cities (*Financial Times*, 13 July 1981). There were more than 4,000 arrests, and over £45 million worth of damage in the areas affected. These predominantly black uprisings could be seen as a response to racism and police harassment, but they were also immediately deployed in broader arguments about economic policy and unemployment. Mr Prior, then arguing for his training package, was to emphasise on 9 July that 'undoubtedly the high level of unemployment is a fruitful breeding ground for the sort of things we are seeing'. The police, local authorities, politicians and other pundits pointed to deteriorating social conditions and prolonged unemployment as primary causes. The media luridly portrayed its fear of the mob, and called for action.

Confronted by this opposition, and in the wake of some damaging by-election results, Mrs Thatcher announced on 27 July a £500 million package of measures. Predictably this was welcomed as an indication of a change of direction, and interpreted by Michael Foot, leader of the opposition, as the first of some necessary 'U-turns'. Unfortunately, the package hardly represented a concession on behalf of the government, as most of his money was to be swallowed up by honouring pledges already made – just keeping the Christmas guarantee, and offering all school leavers a place on YOP, already required extra provision for 100,000 youngsters at a cost of £350 million.

The only significant innovation was the Young Workers' Scheme (YWS), which reflected Mrs Thatcher's conviction that the level of youth wages was one factor causing high youth unemployment. Ignoring the advice of the Think Tank and the opposition of trade unionists, employers were now offered a £15 a week subsidy for any young worker they employed who earned less than £40 a week.[4]

Shortly afterwards Jim Prior was replaced by Norman Tebbit as Employment Secretary in a shift that appeared to signal the full ascendancy of the monetarists over the 'wets' in the Conservative Party.[5] This resulted in a much harder line on trade union reform and in a reaffirmation of the monetarists' financial and economic strategy. Significantly, however, a key element of this strategy now involved a commitment by the government to its own particular version of the NTI. By Christmas a White Paper was promising to invest £1 billion in the creation of a comprehensive, one-year YTS.

This decision to embark on an ambitious and seemingly expensive experiment in social engineering was the end result of two related processes. The economic and wagecutting arguments deployed by the Think Tank gave the NTI an explicitly monetarist rationale; and the inner-city riots had emphasised the necessity for exercising 'political imagination'. As significantly, YOP was itself now encountering acute political difficulties.

By 1981 the consensus on which the MSC operated was starting to fragment. Trade unions were increasingly apprehensive about the abuses and failings of the scheme, and some were to campaign for outright opposition. Significantly, for the first time, an increasing number of young people were refusing to participate, and a stream of complaints about being used as cheap labour began to emerge.

YOP, employers and the youth labour market

YOP was originally defined as an avenue into full-time work, but with the arrival of 2, then 3 million unemployed its credibility was undermined. Not only was it less successful in getting young people into jobs, but the structure and operation of the scheme became subject to a number of powerful criticisms. These developments were to erode public confidence in the scheme and provoke much opposition.

In its first full year, YOP affected one in eight school leavers; by 1982 it was covering one in two. During its five-year existence YOP provided temporary placements for nearly 1.9 million young people. Its gross cost increased from £63 million in 1978–9 to £185 million in 1980–1, and reached £730 million in 1982–3 (Metcalf, 1982, p. 32).

This expansion created a complex structure. Over a quarter of YOP places were provided by local authorities, either directly as employers, or through their colleges and workshops; a further 10 per cent were provided by voluntary organisations. The major part of YOP provision was, however, made up of Work Experience on Employer's Premises (WEEP).[6]

There were some 150,000 WEEP sponsors, predominantly small employers, who would typically provide places for two trainees (Metcalf, 1982, p. 20). By 1981 Youthaid was pointing out that 'the majority of WEEP is concentrated in small, low-paying non-unionised workplaces' (p. 4).

It was precisely this element of the scheme which attracted controversy. Rather than philanthropic employers helping the young unemployed, and providing additional places to their normal workforce, it was increasingly argued that they were using YOP to subsidise their recruitment procedures, if not directly exploiting young trainees as cheap labour. As the programme expanded it became difficult to monitor the scheme effectively, especially as those civil servants expected to police the system were also expected to cultivate the involvement of an ever-growing number of sponsors. The vetting of proposals became more perfunctory and fewer on-site inspections were carried out. A House of Commons Select Committee was told that the 'monitoring of YOP had broken down during 1980–1' and that the MSC had been forced to abandon a comprehensive monitoring system (HMSO, 1983 p. xii). A backlog of 40,000 visits was written off in 1981, but despite redefining their monitoring process and reducing their requirements the backlog was hardly reduced and still amounted to 30,000 visits at the end of October 1982.

Perhaps the most important controversy was the way in which the schemes displaced full-time jobs. In 1981, half the officials of the shopworkers' union, USDAW, claimed that they knew of employers using the scheme as a source of cheap labour (Youthaid, 1981, p. 6). In April of that year the MSC defended themselves against accusations of substitution by pointing to a survey which showed that it occurred in 'only' 30 per cent of WEEP places. In fact, the survey of 302 WEEP sponsors showed that only 30 per cent of those asked had actually admitted that they were breaking MSC guidelines. An earlier survey had shown that most of the jobs displaced would have gone to young people (Network Fact File, 1979).

The real extent to which YOP substituted for, or displaced, proper jobs is difficult to assess, particularly in individual cases.[7] The House of Commons Public Accounts Select Committee, for example, found considerable difficulty in reconciling an admitted substitution rate of 30 per cent with the MSC's evidence that they had closed less than 7 per cent of schemes for substitution (HMSO, 1983, p. 26). The Committee estimated that as a result of 'deadweight, substitution and displacement', between '40,000 and 70,000 jobs enjoying normal pay and conditions may have been lost' (p. 29). They described the MSC's monitoring process as seriously deficient.

As the scheme expanded it also became disproportionately concentrated in certain sectors. In the early period most employers used WEEP to subsidise their recruitment and screening procedures (in effect they used it as a prolonged job interview), but after its expansion amongst small firms it seemed as if employers were able to fill menial jobs with a continual turnover of YOP trainees. The Select Committee observed that while some 30 per cent of approved WEEP places were in the distributive trades and 7 per cent in agriculture, forestry and fishing; these sectors accounted for only 13 per cent and 2 per cent of adult jobs. 'It must be questionable', they concluded, as to whether those industries 'will be able to offer [trainees] subsequent employment in the short term as young people and in the long term as adults' (p. 24).

The success of trainees in obtaining jobs diminished as the scheme expanded. At first the proportion getting jobs or places in education, at over 70 per cent, was high enough to sustain YOP's credibility. Over the next few years, however, the success rate fell dramatically. By mid-1981, only 44 per cent of trainees found jobs or got places in education on leaving the scheme (and this evidence was from a postal survey of only 1 per cent of YOP entrants, less than half of whom replied). In areas of high unemployment, placement rates were even lower.[8]

The structural and cyclical factors eroding youth employment were now being accelerated by a sustained recession. This was having a dramatic impact on the number of jobs and quality of training offered to school leavers. In the manufacturing sector, the number of school leavers obtaining apprenticeships fell from over 236,000 in 1968, to less that 150,000 in 1980. The number of other trainees in manufacturing fell from some 209,000 to 90,000 over the same period. In 1980, the vast majority of school leavers who got jobs received very little training: 35 per cent received no training whatsoever. This collapse of employment was no simple consequence of the free play of market forces. With the evidence that was emerging about substitution and the impact of the recession on employers' recruitment practices, it seemed that YOP actually exacerbated the problem:

> the fact that the gap between youth and adult unemployment rates has widened despite far more resources being devoted to alleviating the former, suggests that British government's solutions may have supplied a classic case of an intended cure aggravating the problem under treatment. State intervention in Britain appears to have accelerated the withdrawal of school-leavers' real jobs as employers have seen the wisdom of obtaining young people's services free of charge and adjusted their recruitment. Simultaneously, work had been transferred from other age-groups thereby ensuring that trainees graduate from schemes to job-starved labour markets (Roberts, 1984, p. 9).

The quality of YOP

Despite the contradictory impact that YOP had on the youth labour market, its creation represented a considerable administrative achievement. It provided places for most unemployed school leavers; and although a decreasing number were able to obtain permanent jobs, YOP helped preserve work habits and motivation and reduced the numbers who would otherwise have been trapped within the vicious circle of long-term unemployment (Roberts, 1984, p. 67).

By 1981, however, young people were becoming increasingly sceptical about the programme. A survey of 'Young People in the 80s' found considerable ambivalence towards YOP. More than 60 per cent of those in jobs, and more than 70 per cent of the young unemployed, felt that YOP provided employers with cheap labour – and more than half of all the young people surveyed did not think YOP helped participants obtain full-time work (DES, 1984, p. 54). In 1980, 11,000 young people refused the offer of a place on YOP, and this refusal rate increased to one in fifteen in 1981 (*TES*, 29 January 1983). In Sheffield, in March 1982, nearly 450 young people – about a quarter of those eligible – refused places on the scheme because they offered 'poor wages and no prospects' (Sheffield Trades Council, 1982, p. 2).

From November 1979 to January 1982, trainees received £23.50 a week even though it was estimated conservatively by the MSC that WEEP trainees added about £12 a week to their sponsor's output (HMSO, 1983, p. 24). Employers freely admitted using trainees as 'an extra pair of hands' (Markall, 1983). Trainees complained about arbitrary disciplinary procedures, conditions at work, and about the level of the allowance.

The subordination of the scheme to the requirements of employers was emphasised by the MSC's insistence of defining young people as trainees on an allowance, rather than young workers on a wage. This excluded young people from the coverage of normal employment, collective bargaining and industrial injuries legislation. This led to real problems in obtaining compensation for injuries at work, and for getting protection against unfair dismissal (Carter and Stewart, 1983). YOP trainees were excluded from the most important sections of the Health and Safety at Work Act 1974, despite an increase in accidents associated with the expansion of the scheme. Between April 1980 and March 1983, seventeen trainees died and over 300 were seriously injured on YOP.[9]

Day release education and YOP

Trainees were entitled to attend off-the-job training for one day a week, but even in 1983 only a third of all YOP participants were offered, and a quarter attended, such courses. Those on WEEP placements were the least likely to be offered day release (Greaves *et al.*, 1982, p. 8); and even among those who took up their option there was a substantial fall-off rate.[10] It seemed that trainees and their employers resisted educational definitions of what they experienced as a temporary work, rather than a training, scheme.

This negative response was fuelled by the material conditions experienced by trainees when they attended colleges, by their antipathy to anything that reminded them of school, and by the assumptions which began to permeate the provision on offer. According to the MSC many of the young unemployed lacked 'some of the basic skills which most of us take for granted' (1976b, p. 1). It developed curricula and schemes to compensate for this and 'help' young people adapt to prevailing conditions at work. One of the central aims of what was called social and life skills training was, according to the original Instructional Guide, 'to adjust trainees to normal working conditions, giving attention to such matters as time-keeping, discipline and the maintenance of satisfactory relations with other trainees and members of staff' (1976b, p. 10).

The assumptions of this new approach were rarely questioned. It offered a convenient exchange for teachers and supervisors inadequately prepared to cope with a new social intake. But Bernard Davies, in a comprehensive defence of what he called *social education*, vigorously questioned whether the fact of unemployment was in itself proof of a need for social and life skills training:

> Does this unemployment really stem merely from personal traits which need to be adjusted or eradicated by such training – from illiteracy or innumeracy, or from laziness, or unpunctuality, or an inability to use the telephone or clock-in at work? Because, during a period of acute economic crisis, they are without a job, have the [young] really forfeited all rights to decide for themselves how they will deal with their unemployment? Must they always, as a price for getting community sympathy or some material support, submit themselves to training programmes aimed at changing their attitudes, their values, their habits, even perhaps their view of themselves? (1979, p. 5).

There may have been young people with various deficiencies in basic skills who had serious learning difficulties, but to suggest that these might be overcome by a dose of work experience, or that they were shared by the major part of a whole new generation of young workers, was a gross distortion which retained some credibility only by constant reiteration. Despite the widespread evidence showing that YOP's growing intake was increasingly *well-qualified*, and that most school leavers were fully prepared culturally and socially to make the transition to work, their unemployment was to be interpreted as a problem of personal inadequacy and skill deficiency (Atkinson *et al.*, 1982).

Moreover, young trainees were not exploited only in the workplace. Ray Newell (head of Occupational Studies at a Liverpool college) showed how the further education sector could use YOP resources to buttress their general provision which had been progressively threatened by expenditure cuts. There were those in colleges genuinely committed to meeting the needs of the young employed, and those who he described as 'empire builders'. For the latter:

> it was discovered that YOP trainees could be accomodated in temporary and often inferior accomodation, possibly segregated from the 'real' students. They were often taught by a much larger proportion of part-time staff, or reluctant full-timers. It has also not been unknown for the materials and equipment supplied to YOP trainees to be inferior to that used by 'normal' students (1982, p. 23).

He also pointed to another ominous development, where the MSC looked at more 'flexible' providers outside the education system and 'turned to less qualified agencies. A whole range of pseudo-training organisations, presenting what could be termed "Mickey Mouse" courses came into being' (Newell, 1982).

YOP and equal opportunites

YOP was proclaimed as offering equal opportunities to all trainees, but it became apparent that the reality was somewhat different. As employers' priorities and recruitment practices began to dominate the programme so it began to take on the divisive character of the labour market. Survey evidence demonstrated the extent of racial and sexual divisions, and test cases confirmed the exclusion of trainees from the Race Relations Act 1976 and Sex Discrimination Act 1975 (Carter and Stewart, 1983, p. 4).

The MSC acknowledged the disproportionate impact of unemployment on black youth but failed to acknowledge, let alone confront, racist practices in the labour market. They explained the concentration of ethnic minority youth on preparatory or remedial courses in terms of their own choices, or as a function of where they lived. The public concern expressed about the plight of black youth was not extended to an examination of the forms of direct and indirect discrimination operating within MSC schemes, nor was there any concerted attempt to tackle the discriminatory practices of employers (Cross, 1985). The MSC also did little to tackle its own image as a 'whites only' employer.

The job prospects of black youth were barely improved by their participation in the programme. Even in 1980, before the full impact of the recession, a survey of YOP entrants found that 40 per cent of West Indian and 30 per cent of Asian youth thought that their participation on YOP would not help their chances of finding a job (Bedeman and Harvey, 1981). By the early 1980s, in many inner cities, over a half of all young blacks were out of work (Roberts, 1984, p. 53).

Evidence also emerged about the extent to which girls still tended to finish up training for women's work and boys for men's jobs (Bedeman and Harvey, 1981, p. 9). In Fife, a report on YOP showed how acute these divisions were. Over 80 per cent of YOP places for girls were in the service sector, and a similar proportion for boys in the manufacturing sector. The report concluded that in effect there were 'two YOPs' in Fife, one for girls and the other for boys (McLeish and Mullin, 1981). By and large YOP placements were divided along traditional lines, boys concentrated in industrial/commercial placements and girls concentrated in placements doing 'typing, general office work and in "caring" activities' (Brelsford, 1983, p. 4). Systematic research showed how young women's choices on YOP were influenced and shaped by staff attitudes and institutional and social processes in ways which tended to circumscribe the effective range of options open to them. It was found that YOP staff frequently betrayed evidence of conscious and unconscious sex discrimination (Brelsford, 1982, p. 31).

Opposition to YOP

1981 witnessed a groundswell of opposition to the schemes. Unions became disenchanted and were less willing to sanction particular programmes: a London trades council argued that 'every major promise that was given by the MSC to the trade union movement has been broken, ignored or manipulated' (Tower Hamlets Trades Council, 1981, p. 11). By September 1981, NUPE had unionised over a thousand trainees in the public sector in its Northern division, and had helped to organise two strikes and a local rally. Right to Work marchers, alongside other socialist and trades union groups, rejected the schemes, especially after the success of the 1981 'People's March for Jobs'. A TUC-sponsored Jobs for Youth campaign attracted national publicity with a Jobs Express train which arrived in London and was followed by a demonstration and a concert. In November 1981, the more militant YOP Trainees Union Rights Campaign was launched by the Labour Party's Young Socialists. Motions were submitted to the annual TUC conference calling for a withdrawal of union co-operation with WEEP schemes, and this growing opposition began to pose important political problems. In discussing the future of special programmes in June 1981, the Commission was informed that 'union support is wavering'. A confidential paper from the Director of Special Programmes argued that:

> A priority must now be to communicate with trade union officers and members at all levels to ensure they understand the objectives of the programmes, the achievements . . . and the situation which will exist if trade unions do not involve themselves in the design and mounting of schemes (SPB, 1981, para. 121).

The 1981 Trades Union Congress went on to accept many of the criticisms of WEEP, but the particular resolutions were eclipsed in a debate about the MSC's NTI. These proposals appeared to secure both the long-standing TUC policy of day release education for all young workers and a new right of access to quality training for unemployed school leavers. The abuses of YOP were admitted, but the focus of attention shifted; after a consultative process, the MSC, voluntary organisations, employers and many trade union officials were to sponsor a concerted campaign to win support for a new training programme – the YTS.

Trade union commitment to the MSC

To explain why the TUC and many individual unions – who were hostile to virtually every other government measure – endorsed these new proposals, we need to grasp the logic behind their involvement with the MSC.

The trade union movement had since the war called for government intervention to impose coherence on the chaotic training arrangements that characterised many sectors of employment. At the same time, the TUC had become involved in a range of corporate organisations which attempted, with varying degrees of success, to modernise the British economy. The high point of this process had been the period of the 'social contract', initiated by the 1974–9 Labour government. In return for wage restraint and a curb on militancy, the TUC and its affiliates were offered legislative concessions and a more direct involvement in the management of the economy.

It was in this context, following the Labour victories in the General Election of 1974, that the MSC developed its work. Its constitution guaranteed union representation, and in contrast to earlier arrangements it was empowered to pursue more vigorous policies for the reform of industrial training. The trade union movement saw within this a major advance, which seemed to be confirmed when the Labour government expanded the direct training services of the MSC, became more heavily involved in supporting the recession-hit apprenticeship system, and developed special programmes for the unemployed.

Ironically, in view of the mounting opposition of some unions, it was actually the TUC which claimed the credit for proposing the original Work Experience Programme (Gregory and Noble, 1982, p. 71). When YOP followed in 1978, the TUC insisted on guarantees that trainees should not be used as cheap labour or as substitutes for other workers. They insisted that 'each scheme must have the support of the appropriate trade unions'.

These guarantees, however, were not enough for some individual unions, such as those in the civil service, who refused to approve WEEP schemes. An important gap emerged between the TUC – which was acting as an executive member of the MSC – and some individual unions who became increasingly critical of YOP's local impact. Pragmatically, most unions adopted policies which attempted to get improvements within the programme, while exerting what pressure they could outside the scheme to secure changes in government policy. Meanwhile, the TUC proclaimed its support for YOP and called on affiliated unions to become more involved.

This support had been threatened by the arrival of the first Thatcher government which was determined to reduce state involvement in these areas. In opposing the original expenditure cuts and policy changes the TUC became more committed, arguing for the MSC's expansion in response to accelerating unemployment. Paradoxically, the TUC was embroiled in an expansion of the special measures at the same time that trade unions were being ousted from the ITBs. In these shifts, the role of trade unions was to be redefined as their influence was eroded. This process was particularly evident at a local level.

Who controlled YOP? Area boards and the civil service

The MSC established a structure of area boards to approve and monitor its special employment measures. They were made up of nominees from the TUC, employers and, to a much smaller degree, the voluntary sector. These boards enabled the MSC to present itself as open and democratic when it actually bypassed established democratic and collective bargaining procedures. Local authorities, for example, had little formal involvement, and could compete for MSC resources only on the same grounds as other sponsors. Many trade union officials and lay members approved schemes without reference to criteria (for instance, rate of pay, job security, discipline, and so on) which they would normally apply in collective bargaining.

Though area boards had formal authority over the scheme, the reality was more complex. In effect, they obscured the ways in which real operational power remained firmly entrenched in the hands of the civil service. The MSC set the agenda, controlled the collection and presentation of data, the monitoring of schemes, the allocation of resources and the construction of policy. In monitoring WEEP schemes, for example, the area boards were effectively bypassed by informal MSC administrative criteria. Dennis Gregory, who was a TUC representative on the Wales Area Board, pointed out:

> From their inception these bodies have only reviewed those individual proposals which offered more than twenty places. This rule, doubtless originally framed with an eye to administrative expediency, has effectively removed from the scrutiny of the area board members the majority of WEEP proposals, and certainly has pre-empted the more dubious ones (e.g., . . . the corner shop, massage parlour or turf accountants), in so far as the trade unions are concerned, from being properly vetted (Gregory and Noble, 1982, p. 80).

Given that two-thirds of the sponsors of WEEP schemes were small private-sector employers with less than ten employees offering one or two YOP places, and that 'as many as 75 per cent of WEEP youngsters' were in non-unionised workplaces, it means that in 1981–2 over 270,000 young people were in placements 'where trade union involvement in approving or monitoring the schemes would have been completely non-existent' (Carter and Stewart, 1983, p. 6).

Even after TUC pressure resulted in a 'tightening-up' of the approval machinery in 1981, the situation did not improve. The MSC continued to approve the vast majority of WEEP schemes without effective trade union involvement (Carter and Stewart, 1981, pp. 6–7).

Colin Ball, one of the civil servants involved in the creation of YOP, described another way in which the MSC was able to exercise political control through administrative means. He (1981) points to a key element in MSC practice, the protection of their central authority by the division of operational responsibility amongst a host of sponsors. Ideologically, because this involved community groups, employers, local authorities, colleges and voluntary organisations, the MSC was able to present itself as involving the whole of the community. In reality, he witnessed a process of divide and rule, where few sponsors could challenge the entrenched power of the bureaucracy.

At grass roots level the MSC became a major source of government funds for any group wishing to respond to the social consequences of mass unemployment. As a direct consequence, educational institutions, voluntary organisations and individual careers became more dependent on MSC funding and the ability of the organisations involved to resist expenditure cuts or harsher government conditions was gradually diminished.

The rise of the MSC into a position of prominence cannot be explained just by pointing to the financial and political autonomies of LEAs, which made them an unpredictable vehicle for responding to youth unemployment. The MSC was an active participant in, as well as a product of, a political struggle about the nature of the state's response to both economic recession and the crisis of mass unemployment. In the prophetic words of Sir Richard O'Brien, then Chairman of the Commission, it offered:

a means whereby we can pursue industrial efficiency and competitiveness without individuals suffering unacceptably, and so becoming casualties of, or perhaps enemies of the society which by failing to give them a chance to work has rejected them (1977).

By the early 1980s, the MSC had become perhaps the key state agency acting to mitigate the political consequences of the return to mass unemployment. The Conservative government had also begun to appreciate, and to use, its strategic importance.

The YTS and youth wages

In December 1981, before the MSC had completed its public consultative process, the recently appointed Employment Secretary (Norman Tebbit) issued a White Paper outlining the government's version of the NTI. This now made public some key elements of the hidden agenda set for training policy in the two Think Tank reports. Shortly afterwards, the Secretary of State took the opportunity of removing the more critical Sir Richard O'Brien as chairman of the Commission, and replaced him with David Young, a close political ally, who was subsequently to be made a Lord, and appointed as Secretary of State for Employment in 1984.

The White Paper supported the broad objectives of NTI, but set them more firmly within the context of the government's overall economic policy. Although it proposed to restructure adult training provision the focus was on young people and the proposed YTS. The government declared its intention of transforming the relationship between working class youth and the labour market.

It was proposed that from September 1983 – ten years after RSLA – unemployed sixteen year old school leavers would lose their entitlement to supplementary benefit. Instead, they would be guaranteed the offer of a place on a new foundation training scheme, which would initially cater for 300,000 trainees. The training would last for a year, with three months off-the-job provision, and trainees would normally be placed with a private employer. To achieve this structural transformation of the youth labour market the government was prepared to invest more than £1 billion in the YTS, and a further £100 million on apprenticeships and vocational preparation. However, this redirection of resources was not just designed to meet the expressed needs of young people for jobs or skills. The new YTS was designed to effect a *qualitative* shift in the nature of vocational training. The government:

> is applying these extra resources to help secure longer term reforms in the quality of training and bring about a change in the attitudes of young people to the value of training and acceptance of relatively lower wages for trainees (HMSO, 1981, p. 13).

Trainees would receive a basic allowance of less than £15 a week. Notwithstanding the empirical weakness of the argument,[11] the reduction of youth wages was now a central plank of government policy and was explicitly connected with the YTS. International comparisons, which had previously focused on the quality of training provision, were now invoked to demonstrate the link between the availability of vocational training and low rates of pay for trainees.

When David Young became chairman of the Commission he brought this argument into the centre of MSC policy-making. He declared that 'youth rates of pay in Britain are far too high', and that the 'young should be a source of cheap labour because they can be trained on the job' (*Observer*, 7 February 1982). Subsequently, he was to invoke comparisons with vocational training in Taiwan, and the Employment Secretary was to suggest that YTS trainees could be used to directly compete with Taiwanese and Korean factories producing components for UK companies (*TES*, 17 September 1982). Early in 1982, the government indicated publicly that it intended removing young workers' pay from protection by Wages Councils.

For the monetarists, the historical market value of youth as cheap labour had been undermined by protective legislation, trade union strength in collective bargaining, and by high rates of supplementary benefit. Tory policy now involved the reconstruction of youth as cheap labour – its cheapness the result not of free collective bargaining, or the free play of market forces, but of direct state intervention and regulation.

The government's strategy of creating a traineeship for all unemployed school leavers had another key, if hidden, element which was concerned with restructuring the relationship of young people with their families. Mass youth unemployment, by delaying the transition to an adult wage, was already having an impact on the structure of the working class family. Government policy now aimed at transforming those patterns of social reproduction. The White Paper assumed that there would be another income, partially subsidising the trainee, who would continue living at home with their family. Invidious comparisons were drawn with the better-off families of young people who continued in full-time education:

> It is accepted that they should continue to be dependent on their parents and that they should not have access to supplementary benefit in their own right. The same will apply to unemployed minimum age school leavers when they are guaranteed a place on this new scheme . . . parents will be expected to provide any necessary financial support to these trainees (HMSO, 1981, p. 9).

This monetarist solution to youth unemployment could not simply be imposed. Not only would the YTS have to win the consent of those who were to be trained, but a whole spectrum of organisations and institutions had to be persuaded to make this new training scheme a material reality (in time, of course, for the approaching General Election of 1983).

The MSC: maintaining the consensus

The proposals outlined in the White Paper provoked substantial opposition. NATFHE, whose members would have to provide the off-the-job provision were immediately hostile; and the Careers Service, who would place young people on the schemes, were also highly critical. Voluntary agencies, youth groups and educational bodies expressed grave reservations. The TUC stated unequivocally that they would not support the scheme unless the allowance was higher and there was no compulsion. For Clare Short, then Director of Youthaid, the future of the programme appeared bleak and uncertain:

If there is not compromise we will see a breakdown of the consensus which has kept alive special programmes for the young unemployed. Such a breakdown might well sweep away the Manpower Services Commission itself which cannot operate without a consensus between CBI and TUC (Short, 1982, p. 2).

It was the MSC, with tacit government approval, which constructed a new consensual approach. However, while its detailed proposals may have involved considerable differences the MSC's response was to be formulated within the costs and constraints outlined in the White Paper.

The Commission had published its own 'Agenda for Action' in December 1981, which contained the results of the consultative process it had launched earlier in the year (1981b). For the MSC's Chief Executive, Geoffrey Holland, the political crisis was to be transformed into a golden opportunity:

We have before us the kind of opportunity which presents itself perhaps only once every 20 years or so – the opportunity to provide a new deal for young people leaving school and entering the world of work. The Government White Paper and the Manpower Services Commission's own 'Agenda for Action', taken together, set the framework within which a new deal could be devised (Holland, 1982, p. 9).

The MSC created a 'high-level' Youth Task Group representing the CBI, TUC and other interests, to report by April 1982 on how to secure this new deal.

In their report, the Task Group completed the policy circle marked by the transition from the JCP to the YTS. They argued, ironically, that their proposals were 'about providing a permanent bridge between school and work'. They were not, it was claimed, 'about youth unemployment' (MSC, 1982). The Task Group proposed the creation of a common 'trainee' status for all young workers, not just the unemployed. Participating employers would be asked to take on an extra three trainees for every two school leavers they normally employed, and they would receive a grant of £1,850 for each of them, out of which they would have to pay a weekly allowance of £25.00.

The YTS would guarantee the offer of a year's broad-based training, including thirteen weeks off-the-job provision, to all minimum age school leavers at a cost of about £1 billion. It redefined the divisions which had characterised YOP. 300,000 trainees were to be placed with employers in Mode A schemes. A further 160,000 trainees would be accommodated in a more expensive mixture of local authority and voluntary provision, called Mode B. This would absorb Training Workshops, Community Projects and a new range of institutions called Information Technology Centres.

Individual schemes were to be approved and monitored by more powerful area manpower boards which were again made up of individuals representing employers and trade unions, with minority representation from the voluntary sector. It was anticipated that YTS would not displace conventional jobs, and that schemes would have the approval of a relevant trade union.

In June 1982, Norman Tebbit offered his self-proclaimed 'olive branch' and accepted the recommendations of the Task Group. He pointed out that the government still thought that school leavers should not be entitled to supplementary benefit, but because of 'the firmly held and clearly expressed views of those on whom the operation of the scheme depends' they had decided not to withdraw such benefits immediately.

Having recreated a corporate consensus around the YTS, the MSC immediately introduced a series of administrative reforms and innovations aimed at making the transition from YOP to the YTS by September 1983. This involved the solution of many complex logistical problems, the creation of new management systems and the crucial development of forms of quality training which would win the assent of the young working class to their new status as trainees.

In effect, the period between 1979 and 1983 had been marked by a working out in practice of new definitions of the rights, opportunities and possibilities for those young people who, despite mass unemployment, still chose to leave school at the earliest possible moment. Under the leadership of the MSC, and in the form of YOP and the YTS, new structural relationships between education, training, employers and young people were explored and created. Internally, a new vocabulary of vocational preparation and social and life skills was to evolve within the programmes, which were presented as meeting the needs of the young unemployed but which, in fact, defined the young as in need of new forms of provision. In this redefinition, young workers were to be effectively separated from the political question of full employment.

Young school leavers were no longer accidental victims of the recession. Having been excluded from the labour market, they were to be redefined as trainees as an aspect of the state's solution to the recession.

7

A New Deal for the Young Working Class? The New Vocationalism and an Employer-led YTS

In their 1983 General Election campaign, and subsequently when creating the two-year YTS, the Conservative Party pointed to their investment in the MSC as evidence of their concern about youth unemployment. On both occasions expensive national publicity campaigns portrayed the YTS as a permanent bridge into work. The impression created was that this training scheme was at the forefront of economic progress, and would prepare all working class school leavers for job opportunities related to new technology, and perhaps even social mobility. Parents, and the general public, were assured that YTS would harness young people's talents and would enable employers to compete more effectively with the UK's international competitors.

The interventions of the MSC can, however, only be partly understood as responses to the skill requirements of international competition, or to the human plight of the unemployed. The Conservatives were also pumping money into the Commission to manage the continuing political crisis of mass unemployment and secure some of their more utilitarian objectives. The YTS, special measures for the unemployed, and the MSC's Adult Training Strategy (ATS),[1] are the product of the supply-side analysis that the monetarists adopted when assessing the labour market of the 1980s. Their vision of an enterprise culture, where a service sector dominated by small firms and new technologies would act as the engine of economic growth and employment creation, pointed to a complete recasting of the education and training system. The YTS was only one – albeit vital – element in this proposed agenda.

Between 1981 and 1985 a variety of training strategies and

plans emerged from government departments. Schools, colleges, polytechnics, universities, skill centres, and adult and youth training, were to be remodelled to service the government's market-led strategy. Radical proposals were outlined to subordinate public education and training provision to the new divisions in the economy brought about by mass unemployment and the impact of the new technologies.

The government had considerable success in imposing its priorities on institutions, but it by no means won unambiguous popular support for its training initiatives, nor did it overcome all sources of opposition or resistance. In particular, the YTS has been bedevilled by two acute contradictions which have persistently undermined its effectiveness. In the first place, young people have obstinately clung to the desire to get jobs, yet as the scheme has expanded youth unemployment has got worse rather than better. For a large cohort of working class school leavers, their time on the scheme has been no more than a prelude to the dole, or to unskilled jobs with little relevance to the training they have received.

In the second place, although YTS has been portrayed as a new right for young people it has, as an employer-led scheme, reduced their already marginal status and rights at work and institutionalised rather than challenged social and economic inequalities. Within a few months of the proposals of the trainee-centred Youth Task Group Report receiving Parliamentary approval, David Young, as chairman of the Commission, was inviting employers to participate in the following terms:

> You now have the opportunity to take on young men or women, train them and let them work for you almost entirely at our expense, and then decide whether or not to employ them (*The Director*, October 1982).

When talking to young people and their parents, however, the government preferred to stress the role that they claimed YTS would play in training for jobs in the new areas of employment growth.

New technologies and service sector employment creation

Government explanations for youth and adult unemployment were not exhausted by blaming the past record of the Labour government, the unrealistic demands of trade unions, world recession, or the inadequate preparation that young people received in schools. By the early 1980s the new technologies based on the silicon chip seemed to be responsible for a revolution in patterns of employment. Yet, at the same time that they were held responsible for causing unemployment, the new technologies were also skilfully used to paint a future of unlimited job opportunities and economic growth. The revolutionary potential of the new technologies became a potent element in the rhetoric of government ministers. In this context, great stress was placed on the fact that all YTS trainees would be getting two weeks' training in information technology; that 5,000 would be getting a year's training in Information Technology Centres; that all schools would be installing microcomputers; and that the MSC was modernising skill training.

However, unlike the overall upward social mobility associated with the upskilling assumption of the 1960s, the Conservatives intended to shape the social and economic inequalities that changes in the labour market were producing. Education and training policies were to be subordinated to this emerging division of labour.

In 1955, 40 per cent of the labour force had been employed in manufacturing industries and 45 per cent in services. By 1984 the proportion in manufacturing had fallen to 26 per cent, while that employed in service industries had increased to 65 per cent. These sectoral shifts were paralleled by occupational ones. In manufacturing there had been a decline in the number of craft and unskilled workers, alongside an increase in demand for new technology-related skills (such as programming), and for multiskilled maintenance workers (Brown and Senker, 1982). The service industries experienced equally complex changes, with the work of typists, cashiers, clerical and shop workers being transformed. Across both sectors, but especially within the electronics industries, crippling shortages of skilled technical and craft workers restricted the development, application and diffusion of microelectronics-based innovations.

The policies of the first Thatcher government accelerated the contraction of manufacturing employment and intensified other fundamental changes in the composition of the labour force. Between June 1973 and June 1983 the numbers employed part time increased by 800,000, while full-time employment fell by 2.5 million. The proportion of part-time workers in the labour force grew from 17 to 23 per cent. Of the 1.8 million vacancies filled by Job Centres in 1984, over 32 per cent were for temporary and 25 per cent were for part-time jobs. A clear trend emerged with employers recruiting peripheral groups of workers rather than hiring conventional full-time employees. These changes were not simply the result of technological innovation, but reflected the shifting balance of power between capital and labour (Massey and Meegan, 1982). In manufacturing in particular, employers rationalised and reorganised their labour requirements by maintaining a diminishing core of skilled and managerial workers – typically enjoying good terms and conditions of employment – supplemented by peripheral workers hired and fired as market demand dictated. These peripheral workers were likely to be employed on temporary contracts, work part time or be employed through subcontractors (Thomas, 1985).

Employment growth was, however, confined to the service sector. Just under 40 per cent of the new part-time jobs created in 1984, for example, were in cleaning, catering, hairdressing and other personal services; 21 per cent were in clerical and 13 per cent were in selling occupations. The jobs were predominantly unskilled, and few part-timers enjoyed security of employment. In 1983, out of 4.1 million part-time women workers, over a third earned less than £34 per week.

For Mrs Thatcher it was the new leisure and service industries which contained most potential for employment growth and, writing in *The Director* in August 1983, she pointed to tourism, the fast food industry, garden centres and theme parks as examples, asserting the value of the 'great industries' to be made in servicing 'other people's pleasures'. The most spectacular example, the fast food industry, was epitomised by the arrival and success of McDonalds (which in the USA employs more people than the steel industry). By 1985 it had established 199 outlets in Britain, employing 15,000 people, mainly part time, over 75 per cent of whom were aged under 21. The success of this industry, one of the few sectors to expand its recruitment of young workers, has been based 'on the systematic exploitation of teenage labour' (Gabriel, 1985, p. 8).

Having wrongly predicted that unemployment would fall after the 1983 General Election, the Conservative Chancellor of the Exchequer was arguing by September 1984 that, if the unemployed wanted to work, then it was these kinds of jobs they would have to accept; in the labour-intensive 'no tech' service industries 'at the lower end of the wage scale'. Market forces, however, were no longer sufficient to create this 'wonder world of short order cooks, waitresses and performing clowns' (Novak, 1985, p. 39). Attention was again paid to what were characterised as 'rigidities' in the labour market, and David Young was promoted to the House of Lords as Secretary of State for Enterprise. The enterprise strategy which evolved required policies designed to weaken the bargaining power of trade unions, reduce labour costs, liberalise employment regulation and protection and stimulate the growth of small businesses. Most dramatically, in 1986 half a million young workers under the age of twenty-one were specifically excluded from the protection of Wages Councils. It was as part of this enterprise strategy that the Conservative government's education and training policies evolved.

Higher education was to be more directly involved in stimulating and developing the practical application of the new technologies, and training was to provide the skilled labour required. Education and training policies were also to focus on jobs at the bottom end of the labour market, especially in the private service sector. In the words of the Chancellor of the Exchequer, in his 'Budget for Jobs' speech in 1985, their policies were designed to create a workforce 'with the right skills: one that is adaptable, reliable, motivated and is prepared to work at wages that employers can afford to pay'.

Within these policies, particular attention was given to the plight of the young working class. In the form of the YTS, the monetarists were creating a social and economic mechanism for integrating early school leavers into the labour market, and they were combining this with a sustained attack on the relative value of youth labour. More generally, though, this enterprise strategy required dramatic changes in the education system. This intensified the pressure for schools, colleges, polytechnics and universities to be directly responsive both to central government spending priorities and to meeting the needs of employers. The MSC was given a key role in forcing through these changes.

The new vocationalism in education

The new ruling elite within the Conservative Party always attached great significance to popular perceptions of the education service. In their self-proclaimed defence of standards and attack on comprehensives and progressive teaching methods they portrayed schools as key examples of all that was wrong with the period of consensus politics. They harnessed parental dissatisfaction with schools and with youth unemployment into a damning critique of the academic insularity of teachers and the irrelevance of much that was taught in schools. In a very effective way, the government and the MSC pointed to real deficiencies and problems in the way that many educational institutions operated, and used these criticisms to justify their own programmes. The central ideological theme around which educational change was orchestrated involved making schools more responsive to employers' and parental needs – which in the government's view of the world became much the same thing. They expressed impatience with the inflexibility of schools and encountered political and educational resistance from local authorities and teachers. This resulted in unprecedented interventions into the curriculum and a struggle to centralise state control of education.

Without consulting the DES or MSC Commissioners, the government launched its Technical and Vocational Education Initiative (TVEI) in November 1982 (Dale, 1985). The TVEI was described initially as a pilot programme aimed at stimulating technical and vocational education for fourteen–eighteen year olds. It was to be administered by the MSC and the courses were to provide a 'variety of skills ranging from manual trades to computer science . . . leading to recognised qualifications'. Within the educational world the initial response was one of confusion, disbelief and opposition; but in a context of expenditure cuts and with the MSC threatening to establish its own technical institutes, many LEAs submitted bids for the available resources. What started as a 'pilot' programme was quickly increased and, apart from some Labour authorities who reject the scheme, by 1986 most LEAs will be directly involved in TVEI.

Some 103 TVEI projects have been established and each will eventually cater for 1,000 young people. About 10 per cent of all secondary schools will be involved. TVEI approaches are to be generalised to all schools, but without the same level of funding. In 1985 the MSC was given a direct role in in-service teacher training so as 'to increase the number of teachers equipped to disseminate the successful elements of the TVEI and thus reinforce the Government's broad objectives for the school curriculum' (HMSO, 1985c, p. 6).

The TVEI represents only one strand in the new vocationalism. Early in 1982, for example, the DES announced the creation of its own specific development projects for lower-attaining pupils – the bottom 40 per cent. These were set up in thirteen LEAs and were preoccupied with out-of-school work experience and job preparation. Many of the curricula and examination changes prompted by RSLA and the Great Debate were caught up in and influenced by these new initiatives. In practice, there has been a complex interplay between more liberal versions of vocational preparation and the more technocratic employer-dominated perspectives pursued by central government.

Teachers and local authorities retained considerable control over the curriculum, and it seems that the additional resources were often used imaginatively and in the interests of the (usually male) pupils selected to benefit from them. What was clear, however, was that TVEI exacerbated curricula divisions by giving some selected pupils, subjects and schools far greater access to scarce educational resources (Chitty, 1986).

Central government initiatives, through their priorities and funding, were the vehicle for imposing a new agenda on comprehensive schools. The MSC and the Department of Trade and Industry (DTI) selectively funded projects in a way that retained central control but exploited locally-generated curricula and new teaching approaches. The concern with new technologies and relevance to employers carried within it a profound change:

in which the liberal humanist goals of social justice and personal development have been severely attenuated in favour of those emphasising vocational preparation and a technically-oriented curriculum, especially for 'low attainers'. The pressure on education to deliver technical competences, skills and respect for workplace disciplines has, outwardly at least, transformed professional concerns and vocabularies . . . [This] has led to the clear prescription for education to service the technological future rather than to engage critically with it (Esland and Cathcart, 1984, p. 5).

The new vocationalism displaced equal opportunity as the *central* reference point for educational change. The guiding philosophy behind educational policy became the creation of appropriate curricula for different groups of pupils, to be derived mainly from their assumed destination in the division of labour. It is not that schools are simply expected to prepare their pupils to get jobs, but they are now required to make them cognitively and attitudinally better potential employees.

There has been opposition to this process from both teachers and local authorities, but the success of the new vocationalism reflects the extent to which comprehensive reform and RSLA failed to meet the educational needs of an important group of working class pupils. Even where comprehensives were most successful, in helping more pupils obtain qualifications, youth unemployment undermined their value in the labour market and undercut the old educational exchange (Payne, 1984).

In this context, the reappraisal of the nature, purposes and content of education was accelerated by the dilemmas of teachers who, confronted by youth unemployment, realised that an academic curriculum, however presented, had little to offer. In place of traditional subjects, the new vocationalism responded to the interest of working class children and their parents in the world of work. It also offered teachers the attractive possibility of being able to overcome the difficulties they had with disenchanted children in school at the same time as meeting the restricted criteria of funding bodies such as the MSC (Grimshaw and Pratt, 1984).

Expenditure cuts and the control of education

The new vocationalism was itself only one element of the changes which were to transform educational politics in the 1980s. Above all, the anxiety expressed by the government about low achievers and academic standards should be seen in a context where nursery provision was contracting and much remedial and specialist work was abandoned because of expenditure cuts. For five consecutive years, HMI warned that educational standards were at risk because of 'the cumulative effects of financial restraint': in 1984 they found that only eleven out of 97 LEAs were providing satisfactory resources for their schools. The neglect of school building stock was not only storing up enormous problems for the future but was 'seriously affecting the quality of work and achievement of many pupils and providing a grim environment for them and their teachers' (DES, 1985).

Patterns of economic inequality were amplified by schools' increasing reliance on parental contributions for books and equipment (NCPTA, 1985). Another kind of hidden transformation of the teaching methods and curriculum of many comprehensive schools took place as a consequence of falling pupils rolls, cuts in staff, equipment and ancillary services. These trends are likely to be reinforced by future planned expenditure cuts.[2] Considerable evidence suggests that these cuts have themselves exacerbated the very deficiencies in information technology skills that the government claimed it was solving (Finn, 1984a, Chapter 7).

The DES played a secondary role in the direct promotion of the new vocationalism, but it embarked on a more general intensification of central government control across the whole range of the education service in England and Wales.[3] A White paper, published in 1985, set out the government's agenda for producing what it called 'Better Schools'. This outlined in some detail what children should learn, how it should be organised and how it should be assessed. The secret garden of the curriculum was now openly cultivated, and the Secretary of State added proposals to reform the examination system, introduce teacher appraisal, and give parents enhanced powers on school governing bodies (HMSO, 1985b).

A sustained crisis erupted in the relationships between the groups upon which the 1944 Education Act relied. Teachers' representation on curricula bodies was summarily ended in 1982.[4] Their living standards fell, their material conditions of work deteriorated, and they were blamed for many of the problems experienced by school leavers. Increasingly authoritarian attempts were made to control their activities and change their conditions of service. The result was a protracted period of industrial unrest in the schools and a near breakdown in the relationship between teachers' unions and the government. The 1985–6 teachers' dispute resulted in a permanent change in the behaviour of teachers and in their role and attitudes in schools.

Local authorities saw key elements of their autonomy disappearing. Central government expenditure cuts and rate capping undermined the ability of many authorities to plan effectively, or invest the resources necessary for implementing progressive educational strategies, and LEAs were bypassed by government initiatives. The MSC was given control of TVEI, and in February 1984 it was unilaterally announced that local authority expenditure would be reduced by transferring control of a quarter of all non-advanced further education to the MSC.

By 1986, senior Conservative education ministers were suggesting that the conflicts and problems within the education service required a re-examination of the relationship between government, the local authorities and teachers. The radical right called for a free market approach, where parents would be given vouchers to spend at schools of their own choice. The government, however, seemed more intent on centralising control over education by giving the Secretary of State direct control of between 10 and 15 per cent of the education budget, and by binding teachers contractually to specific duties (*Financial Times*, 3 March 1986). It was also suggested that a unified Ministry of Education and Training might be created under the leadership of Lord Young who, as Secretary of State for Employment, had already asked the Commission to become more directly involved in planning higher education, to begin to exercise more direct financial and quality control in the educational establishments in which it had a stake, and to make a 'progressively more effective contribution to curriculum change' (*TES*, 7 February 1986).

The Conservatives did experience political setbacks, especially around local and national attempts to reintroduce grammar schools.[5] Their response was to maintain academic hierarchies and increase differentiation within comprehensive schools. In 'Better Schools', the government apparently accepted that pupils should follow a 'broad and balanced' curriculum up to the age of sixteen, but it was to be one which was 'suitably differentiated' to ensure 'that each pupil's programme adequately prepares him for employment' (HMSO, 1985b, p. 23).

Within this framework, reforms which had been working through the system for many years, and which in their turn will set the agenda for educational practice in the 1990s, were reinterpreted in divisive ways. Most significantly, amidst the chaos surrounding its introduction, the common examination for sixteen year olds, the GCSE, will *reinforce* rather than challenge academic hierarchies by retaining clearly differentiated levels of examination within a formally unified system.

In complex ways, education was being restructured to legitimise traditional social divisions, instil the spirit of enterprise, and resocialise working class youth so that it was more acceptable to employers. Brian Simon has pointed out that the preoccupation of Mrs Thatcher's government with educational structure and content reflected its concern to use the ideological and practical role of schooling to reproduce in a stable way new class and social relationships. He quotes, for example, an internal DES memorandum warning that if 'young people drop off the education production line and cannot find work at all, or work which meets their abilities and expectations, then we are only creating frustration with perhaps disturbing social consequences'. The memorandum concluded that people 'must be educated once more to know their place' (1984, p. 21).

The pattern emerging has similarities with the tripartite system. The independent sector has been strengthened and subsidised through the Assisted Places Scheme, which by 1985 was supporting 20,000 pupils. Within the state sector, an academic elite will be separated from a middle tier doing something like TVEI; and the bottom 40 per cent will be suitably differentiated and offered a curriculum which no doubt will more adequately prepare them for employment, or more realistically for places in the two-year YTS.

By 1986, Bryan Nicholson, Lord Young's successor as chairman of the MSC, was berating teachers for their insularity and for their ill-informed opinions and prejudices about the two-year YTS. He spelled out just how far the government intended the MSC to control recruitment to full-time work, and warned that schools were now failing in their responsibilities if they did not adjust to and embrace this new reality:

> Employers will no longer recruit school leavers directly into their workforce, and the school leavers themselves will expect a period of training just as they expect a period of schooling (*The Teacher*, 20 January, 1986).

Many teachers, pupils and parents were to remain sceptical, however, about a scheme which was proclaimed as meeting their needs, yet seemed ever more subordinated to the requirements of employers.

A two-year, employer-led YTS

Government ministers were quick to claim that the one-year YTS had been a great success, with most trainees enjoying the experience and getting jobs at the end of it. The reality for many young people was nothing like that. Moreover, when it became evident that economic recovery was unlikely to reduce levels of unemployment, pressure increased for additional measures to be implemented to manage the continuing crisis of youth unemployment. Authoritative reports continued to criticise the inadequate response of the British vocational education and training system to the pace and demands of technological change. The most significant document, called 'Competence and Competition' (NEDC/MSC, 1984), was produced for the NEDC and the MSC and illustrated the comparative strength of the systems which existed in Germany, Japan and USA. Pressure increased for all sixteen and seventeen year olds to be removed from the conventional labour market by placing them in some form of post-school training.

This concern was seized on by Geoffrey Holland, the MSC's architect of both YOP and YTS, and in a keynote speech (1984b) he called for yet another 'new deal'. This would offer young workers a recognised 'trainee status', but it would have to be responsive to the priorities of a market economy. Trainees, in other words, had to be packaged in ways that would make them attractive to potential employers. In Geoffrey Holland's words, the two-year YTS was not about 'taking young people out of the labour market'; rather, it designed to put 'them in on terms which secure their entry'. One consequence was that, contrary to the original intention, it was decided that the agreement which set out a YTS trainee's conditions and training programme would not be legally binding, and would not extend any contractual rights to the young person.

The two-year YTS was launched formally in January 1986, and took on its first recruits the following April, providing places for all sixteen and seventeen year old school leavers. By 1987 about six out of ten of all the sixteen and seventeen year old age group could be participating in the two-year YTS.

Remarkably, some five years on, the two-year scheme is projected to cost only slightly more than the £1 billion that was originally budgeted for the one-year YTS. In the first year, trainees are paid £27.30 a week, and are entitled to thirteen weeks off-the-job training. In the second year, the allowance is £35 a week with seven weeks off-the-job training. The Commission intends that eventually the transition to the higher rate of pay 'should be related to the individual's achievement'. The scheme will be operated through MSC-approved training organisations, and at the end of two years will provide a certificate and opportunity to obtain a recognised vocational qualification.

The public cost of the extended YTS presupposes that employers will make a much greater financial contribution toward its costs. In turn, it was assumed that employers would recover this cost from the economic value produced by the work of their trainees. The large group of YTS providers who subcontract their work experience were expected to rent out their trainees.

The division between Mode A and B has been abolished. In place of Mode B a smaller number of premium places have been provided to bolster provision for young people with special needs or in areas of high unemployment. In effect, the more expensive, innovative and trainee-centred provision, which had originally been intended to provide a third of YTS places, was more than halved in under three years. The government justified these reductions because they wanted YTS to be more directly employer-led.

However, while the scheme is characterised as employer-led, this does not mean that it is directly organised by employers. A key change made in the transition from YOP to YTS involved the introduction of *managing agencies*. Instead of dealing directly with a multitude of individual employers the MSC now subcontracts most of its training programmes to intermediary agencies. It is these which have the responsibility for delivering quality and making arrangements with individual workplaces.

In 1984–5, some 4,200 managing agents were involved in delivering YTS, and they used in excess of 100,000 different workplaces. Just over half of the YTS providers surveyed by the MSC kept their trainees within their own workplaces; over a quarter subcontracted all their trainees to other employers. At any one time nearly 60 per cent of trainees were receiving work experience from external employers. This was usually provided in relatively small workplaces, with over half having less than ten employees at the sampled workplace. Nearly all these establishments were in the private sector (*Department of Employment Gazette*, August 1985).

Private training agencies were to proliferate. The survey of providers established that 14 per cent aimed to make a profit out of training. Of more than 100,000 employer-based places in major urban areas nearly 30 per cent were controlled by private agencies. In the first phase of YTS some of them – such as KBS and Computotech – were to collapse spectacularly, leaving trainees adrift and the MSC out of pocket (NATFHE, 1984; TURC, 1986).

Alongside these private agencies, a multiplicity of local authority consortiums, voluntary-sector sponsors, and employer-dominated training organisations mushroomed into existence. The arrangements for monitoring individual workplaces became even less effective than they were under YOP. Drawing on the experience of 'agents, sponsors and trade union representatives', independent research carried out by Incomes Data Services concluded that the 'MSC is in no real position to police the scheme thoroughly' and that its 'staff have neither experience nor time to monitor schemes adequately' (IDS, 1984, p. 1).

Area Manpower Boards (AMBs), the independent watchdogs which were supposed to monitor and control the scheme, were less effective than anticipated. Training schemes negotiated nationally by the Large Companies Unit (a division of the MSC), which account for many employer-based schemes, are not subject to the approval or limited scrutiny of AMBs. Further, when visiting schemes, Board members have to be chaperoned and give notice of their intentions. AMBs make decisions on the value of schemes on the basis of one-page summaries provided by MSC officers. In many areas it seems that sponsors need only declare that there is no appropriate or recognised trade union for approval and schemes can proceed unhindered. AMBs have been overruled by the MSC when they tried to prevent the involvement of private training agencies or resist cutbacks in various types of training provision. At best, the role of the AMB has become advisory, approving plans and programmes submitted by MSC officials; at worst, they are a rubber stamp (Youthaid, 1985b; Randall, 1986).

This reduction in scrutiny and control enabled YTS to develop in ways which undercut the assumptions upon which many organisations had given their original approval to the scheme. Originally, the Youth Task Group had envisaged that YTS would cover both employed and unemployed school leavers, but the number of employed trainees anticipated on the scheme was quickly revised downwards from an original one-third of the total to some 5 per cent. Some school leavers continue to obtain jobs outside of YTS, but other employers simply substituted youth trainees for young workers. The MSC's survey of YTS providers found that nearly a quarter of trainees were occupying jobs for young people which had been brought within the scope of YTS, and 7 per cent had been taken on in preference to older workers (*Department of Employment Gazette*, August 1985).

YTS also became an obvious way of screening young people for recruitment. Over half the managing agents, and nearly three-quarters of the other work-experience providers said they were using the scheme in this way. At the time of the survey, however, managing agents anticipated taking on only about 15 per cent of their trainees, and work-experience providers were expecting to take on a quarter. In return for providing rudimentary training employers were able to pick and choose their recruits from a pool of cheap trainees.

An aristocracy of YTS was created in those industries where the scheme was integrated into the declining apprenticeship system. Nearly half of sixteen year old apprentices and other long-term trainees were brought within the scope of YTS. The one in five trainees in employer-based schemes who were classified as apprentices or long-term trainees typically enjoyed better wages (£41 per week) and better quality training, spending on average 32 weeks in off-the-job provision. These trainees were employed mainly in construction and engineering, and were in the first year of a three- or four-year programme (*Department of Employment Gazette*, August 1985). Overall, however, YTS had little impact on the alarming cutback in apprenticeship training (Ryan, 1984).

A dual system within a single training scheme emerged within the first phase of YTS. The majority of trainees were given vocational preparation, which introduced them to some of the experiences and disciplines they would previously have received as young workers. A minority enjoyed the benefits of vocational training along the lines of a conventional apprenticeship. This hierarchy is unlikely to be challenged within the terms of the two-year YTS.

Quality and content of YTS

The early legitimacy of MSC schemes rested on their capacity to provide routes into employment for school leavers. However, as youth unemployment escalated, and as fewer trainees obtained jobs, there was a significant change from defining the young as victims of the recession to locating their employment problem within the inappropriate capacities and aptitudes they were bringing to the labour market. The public emphasis shifted towards the quality of experience offered by YOP. In June 1981, when discussing the future of special programmes, the Commission acknowledged that fewer than half of trainees were then getting jobs, and as a consequence they had 'to find another rationale and the only available rationale is that YOP offers a chance to do something worthwhile'.

As with the long-awaited recovery in employment, however, 'quality' tended to be something to be attained in the near future rather than delivered in the immediate present. Nevertheless, the debate about the quality and content of the training on YTS is now at the core of the programme's public justification.

Crude and educationally naive to begin with, the transition to

YTS was marked by the elaboration of sophisticated curriculum models. These were designed to improve the quality of the scheme by providing an educational and symbolic exchange appropriate to the new social condition of a large number of young school leavers. There was no obvious consensus about what this content should be, and important differences emerged between approaches which had their roots in either education or training. These differences were expressed most clearly in the work of the Further Education Unit (FEU) and the Institute for Manpower Studies (IMS) (Seale, 1984).

Established in 1977 as a DES watchdog around developments in the further education curriculum, the FEU responded to the MSC's developing influence by elaborating curriculum models thought appropriate for the new groups of young people coming into contact with further education. In a comprehensive statement on 'Vocational Preparation' (1981), the FEU set out to construct for the first time 'a coherent curriculum framework alleviating the somewhat divisive response and unequal provision' that characterised college, YOP and UVP courses because, it argued, 'the vocational preparation needs of young people are more or less the same whether they are college-based, unemployed or employed' (accompanying letter, FECDRU, 1981).

In contrast with traditional students whose courses were dominated by the requirements of higher education and 'claimed job demands', this new group – estimated to equal half the sixteen year old age group – required 'a programme based as much on the self-perceived needs of each young person as on requirements defined by professional adults' (p. 17). It would be difficult to derive a curriculum from the jobs they were likely to end up in because of their low skill content. The consequence was the suggestion that these young people now had a very different set of individual social and developmental needs which required a new form of provision.

The proposed curriculum was made up of a series of educational transactions where the trainees would be persuaded to recognise their developmental needs and commit themselves to a programme of vocational preparation. The emphasis was on negotiation and relevance, and on getting young people to assess their own progress:

> Vocational preparation should not be seen as a continuation of
> the normal school experience which inevitably appears to many
> young people as custodial; it must appear as a participatory
> venture requiring responsibility and self-criticism; hopefully
> resulting in increased motivation (FECDRU, 1981, p. 21).

Out of this negotiation would emerge a learning contract,
describing the order and nature of the learning experiences that
would be provided.

At the same time that this learning contract and new exchange
would win the consent of the trainee, this process would also
redefine the role of the 'educators', the lecturers, administrators
and trainers involved, and define the function of the educational
institutions affected. The FEU elaborated one potential way in
which different groups of working class youth who had previously
emerged directly from school on to the labour market could be
absorbed within new forms of education and training. Young
workers could be incorporated into an educational exchange by
sophisticated processes of negotiation and counselling, guidance
and assessment.

The MSC colonised some elements of the FEU approach, but
the stress on personal development and social education was too
reminiscent of the liberal humanism which the government and
elements of the Commission were in the business of changing.
From their standpoint schools offered little of any value to
minimum age school leavers, in fact defined many of them as
failures, and further education colleges in particular were inflexible
and had made an ineffective contribution to YOP. Subsequently,
the MSC was given control of over a quarter of all non-advanced
further education, and the FEU was to find itself increasingly
marginalised, suffering major reductions in its own planned
expenditure. Further education colleges now provide barely half
the off-the-job training for YTS trainees.

The MSC turned instead to the world of work and to the IMS
to develop guidelines on YTS course content, and it invested
considerable resources in a number of work-based projects for
developing teaching materials. The FEU's liberal concern with
trainee's rights to negotiate his or her own programme of work
was given far less priority in the MSC's own thinking, which was

concerned mainly with ensuring that trainees 'understand the purpose of the scheme and their role in it' (Seale, 1984).

The IMS approach attempted to reconcile the needs of employers, who generally wanted trainees to carry out specific tasks, with those of young people who were likely to end up working for someone else or, indeed, be confronted by unemployment. In 'Training for Skill Ownership' (1983), the IMS argued that the key purpose of YTS training should be to ensure that trainees 'own' skills, which could be transferred from one work situation to another. The credibility of the scheme they claimed would rest on this exchange, and the young trainee should be offered a combination of basic and occupationally specific skills.

These latter skills could be grouped into occupational training families (OTFs) which shared common features. Each OTF had distinct learning objectives, but these 'do not incorporate job elements specific to the task or the employer, or specific technical skills'. Instead, 'the focus is on effective and appropriate performance rather than on skills' (Farley, 1983, p. 11). Appropriate performance would be judged by attaining a certain minimum standard which 'is defined as one that is acceptable to the employer in that particular job' (Farley, 1983, p. 12).

All one-year YTS schemes were expected to contain broad-based training across one or more OTFs, eight design elements, and six learning opportunities.[6] Penny Woolcock delivered a withering assessment of the guidelines issued by the MSC:

the bureaucrats have retreated to the world they like best and elaborately administered what was already available to a baffling extent. Instead of making sense of a botched up system and developing its positive aspects they decided to engage in a legitimising exercise by placing a grid over YOP which itemises in ludicrous detail the boring, menial tasks expected of trainees along with many of the daily routines and social intercourse we all engage in as a matter of course anyway (1983).

The harsh realities of low-level skill training, which was intended to socialise young workers to adapt to employers' needs, was obscured behind the complex classifications and concepts first outlined in 'Training for Skill Ownership'. In reality, the concepts developed were difficult to translate into practical curricula, and the whole approach was resisted by employers and young people alike. Employers preferred to train young people in skills which could be used immediately. According to an IDS survey many schemes were 'not broad based but specifically linked to the needs of the industry or company involved – in some cases to the complete exclusion of sections of the MSCs proposals' (1983, p. 2).

An HMI survey of further education courses for YTS trainees found that 'attempts to provide a broadly based introduction to a family of jobs were not readily acceptable' (DES, 1984, p. 6). The best results and most motivated students were found in apprentice-type courses which provided narrower, more specific training. Another HMI survey in Wales found that 'for the most part' trainees were 'anxious to equip themselves as early as possible with a range of saleable job skills which will enable them to obtain jobs' (Welsh Office, 1984, p. 5). Many colleges reported acute behavioural problems with YTS trainees who believed 'college' was the same as 'school' and were thus unwilling to co-operate or participate. Some tutors were 'dogged by discipline and behavioural problems if not consistent absenteeism' (NFER, 1984, p. 25). Even in YTS groups which were sitting for external exams there were motivational problems because trainees were sceptical about the value the qualifications would have in enabling them to obtain work.

The MSC had to respond to these realities, and the two-year scheme will provide some specific vocational training in the second year. The 'outcomes' of the two-year scheme will include:

1. Competence in a job and/or a range of occupational skills.
2. Competence in a range of transferable core skills.
3. Ability to transfer skills and knowledge to new situations.
4. Personal effectiveness.

Trainees will be given the 'opportunity' to take a recognised vocational qualification, but the MSC has acknowledged that these do not yet exist in many occupational areas. Managing agents will be expected to provide these 'designated qualifications' as they are developed by the MSC with employers and validating bodies. These recognised qualifications will, however, only form part of the YTS certificate, which will itself become a recognised qualification.

The certificate will consist of three parts. A summary of the training programme followed; the 'competence objectives' and qualifications achieved; and statements on trainee performance in the four outcomes. Although 'negative remarks should be avoided', trainee performance will continue to be judged largely by the subjective methods of YTS sponsors and managing agents. Terry Edwards has emphasised that this certificate will become a sophisticated label 'distinguishing those more likely to make suitable employees' (1984, p. 158). In schemes which offer the direct possibility of employment, 'those "passing" will get the jobs, those "failing" will get YTS certificates' (p. 152).

The MSC hopes that eventually the YTS certificate will amount to a work-based alternative to conventional qualifications. David Young, when chairman of the Commission, claimed that the YTS certificate will be 'more important in employment prospects for young people than even O levels or A levels' (HMSO, 1983, p. 41). However, the Review of Vocational Qualifications, which has been instituted to rationalise employment-related qualifications and integrate the YTS certificate into them, is likely to intensify and institutionalise academic and vocational differences. An arbitrary barrier is being drawn across the structure of qualifications, with the vocational system organised around the needs and interests of employers and academic qualifications even more narrowly geared to meeting the requirements of higher education.

The educational pretentions of the YTS were crudely exposed in its early history when the Department of Employment issued Ministerial guidelines for the content of off-the-job training. These specifically excluded trainees from considering matters 'related to the organisation and functioning of society in general'. It appeared that young people could be taught how to complete application forms, but would not be allowed to discuss why they were unemployed! The guidelines were revised after an outburst of criticism, but they signalled the government's intention of maintaining strict control over the content and methods of YTS. For the government, the objective of the two-year YTS was to enable:

young people to acquire the practical skills they need for finding jobs, to form the attitudes that will make them useful and employable, and to demonstrate their capabilities to employers (HMSO, 1985a, p. 15).

The key assumption was that in return for the training offered on YTS the young working class would quiescently accept the constraints of its new social condition. Yet as we began to glimpse in the response of trainees to broad-based training, and as was to be evident in the school strikes of 1985 – when up to 200,000 school students in over 60 towns and cities staged demonstrations and strikes against YTS and the suggestion that it would be made compulsory – it is by no means certain that the young unemployed will simply defer to the new role allotted them.

The experience of trainees

The MSC has gone to great lengths to demonstrate how popular its schemes are, and the general public have been treated to technicolour literature and advertising campaigns which have shown happy, smiling faces and recorded young people's gratitude for the opportunities created. This material has been deployed, with great effect, to allay the fears of those whose reservations have increased as youth unemployment has persisted.

Survey evidence has been regularly produced to show that trainees react favourably to their experiences on YTS; that they thought participation increased their chances of getting a job, improved their self-confidence, helped them to get on with other people; and that the training on offer would be useful to them in obtaining work. Yet the criteria by which the MSC asked trainees to judge schemes have hardly been demanding. At best they suggest that 'the main value of the scheme represent[s] the provision of experiences which even unskilled jobs would offer' (Watts, 1983, p. 30).

When this surface approval is interrogated a different reality emerges. In the first year of YTS only 350,000 places were taken up; less than three-quarters of the anticipated number. One in five trainees dropped out of the scheme prematurely, a third of whom became unemployed. Between April 1984 and March 1985 55 per cent of those who left finished with YTS more than four weeks before the end of their course. A quarter of early leavers complained about their schemes, and one in five blamed the low level of the allowance. At least 10 per cent of eligible unemployed school leavers were not participating in YTS (Horton, 1986).

This was occurring in a context where Job Centres and Careers Officers had resorted to sending threatening letters to unemployed school leavers. In the first eighteen months of YTS up to a thousand young people a month were having their supplementary benefit reduced for leaving the scheme early or for refusing to take up a place. Within a year, what had been proclaimed as a voluntary 'quality' training scheme was beginning to look like a compulsory dose of work experience. By December 1984, Mrs Thatcher again announced that she would like to take steps to remove their right to supplementary benefit. She declared that 'young people ought not to be idle', and 'should not have the option of being unemployed'. The subsequent creation of the two-year scheme constituted 'a major step towards our objective of ensuring that unemployment among young people under 18 becomes a thing of the past' (HMSO, 1985c, p. 7).

Irrespective of the presentation of YTS as quality training, it was evident to the HMIs who inspected it that trainees saw the scheme primarily as an avenue into employment. For many young people YTS was a *substitute* for paid employment, and they 'rarely' stayed on the scheme when jobs became available (DES, 1984, p. 5).

The vital element of the scheme for many trainees was the work placement, which gave 'a foot in the door' with employers. Where the YTS had become an agreed mechanism for recruitment into an occupation, such as construction or agriculture, trainees now saw participation as an appropriate first step. But, according to the HMIs, other trainees viewed the YTS in a very different light. Those whose relatives or friends were unemployed, or who themselves had joined the YTS after losing a job, often viewed the programme with some scepticism. In areas of high unemployment, it seemed that the training allowance was as much the incentive to join as was the prospect of getting work.

Despite moral panics portraying the young unemployed as

living it up on the proceeds of crime or on illicit incomes obtained in the hidden economy, the reality was that most school leavers had little access to other sources of income and desperately wanted to work and obtain a wage (Roberts *et al.*, 1981). In many working class families, some of which were themselves experiencing unemployment and declining living standards, the option of not going on YTS was hardly realistic. For other young people staying on the dole would be pointless and boring, and many parents would put pressure on their children to take what was available.

Nevertheless, when travel costs and meal expenses were deducted from the allowance it hardly provided a generous standard of living. Almost universally, YTS trainees (and refusers) complained about the low level of the allowance, and this feeling was particularly acute amongst those trainees who were doing similar work alongside employees on normal rates of pay.

This sentiment was reinforced for many trainees by the nature of the work they were required to carry out. It often involved tasks which were 'mundane, and repetitive, reflecting in fact the reality of much working life' (Welsh Office, 1984, p. 28). The MSC's survey of providers found that only 30 per cent of trainees, mainly apprentices, were predominantly involved in on-the-job training which produced little or no output. 40 per cent of trainees spent most of their time assisting other workers to do their normal jobs, and 30 per cent did work that was similar to that done by ordinary employees (*Department of Employment Gazette*, August 1985).

There were indications that it was not just colleges which experienced problems with discipline. Scheme managers warned that unqualified school leavers with no hope of a job at the end of their placement would have a 'real shock', and that their 'discipline, regular attendance and reliability' could not be guaranteed (IDS, 1983, p. 7). Even an employer like GEC, in an area of high unemployment, noted that 'discipline without a shadow of a doubt was the biggest problem of the lot'. Bryan Wilson, the company's senior training officer, pointed to the realities which undermined their authority: 'the trainees were not necessarily interested in all the jobs; there was no thought of the sack; the money was not much more than the dole; and there was no guarantee of a job at the end' (NATFHE, 1983, p. 11).

The lack of enthusiasm for YTS displayed by many school leavers was not the product of irresponsibility or feckless idleness. Despite the attractive images of MSC publicity there were enormous variations within the scheme. Some employers may have offered good training, with the chance of a job at the end, but other sponsors clearly offered what school leavers saw as an extension of YOP, and experienced as a spell of cheap labour. Those who refused to join the scheme saw it as a poor substitute for a job and dismissed it as 'slave labour' doing menial work which offered no real training (Fawcett Society, 1985, pp. 32–3; Roberts and Kirby, 1985; Horton, 1986).

YTS and the labour market: a permanent bridge to work?

YTS has transformed the way that young people can inhabit the labour market, but it had little impact on employers' recruitment practices. Many organisations used their 'normal recruitment methods and selection procedures' (IDS, 1983, p. 1). Where YTS was the first year of an extended period of training, or was used to select people for permanent employment, then entry standards were that much more stringent. One in ten managing agents required prospective trainees to have at least three 'O' levels, and just over a quarter used tests of skills such as numeracy, literacy and manual dexterity when selecting trainees.

These recruitment patterns, in combination with the other employment practices which create direct and indirect discrimination in the labour market, led to the emergence of clear racial and sexual divisions between the different types of provision. Young women were recruited to traditional areas of work, with few opportunities for long-term skill training. Even when they participated in the high-technology elements of YTS they were often given more limited training (Thorpe, 1984; Fawcett Society, 1985). In 1984–5 the Construction Industry Training Board took on more than 10,000 young people, but apart from 190 clerical and administrative trainees, just over 40 were young women.

Black youngsters were far less likely to get on employer-based schemes or obtain full-time work, and when the Commission for Racial Equality, for example, investigated fifteen major employers (CRE, 1984) it found that virtually no black youngsters had been recruited. A detailed study of racial discrimination on YTS concluded that:

> For all its talk of equal opportunities, the MSC has not implemented any policies which will break the mould of racial inequality or seriously challenge racial discrimination. Not only is YTS reproducing racial disadvantage in the labour market and training, but its selective, hierarchical structure is channelling, institutionalising and entrenching inequality (TURC, 1985, p. 46).

Other social divisions were evident in the job prospects of trainees, which varied widely by region, occupational training area, and previous levels of qualification. Those with the best job prospects were found in administrative and clerical areas working for large employers. Those with the worst prospects were unqualified trainees working in areas of high unemployment. Instead of ameliorating inequalities, YTS apparently compounded them.

Towards the end of the first year of operation local publicity extolling the virtues of particular schemes, and the first indications that employers were taking on trainees, were greeted with enthusiasm by government ministers. The Chancellor of the Exchequer claimed that 'about 70 per cent of youngsters leaving the scheme' were going 'straight into work or other training', a claim he repeated in his 1985 Budget. It did not seem to matter that many of these young people had obtained unskilled work in areas completely unrelated to their YTS training, just as long as they had got jobs.

Furthermore, within days Youthaid had shown that these figures were exaggerated. Overall, between 55 and 60 per cent of trainees were obtaining jobs, but this applied to only one in three black trainees. A third of the young people coming out of YTS (more than 100,000) were going straight into the dole queues. Even with a two-year scheme, the Chairman of the Commission anticipates that only some 66 per cent of trainees will get jobs after YTS.

Armed with their YTS certificates, unemployed trainees were left to enter a depressed labour market where their job prospects were squeezed by competition from experienced adult workers and new batches of subsidised school leavers. After those aged over fifty, under-twenty-five year olds had become more vulnerable to prolonged unemployment than any other age group.

By 1986 more than half of under-eighteen year olds and a quarter of under-twenty-five year olds were unemployed. One in three young men aged eighteen and nineteen were without work. Over 600,000 under-twenty-five year olds had been unemployed for more than six months, and just under 350,000 had been continuously out of work for more than a year. There were over 300,000 young adults who had never had a job since leaving school. It was these realities, and the quality of many YTS places, not young people's alleged idleness, which were seriously undermining the credibility of the scheme, and provoking the different reactions of young people to it. For many, the YTS was a preparation for the dole, not a permanent bridge to work.

A new social condition

Many young people have been sceptical about YTS and have rejected the ideology going with it, but they have negotiated their labour market realities and opportunities for education and training in a variety of undramatic ways. It seems that this adaptability of young people, in combination with the training schemes, has confounded the apocalyptic predictions made in the early 1970s. Increasing numbers of young people have chosen to continue their full-time education and, as Ken Roberts has pointed out, many school leavers are likely to experience unemployment only *intermittently*. Rather than a particular group being condemned to permanent idleness in many districts the joblessness was spread around and 'absorbed within sub-employed biographies'. As the jobs available in their local labour markets were frequently monotonous and low paid, young people were likely to settle for working sporadically; a 'common view is that neither work nor unemployment are tolerable for long unbroken periods' (1984, p. 65).

Within such a career of subemployment a transition to adulthood can still be secured. This is especially the case for those whose families enjoyed some economic security or in those parts of the country least devastated by the recession. However, in other areas the old transitions may now be shattered. Once youth unemployment rises above 30 per cent, as it has done in many inner city areas and on many housing estates, long-term unemployment spreads rapidly (Roberts, 1984, p. 7).

Paul Willis (1984) has argued that it is in these areas that we are witnessing the emergence of a 'new social state'. In a comprehensive survey of the social condition of young people in Wolverhampton he found that the long-term unemployed became increasingly pessimistic and were left in a state of 'suspended animation', cut off from anticipated futures of leaving home, material consumption and marriage. In place of the traditional, employment-related passage to adulthood, there was now a period of extended dependence on the state, on state welfare, on temporary training and employment schemes, and on a sometimes unwilling family.

In this changing world some of the young unemployed were developing new ways of growing up working class. In her 1980s experiences on the road to Wigan Pier, for example, Beatrix Campbell (1984) found a baby boom and what she called a wave of 'dole queue mothers'. Single parenthood got these young women off the unemployment register and cut out the demoralising failure to find a job. It could end the monotonous experience of badly-paid work or provide a way out of the parental home. Significantly the young women were creating a future that no longer presupposed dependence on the male wage. Single parenthood offered young women maturity, some independence, and the positive experiences of motherhood. Their new independence, however, could also produce its own isolation and oppression. For one group of young mothers:

> With the glitter of a modern youth culture within easy view, their reality is one of shared rooms and continual struggles with the authorities to discover what their rights are, and then try to assert them . . . For the young mothers, instead of the gradual move from schoolgirl to worker, to fiancée, to wife and finally to mother, they were suddenly ripped away from their friends and their existing way of life and flung into the blurred existence of the single mother. For them there was a feeling of lost youth, of not being part of something they should have been, or of growing old too quickly (Presdee, 1984).

The dominant experience of long-term unemployment is still that of poverty, social isolation, and depression both for the unemployed and their families. It is often a world of social crisis, of domestic breakdown, violence, ill-health and even suicide. Temporary training and employment schemes were the only lifeline extended to this lost generation.

Another new deal in the making: a job guarantee for the long-term unemployed

In response to the continuing crisis of youth unemployment another generation of government measures were beginning to evolve. By 1986 the Community Programme (CP), which provides part-time temporary jobs for the long-term unemployed, was expanded to provide more than a quarter of a million places. This would cost over £1 billion a year, and was introduced at the same time that the attack on the pay and conditions of young workers was intensified. Young people were removed from the protection of Wages Councils, and employers were offered subsidies for paying some 70,000 eighteen and nineteen year olds below trade union rates of pay.

More than 65 per cent of the workers on CP were aged under twenty-five, were predominantly male, and were paid less than £60 a week – many were graduates of YOP and YTS. In the way that YTS transformed the world of education, CP was creating dilemmas about job substitution and services in the construction industry, health and local authorities and voluntary agencies.[7] By 1986 half a million of the long-term unemployed had joined CP. At the end of their year on CP 70 per cent went straight back to the dole queue.

In the absence of an effective strategy for creating jobs, political pressure increased for a further expansion of the programme. In response to the human crisis of unemployment, and the waste it represented, pressure groups, voluntary organisations, political parties, and even the government's own supporters demanded a job guarantee for the long-term unemployed. However, in the same way that the Christmas guarantee of a place on YTS for school leavers could look very different to the young person receiving it, so too this guarantee for many of the long-term unemployed would be experienced as a temporary stay on a low-paid scheme doing unskilled work, likely to be followed by yet another period on the dole. As it was cheap, and could be used to further their overall strategy of reducing wage levels and people's expectations, it appeared that the government would expand CP to more than 400,000 places in time for the next General Election (Finn, 1986).

The double and partly contradictory aim of the YTS – and increasingly of CP – is to produce a generation of young people who are basically skilled and willing to work, but who can also maintain these qualities in suspended animation through any periods of unemployment they experience. Having been suitably differentiated at school, and taught to know their place, these new model workers are to be instructed, through their training and work experience, and through the discipline of unemployment, to transcend the narrow trade practices and occupational loyalties of a now unwanted division of labour. They will, it is hoped, become highly mobile and individualistic, infinitely adaptable to technological change, possessing all the traditional virtues of the work ethic.

What started out as a demand for day release education, to protect the young working class from blind alley work, has now been secured in the unrecognisable form of a near-compulsory two-year traineeship. In place of programmes which would extend the rights of school leavers and develop *all* their potential, are schemes which at their heart are involved in the systematic reduction of young people's expectations. Working class youth is being given its first harsh lessons in the political and economic realities of 1980s Britain.

8

Conclusion: Training Without Jobs

The campaign to protect young workers from exploitation and create equal educational opportunities has reached a new and dramatic stage. Secondary education for all, a higher leaving age and comprehensive reorganisation have been secured, but they have failed to deliver all that was promised, they have been experienced by many pupils and parents as irrelevant or oppressive, and they have been undermined by the collapse of youth employment.

The political assumptions and economic circumstances which underpinned the period of educational expansion and reform have been shattered by relative economic decline and by the successful campaigns launched by the Black Paper writers, which mobilised and directed the dissatisfaction felt by both parents and pupils. When the 1974–9 Labour government, however, responded to this popular discontent it launched its Great Debate on education within the terms of reference propagated by the radical right and by employers. Schools were blamed for youth unemployment and school leavers, contrary to the evidence, were accused of lacking even basic skills and of being ignorant about the world of work. Schools had to change, and in combination with a new generation of special employment schemes, were now expected to provide the work socialisation that had been a normal part of leaving school and getting a job.

The Conservatives have since extended this transformation of the relationship between education, training and work. After 1979, they used the strategic power of the MSC to engineer a new economic role and status for young school leavers. The YTS, and the new tripartitism, represent their distinctive attempt to grapple with the legacy of RSLA and other social democratic reforms *and* manage the consequences of profound economic changes. They have embarked on an ambitious attempt to remake the attitudes and skills of the young working class so that they become more acceptable to potential employers. The Tories have captured the language of reform.

Although this strategy is encountering new forms of opposition from young people, parents, trade unions and local authorities, the central assumptions of the new vocationalism have not yet been challenged. The Conservatives could still win extensive popular support by presenting the two-year YTS, and a differentiated and vocational curriculum in schools, as the best efforts of a government responding successfully and creatively to the demands of the new technologies and the crisis of mass unemployment.

An alternative strategy must start from a clear analysis and rejection of the monetarists' ambitions. Attention should be given to the harsh realities of the youth labour market and to young people's relative knowledge about working life, rejecting any simple identity of interest between what employers say they want and what should be provided for young people. Objectives must be formulated which more adequately respond to the new social and economic condition of young people in the 1980s. A purely defensive response provides no answer to the immediate political problems posed by the MSC, or to the central issue of the relationship between education, training and work.

A renewed socialist policy for education and training involves more than the recreation of some mythical golden age of comprehensive education or full employment. Preserving or restoring the status quo is neither feasible nor, as I have shown, desirable. Economic growth and the recreation of full employment may be fundamental preconditions of future progress, but without a coherent strategy the jobs created will simply reproduce the exploitation and the blind alleys and racial and sexual inequalities which awaited school leavers in the secondary labour market of the 1960s. The following discussion does not provide some magical or immediate resolution to the long-term conflicts between state schooling and growing up working class. Instead, through absorbing some of the historical lessons of the book, it points to ways in which demands for equal educational opportunities and the protection of young workers from exploitation can be advanced in the changed circumstances of the 1980s.

Comprehensive schools

Education in Britain has entered a deep crisis. The radical right has exposed the failures of social democratic reform and effectively blamed comprehensive schools for unemployment. The Conservatives have exploited popular discontent with schooling, reduced its material resources, and are now creating a new tripartitism.

The stated objectives of the Labour Party and trade union movement are, however, still preoccupied with restoring levels of expenditure and opening up access to post-compulsory forms of education. Little has been said about the content of the curriculum or the objectives of a socialist educational strategy. In continuing to ignore this ground of educational content and purpose, their alternative looks very much like a better-funded version of the new vocationalism for all. Yet the fundamental perspectives which inform the new vocationalism are highly misleading. Ideologically distorting the experiences involved in growing up working class (by portraying young people as both ignorant about the world of work and as unwilling to subject themselves to its disciplines), they have helped pathologise the quite reasonable responses of young people to the realities of the juvenile labour market.

Nevertheless, while the new tripartitism must be rejected, it will be important to extend and draw on those elements of its vocational curriculum which address the aspirations and destinies of many school leavers. There is nothing inevitable about a more work-related curriculum being restricted to an employer-dominated version of work preparation. As early as the 1920s, John Dewey, an American advocate of vocational education, stressed its radical potential:

> The kind of education in which I am interested is not one which will adapt workers to the existing industrial regime; I am not sufficiently in love with the regime for that. It seems to me that the business of all those who would not be educational time-servers is to resist every move in this direction, and to

strive for a kind of vocational education which will first alter the existing industrial system, and ultimately transform it (quoted by Reeder, 1979, p. 117).

While few people retain any illusions about the ability of educational change to transform society on its own, it is still vital to counterpose an alternative vision of its purposes and functions, and of its content.

A central starting point of any new curriculum is the heightened stake and interest that *young people themselves* have in employment. However, instead of creating an instant or superficial relevance, which in its desire to meet 'kids where they're at' could end up leaving them exactly where they started from, this curriculum would challenge prevailing assumptions (Green, 1986). It would evaluate the differences between employment, work and leisure, and question the domestic division of labour which underpins them. It would allow for a critical engagement with – rather than mere subservience to – the processes and products of technical change. For the many thousands of young people who continue to leave school at the earliest opportunity, such a 'really useful knowledge' would pose the problem as to why they were likely to be unemployed, as well as attempt to develop the capacities needed for coping with and challenging that situation (Waugh, 1982).

Although the 'world of work' should be a point of reference across the curriculum, the insertion of a strong vocational element before the age of sixteen should be resisted. It directly threatens the comprehensive principle of a broad, common curriculum for all pupils during the period of compulsory education, and it will effectively restrict young people's future choices rather than keeping them open. Ruth Johnathan (1982) has pointed out, in her critical assessment of the educational claims of the new vocationalism, that 'we must resist moves to replace a system which leaves people insufficiently equipped for their economic role with one which seeks to equip them for little else'.

A modern curriculum must respond to young people's needs as citizens and as potential parents, as well as future workers. Just as new technology and keyboard skills should be part of every pupil's education, so should an introduction to other cultures, to the workings of the mass media, and to the social processes that characterise modern societies. As part of the creation of a more active, democratic relationship between parents, comprehensive schools and their communities, young people should be offered a political education which involves extensive practice in democratic procedures, including meetings, negotiations and the selection and conduct of representatives and leaders (Williams, 1975, p. 175).

At the heart of any future strategy must be the right of *all* pupils to equal treatment in their educational and personal development. This is unlikely to be secured by imposing a one-dimensional uniformity of provision on pupils with different needs and interests. The role of comprehensive schools in challenging the alienation and systematic underachievement of girls, of black pupils, and of working class boys can be secured only through provision which is sensitive to their different needs and experiences. The contradictions and antagonism between the demands of compulsory schooling and the material and social realities of many working class families will not be magically resolved, but when placed at the forefront of policy objectives, and given adequate resources, considerable improvements can be secured *within* a common, broad-based education (ILEA, 1984).

A renewed vision of comprehensive education would be hopelessly inadequate without continuing efforts to minimise and erode the harmful consequences, and self-fulfilling prophecies, associated with streaming and selection. The further extension and full development of mixed ability teaching requires adequate resources, and breaking the stranglehold on curriculum development exercised by the university-dominated examination boards (Jones, 1983). Mixed ability teaching does not represent a panacea, but it would be a key element of future relationships within schools. It could help begin the task of recapturing the once denigrated 'progressive' methods, especially around pupil-centred forms of assessment and negotiation, which have since been colonised by the new vocationalism.

This renewed development of the comprehensive principle would enable schools to respond to the trends, changes and realities of the 1980s. In addition to providing adequate resources and pay for teachers, government policy would also need to secure the basic organisational and material reforms still required to achieve a formally comprehensive system: a redistribution, as well as expansion, of educational resources and equipment; the withdrawal of state support for the private sector; and the introduction of a mandatory system of educational maintenance allowances.

It is vital that those young people who are now forced to leave school because of economic circumstances should, like their better-off contemporaries, be entitled to independent income support so that they can choose to extend their education and defer their entry into the labour market. The continuing increase in staying-on rates is already raising fundamental issues about the nature of what is called 'tertiary' education. However, an educational choice represents only one option, and we should resist the bureaucratically convenient solution of excluding all sixteen and seventeen year olds from the formal labour market.

Many young people still want to start work as soon as they can, and this experience is vital to their self-development. A progressive policy must recognise their right to work and address the conditions and possibilities they are now likely to experience as trainees in the labour market. However, in the same way that creating a popular demand for educational progress requires more than sitting back and awaiting the arrival of a change of government, so too transforming the YTS and improving the prospects of young workers requires an immediate and continuing response. In addition to resisting attacks on the pay and working conditions of young people, there must be a fundamental reappraisal of the activities and directions of the MSC, and of the role of the labour movement within it.

Opposition to the MSC

There has been intermittent opposition to the MSC. Individual trade unions, and many workplaces, have negotiated improvements or alternatively will have nothing to do with the YTS; some of the unemployed refuse places on the Commission's various schemes. In April 1985, tens of thousands of school children took to the streets in protest against the suggestion that YTS would be made compulsory. The resistance has, however, been fragmented and localised. This has partly been the result of the TUC's unwillingness to question its commitment to the MSC, but more realistically has reflected the success of the Conservatives in exploiting the plight of the unemployed.

The lengthy debate about how trade unions and other progressive forces should respond to these political realities has been polarised between those advocating a boycott of MSC programmes and those who claim that existing arrangements, though underfunded, are sufficient. In place of the pragmatism which has guided official attitudes, many trade unionists argue that involvement in the MSC has been largely ineffectual, has given a TUC seal of approval to cheap labour schemes, and has made it very difficult to create a strategy of opposition.

The call for a boycott has, in its turn, created a gulf between those working within and those working outside the MSC, and among many active trade unionists. The argument creates divisions because it avoids the reality that MSC programmes, however inadequately, do respond to some of the needs of the unemployed. A boycott could easily become a simple defence of the position of those in work, or those who already have a monopoly of access to training. It would offer little to the workers and activists involved in MSC schemes, or to the young people and unemployed who have few other choices.

As the TUC is unlikely to withdraw from the MSC, it is vital that its role is transformed from one of consensual partner to that of advocate of the interests of trainees and the unemployed. Such a change in perspective would have an immediate effect and would give a great boost to grass roots campaigns and to the beleaguered TUC representatives on local AMB's (Eversley, 1986).

Existing TUC policy calls on trades unionists to report abuses of individual schemes to area boards, to negotiate improvements, to recruit trainees and to monitor the impact of the YTS. These are important activities which, without more resources and a broader campaign, are unlikely to be translated into reality, even in organised workplaces. Nevertheless, with the support of some local authorities, YTS monitoring projects have drawn attention to the inadequacies and abuses of the scheme, and in alliance with groups like Women in Youth Training and trade union resource centres, have begun to create ways of exposing the effects of MSC policy (LMI, 1984–5; Benn and Fairley (eds), 1986). Little headway has been made, however, in creating an active relationship between young people and the labour movement.

There is an urgent need for the TUC, and those other groups working directly with young people, to establish the conditions in which trainees are able to organise collectively and be represented at all levels within the MSC.

At an ideological level, the duplicity of the Conservative government, which is using unemployment to discipline the working class, has to be exposed. This involves more than the espousal of an alternative economic policy which would create more jobs. It means highlighting, with all the means at the disposal of the labour movement, the bankruptcy of a training policy without jobs. It also requires immediate opposition to policies which are subordinating education and training provision to a narrow view of employers requirements.

The MSC and training for social advance

There is a compelling economic case for more public investment in education and training if the UK is to exploit the new technologies and keep pace with major international trading rivals. But the reliance on an employer-led strategy defies our historical experience which has consistently shown that employers take a shortsighted view of training and are not prepared to invest the necessary resources in it (Perry, 1975). The shortages in specific skills which are even now constricting the pace of technical change can be largely blamed on industry itself which, during the recession, cut back capital investment and skill training.

According to the Industrial Society (1985), two-thirds of British employers spend less than 0.5 per cent of their annual turnover on staff training. A survey of 500 companies found that employers spent a marginal 0.15 per cent of turnover – or under £4 per week per employee – on training and retraining their adult workers. The average amount of time spent on training worked out at just five days a year, only two of which were spent off the job (IFF, 1985). A Coopers and Lybrand report on British employers' attitudes (1985) showed that British firms were not just backward in investing in training and every other human resource, but they were complacent about it too. Few employers think training is of central importance in their business, and few of the chief executives interviewed saw lower wages for young people while training as a realistic strategy to get them to increase their intake. YTS has had little effect on the cutback in long-term skill training. In 1983, less than 40,000 apprentices were recruited, compared with 100,000 in 1979 (Holland, 1984a, para. 23).

The evidence is that most employers, even when they can predict their needs with any coherence, will not train sufficient numbers, in sufficient quality, to meet either economic or technical requirements. To provide them with an enormous public subsidy, in the form of a two-year YTS, without any rigorous attempt to define and establish the needs of the labour market, or police standards, is a receipt for a 'great training robbery' (Kaufman, 1986). For these reasons a statutory and public training system is essential. But, in contrast with the centralised corporatism of the MSC, a progressive strategy would create a decentralised training system made up of democratic and accountable structures operating on a local, area or sectoral basis. In addition to servicing the immediate requirements of the economy, and providing opportunities for school leavers, such a training strategy could draw on the innovative projects that now exist (in local authorities, for example). A legal framework is required within which the many groups who have traditionally been marginalised by employers would be given the resources to explore, define and meet their own training needs, which would be identified and planned for according to a far broader definition than employers' immediate requirements. This would require a major transformation of the priorities of the MSC.

In the context of an expanding economy and employment creation, such a training policy would be a powerful weapon for securing other elements of social change. Through positive action programmes, a flexible range of educational and training provision could begin to release the talents and energies of married women, the ethnic minorities, and the older and younger unemployed who are frequently written off as unskilled. Training for social advance must involve a significant expansion in funding for adult training and education, with an adequate system of income support, which would equip people with the ability to criticise and shape technical change rather than simply respond to it (GLC, 1984).

A more adequate foundation training for school leavers would look very different from the two-year YTS. It would have structured into it the acquisition of practical skills, democratic participation, equal opportunities, and properly negotiated rates of pay. Above a basic minimum these would reflect the value of the work performed by young people.

Such a foundation training would not just be concerned with the acquisition of technical skills, nor would it promote an employer-defined version of work socialisation. It would start from the reality that even those going into unskilled jobs requiring little or no training do continue their 'education', as do those consigned to unemployment. In that process of growing up working class most of the lessons are harsh, negative and alienating. It is time that the entry into work of the vast majority of young people was designed consciously so that the experience encountered and the skills developed can be integrated and extended as part of their *general education*. Britain needs highly-skilled and educated young workers, it does not need spare parts or 'cannon-fodder' for employers.

These suggestions may seem utopian in a context of continuing expenditure cuts, where political power remains firmly in the hands of a government which is using unemployment and the mechanism of training schemes to secure a permanent change in the skills and attitudes of the British working class. However, the ambitions of the Conservatives are unlikely to be realised in the form in which they are proposed. In this climate it could now be possible to win support for an alternative which would lead to a genuine advance. For the young working class, *and* their parents, are becoming increasingly disenchanted with the MSC's 'new deal' of training without jobs.

Notes

1 Introduction: New Deals and Broken Promises

1. Self-consciously adapting the language of the New Deal era in American politics, successive Employment Ministers have described each expansion in provision as 'a new deal' for the young unemployed. The phrase was first used by Albert Booth, Secretary of State for Employment, when introducing YOP for the Labour government in 1978. It was used again by Jim Prior, then Conservative Secretary of State for Employment, when announcing a substantial expansion of YOP in November 1980. Geoffrey Holland, a career civil servant who has become Director of the MSC, has used the expression to describe each qualitatitive shift in youth training.

2. In describing the social reaction to the activities of youth groups in the 1950s and 60s – the 'Teddy Boys' and 'Mods and Rockers' – Stan Cohen described moral panics as follows:

> Societies appear every now and then to be subject to periods of moral panic. A condition, episode, person or group of persons emerges to become defined as a threat to societal values and interests; its nature is presented in a stylised and stereo-typical fashion by the mass media; the moral barricades are manned by editors, bishops, politicians and other right-thinking people; socially accredited experts pronounce their diagnoses and solutions; ways of coping are evolved, or (more often) resorted to; the condition then disappears, submerges, or deteriorates and becomes more visible. Sometimes the panic is passed over and forgotten . . . at other times it has more serious and long-term repercussions and might produce changes in legal and social policy or even in the way society conceives itself (Cohen, 1973, p. 9).

3. There is an important debate about the precise nature of the
    relationship between the social division of labour and the education
    system. The formulation adopted here draws on the work of Bordieu
    who, in his analysis of social reproduction, provides many insights
    into the social and cultural mechanisms through which the education
    system translates and recreates forms of economic and social privilege
    (Bordieu and Passeron, 1977).
4. Empirical research has concluded, time and again, that despite
    internal and external changes in British schooling, class inequalities
    have persisted. From the purchased privilege of private education
    (Tapper and Salter, 1981, Chapter 8), to the failure of comprehensive
    reform, the educational chances of young people are still dominated
    by their class of origin (Halsey *et al.*, 1980). Moving beyond the
    white, male focus of traditional mobility studies other research has
    shown the extent to which educational outcomes are determined by
    gender (Deem, 1978), and by race (Eggleston *et al.*, 1985).
5. In 1893 the minimum leaving age was increased to eleven years of
    age, and this had a marked impact on the number of half-timers
    employed, who had become concentrated in the textile mills of
    Lancashire and the farms of East Anglia. From over 200,000 in
    1876, the number of half-timers had fallen to 175,437 by 1890, 52 per
    cent of whom were in Lancashire, and to 110,654 by 1897, 54 per
    cent in Lancashire (Simon, 1974, p. 290). When the school leaving
    age was subsequently raised to twelve without exemption in 1899
    and School Boards were permitted to raise the upper leaving age in
    their areas from thirteen to fourteen, all such by-laws had to contain
    some provision for either total or partial exemption. Having satisfied
    minimum attendance requirements, children between twelve and
    fourteen years of age could work in textile factories for up to 27.75
    hours per week, and in other factories for 30 hours per week
    (Gollan, 1937, p. 17).
    Consequently, while more children were compelled to attend school
    for longer periods, it had the effect of increasing the number of half-
    timers, who grew from just over 47,000 in 1906 to over 84,000 in
    1907 (Simon 1974, p. 290). Even in 1922, after the Fisher Act of
    1918 had called for the end of exemptions, there were still about
    70,000 half-timers.

2   'Secondary Education for All': Raising the School Leaving Age and Juvenile Unemployment Between the Wars

1. There is no simple 'history' of the period spanned by this chapter,

and there are intense arguments about the impact of mass unemployment. Stevenson and Cook, for example, have argued with great conviction and much evidence against a left-inclined version of events:

> It would, of course, be fatuous to suggest that the 1930s were not for many thousands of people a time of great hardship and personal suffering. Alongside the pictures of dole queues and hunger marches must also be placed those of another Britain, of new industries, prosperous suburbs and a rising standard of living (1977, p. 4).

2. For an extended discussion of the nature of the relationship that developed between the universities and British industry see Sanderson (1972). For a more general appraisal of the education and industry debate in the interwar period see Reeder (1979).

3. Stephen Humphries emphasises that it wasn't just boys who resisted the formal demands of schooling:

> Interviews clearly indicate that girls were as likely to resist authoritarian control as boys. This may seem surprising in view of the orthodoxy which portrays working class girls as much more passive, subservient and deferential . . . [but] . . . there is evidence to suggest that inside school girls were as disobedient as, or even more disobedient than, boys. This defiance was occasionally reflected in higher expulsion rates . . . but because girls often employed more subtle and devious techniques of resistance than boys, much of their misbehaviour has remained hidden and unrecorded in school log and punishment books (1981, p. 76).

4. The most important legislation was the Shops Act 1934, the Factories Act 1937, and the subsequent Young Persons (Employment) Act 1938.

5. From the economic dislocations generated by demobilisation and the industrial struggles that marked the immediate postwar period, registered unemployment reached over 2.5 million in 1921, and while it fell relatively rapidly it never went below a million in the 1920s and was to jump again to 2.7 million in 1932. It did not fall below 2 million until 1936 and in 1939 still totalled over 1.5 million. Because of the restricted scope of unemployment insurance, the totals unemployed in the 1920s and 1930s were higher than the official figures would suggest. Groups excluded were as diverse as the self-employed, domestic servants, agricultural workers and married women. The totals are the 'official' ones, extracted from a table in Stevenson and Cook, 1977, p. 286.

6. The Insurance Act 1934 established a network of labour camps which were designed to secure the physical and moral regeneration of the ablebodied male unemployed. The men who were recruited to the labour camps were removed many miles from their homes and families; they lived under semi-military discipline; 'out of bounds' areas were laid down and curfews imposed; they would have to perform a full week's work on road making (for example, sections of the North Circular Road in London), land drainage, irrigation systems, new sewerage schemes, afforestation, improvement of canals and bridges, brickmaking, building Whipsnade Zoo, and so on. For this labour they received no wages, but would get their meals in the camp plus 4 shillings a week pocket money. Their dependents, if any, had to exist on the scale of allowances provided by the unemployment board. At their high point there were thirty-six residential camps with between 150 and 200 inmates in each. Up to 1939 just under 190,000 unemployed men had been sent to the camps for three-month stretches. It speaks volumes about the conditions in the camps that over 37,000 men walked out of them knowing that they would be disqualified from benefit. The camps were closed at the outbreak of war when most inmates 'volunteered' for the forces (Colledge and Field, 1983).

7. During the 1930s there were a number of political groups propagating a 'middle' path out of economic crisis and mass unemployment, defining a new role for the state in the economy. The Next Five Years Group was formed in 1934, and was supported by members of all political parties (notably Harold Macmillan) and by numerous writers, scientists and educationalists such as Hadow and Percy Nunn. Their plans for reconstruction gave an important place to the education system which was to create the democratic citizens of a new society:

    The principle of government by consent and free discussion must be made more fully operative through the extension of education – that cardinal function of a democratic state; through the improvement of the system of representation, and through the further breaking down of barriers of class and privilege (quoted in Education Group, 1981, p. 52).

8. Although intelligence testing has been associated with the rise of the tripartite system, and with the earlier scholarship system, it is important to note its early use by reformers. They were able to demonstrate that in its own terms the distribution of tested intelligence and school places was at variance. Initially, this was used by Kenneth Lindsay, from the London School of Economics, to

demonstrate the inadequacy of the scholarship system. Subsequently, it was used by sociologists, such as Halsey and Flood, to demonstrate the inadequacy of the eleven plus as a mechanism for differentiation in the 1950s. For a full discussion of the debates around intelligence testing and psychology in education, see Brian Simon, 1971.

3 Raising the School Leaving Age to Sixteen: School and Work in the 1960s

1. Colin MacInnes, in 'Absolute Beginners', published in 1959, described what was involved in the 'teenage ball'. It:

   > had a real splendour in the days when the kids discovered that, for the first time since centuries of kingdom come, they'd money, which hitherto had always been denied to us at the best time of life to use it, namely, when you're young and strong, and also before the newspapers and telly got hold of this teenage fable and prostituted it as conscripts seem to do to everything they touch. Yes, I tell you, it had a real savage splendour in the days when we found that no-one couldn't sit on our faces any more because we'd loot to spend at last, and our world was to be our world, the one we wanted and not standing on the doorstep of somebody else's.

2. During the 1950s the assumption that widespread material poverty had been widely ameliorated became so widely accepted by politicians, social commentators and the general public alike that for over a decade, public controversy and political discussion were engrossed by the new problems of what people called the 'Affluent Society'. The fallacies at the heart of this debate are described in a pioneering critique written by J. H. Westergaard in 1964 (1972).

3. In preparation for the Second World War the government introduced national service under the Military Training Act, which became law in August 1939. In contrast with events following the First World War, national service was not abandoned immediately. The Cold War which merged into the Korean conflict, plus the seemingly endless succession of colonial emergencies which accompanied the collapse of the empire, made governments reluctant to end conscription. By the mid-1950s, labour shortages which economists argued were hindering economic growth, and the growing attachement of the military to the idea of an all professional career army, combined to convince politicians to end conscription. In May 1957, call-up duty ceased (see Jeffs, 1982, pp. 14–15).

4. Many of the 1960s and 1970s studies of young people were

preoccupied with the most spectacular, most deviant forms of youth culture. Many young workers, whose involvement in such groups was limited or constrained, were by and large marginalised. This focus on the most visible youth groups and their delinquent activities also had the effect of excluding young girls from such investigations, and youth culture became almost synonymous with assertive expressions of masculinity – hooliganism, certain crimes, certain acts of violence, and so on (McRobbie and Garber, 1975; Griffin, 1985b). Moreover, as Frith (1978) points out, the focus of investigation was on delinquency and tended to give scant attention to other areas in the lives of the young. It became a sociology of leisure, a sociology of those areas where delinquent acts were likely to occur – the street corner, in pubs, at night or the weekend.

5. The question in relation to upskilling was whether the forms of labour associated with the application of science and technology to the production process tended towards *averaging* the skill required, or on the contrary, tended toward *polarisation*. As Braverman makes the point:

> The mass of workers gain nothing from the fact that the decline in their command over the labour process is more than compensated for by the increasing command on the part of managers and engineers. On the contrary, not only does their skill fall in an absolute sense (in that they lose craft and traditional abilites without gaining new abilities to compensate the loss), but it falls even more in a *relative* sense. The more science is incorporated in the labour process, the less the worker understands of the process; the more sophisticated an intellectual product the machine becomes the less control and comprehension of the machine the worker has. In other words, the more the worker needs to know in order to remain a human being at work, the less does he or she know. This is the chasm which the notion of 'average skill' conceals (1974, p. 425).

6. One example of the new primacy accorded to educational reform and expansion by the Labour Party can be seen in their 'Signposts for the Sixties', a manifesto issued in 1963:

> Children are the nation's most valuable asset. What we spend on their schooling earns a bigger return in the quality of our national life than any other expenditure. This is more true than ever in the age of a scientific revolution, when the improvement of our living standards and our survival as a free democracy depend largely upon the quality of our scientific, technological and technical education (1963, p. 28).

7. In Coventry, in 1973, only one in-service training course for RSLA had been arranged; only one school was setting aside special accommodation for RSLA pupils (called for in DES building Bulletin No. 32); school equipment and materials were in short supply, a position which deteriorated following a 10 per cent cut in spending in the November, and pupil–teacher ratios were just being maintained at pre-RSLA levels. The extent of planned curriculum change was, at the most, an attempt to get RSLA pupils to take one or two Mode III CSE examinations, telling pupils to take part in linked courses with technical colleges or, as in the majority of cases, asking pupils to do an afternoon's community work such as visiting old age pensioners or looking after the under-fives (Finn, 1975).

8. The 'New Right' were initially an extra-parliamentary grouping of academics, businessmen, MPs, and leader writers, whose critique of all aspects of the Welfare State and the consensus politics of the 1960s – at first ridiculed – gained increasing prominence in the Conservative Party in the early 1970s. Following the electoral defeat of the Heath government in 1974, and the subsequent fusion with monetarism, this political tendency, in the form of Thatcherism, came to power in 1979, in a new phase of what has been called 'authoritarian populism'. These political developments are discussed in some detail by Stuart Hall and others (1978).

4 The Impact of RSLA: Growing Up and Leaving School

1. The research drawn on in this chapter has been fully written up in my unpublished Ph.D. thesis: *New Deals and Broken Promises: Young Workers, the School Leaving Age and Youth Unemployment*, Centre for Contemporary Cultural Studies, Faculty of Arts, Birmingham University, 1982.

2. The choice of *entry* to four 'O' levels or equivalent reflected a number of important considerations. In the first place, four 'O' levels represents the bottom end of a significant cutoff point in relation to access to sectors of the youth labour market and to forms of higher education (Markall and Finn, 1982; Ashton and Maguire, 1982). Secondly, although CSEs are of considerable importance in internal school hierarchies they are largely discounted by employers, save for the elusive grade 1 (Hunt and Small, 1981; Freedman, 1981).

3. Between 1977 and 1979 research in an ex-mining community in Durham found that the majority of school children were involved in paid work before leaving school (James, 1984). In Birmingham,

there was a significant increase in registered child employment in the late 1970s and it seemed that unemployment and the pressure on living standards was forcing more young people to look for part-time work to get some independence from their parents and obtain the commodities which their parents would not, or could no longer afford to, supply (Forester, 1979, p. 259).

Ron Jeffries, a youth worker writing in the journal of the National Youth Bureau in 1982, registered surprise at the extent of child labour, and after conducting a survey with the help of over seventy youth leaders, parents and teachers, recorded the rates of pay and conditions of work of young children and expressed his horror at the lack of protection and degree of exploitation uncovered.

Early in 1985, the Low Pay Unit published results of a survey of 1,700 children which found that 40 per cent were working at the time of the investigation, and over two-thirds had worked recently in some employment other than running errands or babysitting. The majority were working illegally, either because they were under-aged, working the wrong hours, or were working in jobs they should not have been doing. Many of them had suffered from accidents at work (MacLennan *et al.*, 1985).

5   The Great Debate on Education, Youth Unemployment and the MSC

1. The government had wanted to eliminate the levy-grant system entirely, but met resistance from the TUC and CBI who feared a total loss of control over training to a centralised state agency. The compromise was the levy-grant exemption system which formalised small company eligibility for grants and state provision without a levy obligation. In addition, companies could win levy exemption by internal evaluation of their training activity compared with company requirements. That is, company-specific criteria for training quality replaced industry-imposed standards. The 1973 Act marked a retreat from the position of 1964, and undermined the ability of ITBs to provide counter-cyclical training when individual employers were experiencing financial constraints (Goldstein, 1984, p. 97).

2. The Job Creation Programme came to an end in December 1978, and was replaced by YOP for sixteen–eighteen year olds, and the Special Temporary Employment Programme for unemployed adults. STEP was to provide 25,000 places and was open to people aged nineteen–twenty four who had been unemployed for more than six months or those aged over twenty-five who had been continuously unemployed for more than a year. Participants were to be employed

by sponsors, normally for a maximum of 52 weeks, on projects of benefit to the community, which would not otherwise be carried out.

6 Mrs Thatcher's U-turn? From Youth Opportunities to Youth Training

1. One of the Conservative government's first educational initiatives was to create an 'Assisted Places Scheme' which was to subsidise places at private schools for 'bright' children from less well-off families who performed well in a competitive selection process. Individual children have all or part of their fees paid by the DES, according to parental income. There has been resistance to the scheme by Labour authorities, but by 1983 223 private schools were participating.
   When the scheme is in full operation 44 private schools will have more than 40 per cent of their pupils on assisted places. In all, 142 private schools will have over one in five of their pupils on assisted places, many of them being the ex-direct grant schools which abandoned the state system rather than contemplate comprehensive reform. By 1988, over 30,000 children will be on assisted places at a substantially increased cost than the £22.5 million it was costing in 1984.

2. Although it is not a dimension I have the space to explore, it should be stressed that international organisations such as the EEC and OECD played an important role in setting the agenda for debates about education, training and manpower policy (Wickham, 1981).
   Most directly, the EEC's continuing refusal to accept the work experience element of YOP as a genuine contribution to vocational training – as against simple temporary job creation – affected the amount of grant it could attract. In 1979, nearly £39 million of the £116 million that YOP cost was recovered from the social fund. In 1980 the British government requested £78 million, but for the same reasons, was granted only £48 million. In the first year of the YTS, however, the government was able to recover nearly £140 million from the social fund towards the gross cost of £770 million.

3. The most important objection to the CP was that it would provide only low-paid part-time work when for the same *net* cost 130,000 full-time jobs paying up to £89 a week could have been created. The second major objection was that the wages were so low that very few people would be better off than they would have been on supplementary benefit. The third objection was that CP contained no real provision for training. The Unemployment Unit argued

(1982) that the scheme was designed to help 'cut wage levels', and that sponsors were 'being used by the MSC to implement a scheme which exploits the long-term unemployed'.

4. Government-sponsored research, by the Institute of Manpower Studies, showed that of the first 163,000 successful applications for the Young Workers Subsidy, 90 per cent of the jobs would have been created by the employer without the subsidy. Of the 16,000 odd jobs created, the Institute estimated that about 6,500 would have been occupied by adult workers but for the subsidy. In other words, the scheme created about 10,000 low-wage jobs at a cost of £60 million or £6,000 a job.

5. During the summer of 1981, clear divisions emerged within the Conservative Party. Critics within the Cabinet became increasingly vocal about their opposition to monetarism and the consequences it was having on unemployment. They publicly acknowledged their commitment to a 'one nation' conservatism. They were swiftly dubbed the 'wets', and rather than securing any changes in policy were effectively marginalised by a Cabinet reshuffle in September 1981. Their most prominent leader, Jim Prior, who was threatening to resign if he was moved from the Department of Employment, capitulated and was moved to the more onerous task of Secretary of State for Northern Ireland (Gamble, 1981).

6. *Composition of YOP, 1978–83*

	1978–9	*79–80*	*80–1*	*81–2*	*82–3*
Work experience (WEEP)	128,200	182,100	304,500	461,500	393,400
(% with private employers)	(84.5%)	(76.2%)	(79.5%)	80.4%)	(78.6%)
Work preparation	34,000	34,300	55,500	91,500	67,800
Pilot YTS places (12 months long)					81,900
TOTAL – ALL YOP	162,200	216,400	360,000	553,000	543,100

Source: MSC Annual Reports.

7. For a detailed analysis of MSC operational guidelines around substitution and displacement, and their actual application in WEEP schemes, see Markall, 1983, Chapter 1.

8. In Cleveland, in the North East, for example, a mere 16 per cent of 'graduate' trainees found proper employment in 1980–1. In Sheffield, in 1982, the Careers Service reported that only one in five YOP entrants could expect their schemes to lead to jobs (Roberts, 1984, p. 85).

9. Youthaid has estimated that trainees on YOP were especially vulnerable to accidents at work; and in an evaluation for the MSC, Aston University reported that 'a problem of trainee supervision and control could lie at the root of some of the more serious problems'. Youthaid, in their October 1984 Bulletin, produced the following table, charting the health and safety record of YOP and YTS:

Accidents to YOP/YTS trainees

	1980–1	81–2	82–3	83–4[a]	84–5[b]
Minor	1,530	2,968	3,565	1,662	395
Major	176	271	311	183	38
Fatal	4	6	7	6	0
Average no. of trainees	127,508	188,383	256,850	235,055	241,312
Rate of major injury per 100,000 trainees	138	144	121	78	63

a   A new system of recording accidents began during 1983. Figures for 1983–4 and later figures are *not* comparable with earlier figures.
b   1st quarter.

10. In a Gateshead technical college, to take one example, of 400 eligible YOP trainees only 259 attended induction sessions and only nineteen completed the course (Gould, 1982).

11. An Unemployment Unit Briefing on 'Youth Wages and Unemployment' examined the available evidence and concluded that the argument that youth unemployment was the result of narrowing youth/adult earnings differentials was 'substantially unfounded', and 'was at variance with the available statistical evidence' (1983, p. 8). For an excellent critique of the economic arguments on which the 'pricing into work' thesis is based, see the Low Pay Unit discussion paper by Henry Neuburger (1984).

7   A New Deal for the Young Working Class? The New Vocationalism and an Employer-led YTS

1. The Adult Training Strategy represents the third arm of the NTI and will be funded by a reallocation of the money already spent on adult training. It is intended to train over 250,000 people a year, and the MSC has stated that its main tasks are:
    1. To act as a focus for national priorities and objectives for adult training and improving awareness of its importance.

2. Working with others to encourage agreement on broad aims and objectives and ways of achieving them.
3. To use its resources both nationally and locally to help form opinion, provide information and act as a broker to help secure action to tackle common and urgent problems.
4. To work with others in encouraging improvements in access to and the attractiveness of training and continuing education.
5. To make the most effective use of its resources (money and staff) drawing on its experience of other programmes (e.g., TVEI and Open Tech) where marginal resources make maximum impact.
6. To make its own programmes and offerings more adaptable and responsive and to encourage others to do likewise.
7. To play an important (perhaps the lead) part in making relevant information on employment and training available to those who need it.

The MSC's principal recommendations, which were accepted by the government, were for:

1. A National Awareness Campaign – to raise the profile on the importance of adult training.
2. Action at a national level – to establish a funding framework and to remove obstacles to institutions providing for individuals' needs.
3. Achieving and measuring competence – action with examining and standard-setting bodies in line with objective 1 of the NTI.
4. Local level collaboration – helping training providers and employers to work together and some small-scale funding to encourage such work with larger projects to 'sow the seed' in areas where there are no such initiatives but considerable problems to be tackled.
5. Working with the market – providing better information and developing new forms of delivery, as well as stimulating and strengthening the training infrastructure.
6. The Commission's own programmes (considered marginal in relation to the total volume of adult training) consisting of two main categories – an industry-focused programme of job-related training directed to known employment needs and to helping the creation and growth of businesses, and a programme specifically to help unemployed people to improve their basic skills, retain their employability and cope with the changing content of jobs and pattern of work.

7. A National Loan scheme – to look at the practicability of such a scheme for adult trainees.

Despite the rhetoric of the MSC, Lucia Jones, General Secretary of the Association for Adult Education, remains sceptical about its likely effects:

> It remains to be seen how far the redeployment of about half of the TOPs money, a reshaping of the existing TOPs programmes, and a limited amount of pump-priming and a glossy advertising programme will be effective in delivering this ambitious new training package for adults (1984, p. 29).

2. From reaching 6.25 per cent of Gross National Product in 1975, educational expenditure had fallen to just under 5.25 per cent in 1982, and was to be reduced even further to 4.5 per cent by 1986. According to John Hughes, principal of Ruskin College, when inflation is taken into account, these projections 'imply a violent acceleration of real cuts in education' (1984).

3. Many of the developments described in this chapter are specific to England and Wales. The Scottish system is not only historically different but is now in the process of a major reform prompted by the Scottish Education Department's 16 Plus Action Plan. All non-advanced courses in further education and all non-adademic courses for sixteen–eighteen year olds in schools are to be replaced by a system of modular courses assessed by a single certificate. These changes are a response to the general pressures operating on schools and colleges, but according to David Raffe they also 'owe much to specifically Scottish circumstances'. In an excellent analysis, he goes on to emphasise that we should be very cautious in assuming that modules will somehow magically dispose of the problems of difficulty, selection and motivation: 'the apparent abolition by the Action Plan of structural constraints upon educational change is largely illusory' (1985, p. 32).

4. The Schools Council, which gave advice to government on examinations and the school curriculum, had a considerable proportion of teacher union representation on its committees and governing body. Despite the recommendations of a hostile review, which concluded that the Council should be retained, in 1982 Sir Keith Joseph decided to replace it with two small, nominated bodies, one for exams and another for the curriculum. Teacher unions were excluded from membership.

5. In the autumn of 1983 an opinion poll was published, indicating that a majority of those questioned supported the selective grammar–modern school set-up in preference to comprehensives. The outcome was predictable. Sixty Tory MPs called for the reintroduction of

selection, and a junior education Minister supported their call. Solihull was the most notable of a number of Tory local authorities which took up the suggestion, only to encounter a wide range of opposition which made them back down. Concurrent attempts in Berkshire and Wiltshire to extend selective procedures also met with opposition from parents and teachers.

Asked about these events on a TV programme, Sir Keith Joseph concluded: 'If it be so, as it is, that selection between schools is largely out, then I emphasise that *there must be differentiation* within schools'. As Brian Simon concludes, this was 'a clear statement of the tactic to negate the move towards the unification of secondary education – the main objective of the comprehensive reform' (1984, p. 21).

Press reports in 1986 suggested that the Conservatives would be going into the following election with the reintroduction of direct grant grammar schools as a central element of its manifesto.

6. The occupational training families, eight design elements, and six learning opportunities for the YTS are as follows:

A   The eleven occupational training families

OTF No.	Occupations	Key Purpose
1	Administrative, clerical and office services	Information processing
2	Agriculture, horticulture, forestry and fisheries	Nurturing and gathering living resources
3	Craft and design	Creating single or small numbers of objects using hand or power tools
4	Installation, maintenance and repair	Applying known procedures for making equipment work
5	Technical and scientific	Applying known principles to make things work or usable
6	Manufacturing and assembly	Transforming metallic and non-metallic materials through shaping, constructing and assembling into products
7	Processing	Intervening in the working of machines when necessary
8	Food preparation and service	Transforming and handling edible matter

9	Personal service and sales	Satisfying the needs of individual customers
10	Community and health services	Meeting socially defined needs of the community
11	Transport services	Moving goods and people

B The eight design elements
(a) induction
(b) occupationally-based training
(c) a minimum of thirteen weeks off-the-job training/education in a scheme lasting about twelve months
(d) planned work experience
(e) core areas, which are:

  1. number and its applications
  2. communication
  3. problem-solving and planning
  4. manual dexterity
  5. introduction to computer literacy/information technology.

(f) guidance and counselling
(g) assessment
(h) reviewing and recording of progress/achievement and certification.

C The six learning opportunities
(a) basic skills and additional skills such as computer literacy/ information technology
(b) the world of work
(c) the world outside employment, including trainees' interaction with the community
(d) job-specific and broadly related skills
(e) personal effectiveness, planning and problem solving, inter-personal skills
(f) ability to transfer skills, skill ownership and learning to learn.

7. Elements of the voluntary sector have been transformed by CP. Many organisations have become dependent subcontractors of the MSC and their traditional activities and ways of working have been increasingly affected by their new role in the management of unemployment. The CP has also impinged on the activities and jobs of those working in hardpressed local authorities and health services. What appears to be happening is that through CP, the MSC is acquiring responsibility for a considerable segment of local social

policy and service provision. It has also acquired considerable power to define what are, and what are not, acceptable forms of community benefit (Scott and Wilding, 1983).

Bibliography

Aaronovitch, S., 'Unemployment – Halting the Slide', *Marxism Today*, May 1981.

Abrams, M., *The Teenage Consumer* (London Press Exchange, 1959).

Albury, D. and Schwartz, J., *Partial Progress: The Politics of Science and Technology* (Pluto Press, 1982).

Ashton, D. N. and Bourn, C. J. (eds), *Education, Employment and Young People*, Vaughan Papers in Adult Education, University of Leicester (1981).

————— and Maguire, M.J., *Youth in the Labour Market* (DE, 1982).

————— and Maguire, M., *The Vanishing Youth Labour Market*, Youthaid Occasional Paper no. 3 (1983).

Atkinson, P., Rees, T., Shone, D. and Williamson, H., 'Social and Life Skills: The Latest Case of Compensatory Education', in Rees, T. and Atkinson, P. (eds), *Youth Unemployment and State Intervention* (RKP, 1982).

Ball, C., 'Here Comes Super YOP', *New Society*, 20 August 1981.

Baker, K., *New Jobs from New Technology* (Conservative Political Centre, 1982).

Banks, O., *Parity and Prestige in English Secondary Education: A Study in Education Sociology* (RKP, 1955).

—————, *The Sociology of Education* (Batsford, 1976).

Barker, R., *Education and Politics 1900–51: A Study of the Labour Party* (OUP, 1972).

Bates, I., 'From Vocational Guidance to Life Skills: Historical Perspectives on Careers Education', in Bates, I., *et al*, *Schooling for the Dole? The New Vocationalism* (Macmillan, 1984).

Bedeman, T. and Harvey, J., *Young People on YOP: A National Survey of Entrants to YOP*, Research and Development Paper no. 3 (MSC, 1981).

————— and Courtenay, G., *One in Three*, Research and Development Paper no. 13 (MSC, 1983).

Bellaby, P., *The Sociology of the Comprehensive School* (Methuen, 1977).

Benn, C., Fairley, J. (eds); *Challenging the MSC on Jobs, Education and Training: Enquiry into a National Disaster* (Pluto, 1986).

Berg, I., *Education and Jobs: The Great Training Robbery* (Penguin, 1977).

Bernbaum, G., *Social Change and the Schools 1918–1944* (RKP, 1971).

Beveridge, W. H. , *Full Employment in a Free Society* (Allen & Unwin, 1944).

Blackburn, R. M. and Mann, M., *The Working Class in the Labour Market* (Macmillan, 1979).

Boffey, R., 'Some Thoughts on Year One', *NATFHE Journal*, October 1984.

Bordieu, P. and Passeron, J., *Reproduction in Education, Society and Culture* (Sage, 1977).

Brannen, P., 'Industrial and Economic Change and the Entry into Work', in Brannen, P. (ed.), *Entering the World of Work; Some Sociological Perspectives* (HMSO, 1975).

Braverman, H., *Labour and Monopoly Capital: The Degradation of Work in the Twentieth Century* (Monthly Review Press, 1974).

Brelsford, P., 'Give Us A Break', *Youth Training News*, no. 1 (MSC, 1983).

————, Smith, G. and Rix, A., *Give us a Break: Widening Opportunities For Young Women within YOP/YTS*, Research and Development Paper no. 11 (MSC, 1982).

British Youth Council, *Youth Unemployment: Causes and Cures* (BYC, 1977).

Brown, E. and Senker, P., *New Technology and Employment*, Manpower Intelligence and Planning (MSC, 1982).

Bruce, M., *The Coming of the Welfare State*, B. T. Batsford Ltd., 1972.

Callaghan, J., 'What the PM Said', *Times Education Supplement*, 22 October 1976.

Campbell, B., *Wigan Pier Revisited: Poverty and Politics in the 80s* (Virago, 1984).

Carter, D. and Stewart, I., *YOP, Youth Training and the MSC: The Need for a New Trade Union Response* (Manchester Employment Research Group, 1983).

Carter M., *Into Work* (Pelican, 1966).

Casson, M., *Youth Unemployment* (Macmillan, 1979).

————, 'Youth Unemployment – Past, Present and Future', *Youth in Society* 40, March 1980.

Central Advisory Council for Education (England), *School and Life* (HMSO, 1947).

————, *Fifteen to Eighteen* (Crowther Report) (HMSO, 1959).

————, *Half Our Future* (Newsom Report) (HMSO, 1963).

Central Policy Review Staff (Think Tank), *Education, Training and Industrial Performance* (HMSO, 1980).

Chitty, C., 'TVEI: The MSC's Trojan Horse', in Benn, C. and Fairley, J. (eds), *Challenging the MSC on Jobs, Education and Training: Enquiry into a National Disaster* (Pluto Press, 1986).

Clark, G., 'Recent Developments in Working Patterns', *Department of Employment Gazette*, July 1982.

Clarke, L., *The Transition from School to Work: A Critical Review of UK Research Literature*, Report no. 49 (Employment Services Agency, 1978).

Cohen, P., 'Subcultural Conflict and Working Class Community', in *Working Papers in Cultural Studies*, no. 2, Spring 1972.

————, 'Against the New Vocationalism', in Bates, I. *et al.*, *Schooling for the Dole? The New Vocationalism* (Macmillan, 1984).

Cohen, S., *Folk Devils and Moral Panics* (Paladin, 1973).

Colledge, D. and Field, J., 'To Recondition Human Material . . .': An Account of a British Labour Camp in the 1930s. An Interview with William Herd, *History Workshop* 15, Spring 1983.

Coopers and Lybrand Associates, *A Challenge to Complacency: Changing Attitudes to Training*, A Report to the Manpower Services Commission and the National Economic Development Office (MSC, 1985).

Corrigan, P., *Schooling the Smash Street Kids* (Macmillan, 1979).

CRE, *Looking for Work: Black and White School Leavers in Lewisham* (CRE, 1978).

————, *Ethnic Minorities and the Youth Opportunities Programme* (CRE, 1980).

————, *Racial Equality and the Youth Training Scheme* (CRE, 1984).

Crosland, C. A. R., *The Conservative Enemy* (Cape, 1962).

Cross, M., *Equality of Opportunity and Inequality of Outcome: the MSC, Ethnic Minorities and Training Policy* unpublished paper (Centre for Research in Ethnic Relations, Warwick University, 1985).

Dale, R., 'The Background and Inception of the Technical and Vocational Education Initiative', in Dale, R. (ed.); *Education, Training and Employment: Towards a New Vocationalism?* (Pergamon Press/Open University, 1985).

Daniel, W. W., *Racial Discrimination in England* (Penguin, 1968).

Davies, B., *In Whose Interests?*, National Youth Bureau Occasional Paper 19 (NYB, 1979).

DE, *Training for the Future: A Plan for Discussion*, Department of Employment (HMSO, 1972).

————, 'First Employment of Young People', *Department of Employment Gazette*, October 1984.

DE/DHSS, *Payment of Benefits to Unemployed People*, Department of Employment (DHSS, 1981).

Deem, R., *Women and Schooling* (RKP, 1978).

DES, *Report of the Committee on Higher Education* (Robbins Report), Cmnd 2154 (HMSO, 1963).

————, *Raising the School Leaving Age*, DES Circular 8/70 (DES, 1970).

————, *Progress Report on RSLA*, Report on Education no. 73 (DES, March 1972).

————, *The First Year After RSLA* (DES, April 1975).

————, *Unified Vocational Preparation: A Pilot Approach, A Government Statement* (DES, 1976).

————, *Education in Schools: A Consultative Document*, Cmnd 6869, (HMSO, 1977).

————, *RSLA Four Years On*, Report on Education no. 95 (DES, October 1979).

————, *Young People in the 80s* (HMSO, 1983).

————, *The Youth Training Scheme in Further Education 1983–84; An HMI Survey*, report by HM Inspectors (DES, 1984).

————, *Report by HMI on the Effects of Local Authority Expenditure Policies on Education Provision in England in 1984* (DES, 1985).

————, DE, *16–18: Education and Training for 16–18 Year Olds*: a consultative paper presented by the Secretaries of State for Education and Science, for Employment and for Wales (DES, 1979).

DHSS, *Opportunities for Volunteering: A Consultation Paper by the Department of Health and Social Security* (DHSS, 1981).

Downes, D. M., *The Delinquent Solution* (RKP, 1966).

Education Group, *Unpopular Education: Schooling and Social Democracy in England since 1944* (CCCS/Hutchinson, 1981).

Edwards, T., *The Youth Training Scheme: A New Curriculum? Episode One* (Falmer Press, 1984).

Eggleston, S. J., Dunn D. K. and Anjali M., *The Educational and Vocational Experiences of 15–18 Year-Old Young People of Minority Ethnic Groups* (Department of Education, Warwick University, Coventry, 1985).

Esland, G. and Cathcart, H., 'The Compliant Creative Worker: The Ideological Reconstruction of the School Leaver', *Proceedings of the Standing Conference on the Sociology of Further Education*, Paper no. 84/22e (Blagdon, Coombe Lodge, 1984).

Eversley, J., 'Trade Union Responses to the MSC', in Benn, C. and Fairley, J. (eds); *Challenging the MSC on Jobs, Education and Training: Enquiry into a National Disaster* (Pluto Press, 1986).

EWO, 'The Educational Welfare Officer', *Journal of the Association of EWOs*, September 1971.

Farley, M., 'Training for Skill Ownership', *NATFHE Journal*, November 1983.

Fawcett Society and the National Joint Commission of Working Women's Organisations, *The Class of '84: A Study of Girls on the First Year of the Youth Training Scheme*, 150 Walworth Road, London (1985).

Fenwick, J. G. K., *The Comprehensive School 1944–1970: The Politics of Secondary School Reorganisation* (Methuen, 1976).

Fenton, S., Davies, J., Means, R. and Burton, P., *Ethnic Minorities and the Youth Training Scheme*, MSC Research and Development, no. 20 (MSC, 1984).

Finn, D. J., *Education, Class, Experience and the Former Early School Leaver*, unpublished paper (1975).

————, *The Employment Effects of the New Technologies: A Review of the Arguments* (Unemployment Unit, 1984a).

————, 'Leaving School and Growing Up: Work Experience in the Juvenile Labour Market', in Bates, I. *et al.*, *Schooling for the Dole? The New Vocationalism* (Macmillan, 1984b).

————, *Half Measures: Recent Developments in Special Measures for the Unemployed*, Unemployment Unit Bulletin, no. 19 (February, 1986).

Forester, T, 'Children at Work', *New Society*, 1 November 1979.

Freedman, S., 'The Certificate of Secondary Education and the Employer', in Ashton, D. N. and Bourn, C. J. (eds), *Education, Employment and Young People*, Vaughan Papers in Adult Education, University of Leicester (1981).

Friend, A. and Metcalfe, A., *Slump City: The Politics of Mass Unemployment* (Pluto Press, 1981).

Frith, S., 'Socialisation and Rational Schooling: Elementary Education in Leeds 1800–1870, in McCann, P. (ed.), *Popular Education and Socialisation in the Nineteenth Century* (Methuen, 1977a).

————, *Education, Training and the Labour Process*, unpublished paper given to the CSE Education Group, Birmingham (November 1977b).

Frith, S., *The Sociology of Rock*, (Constable, 1978).

————, 'Youth and the Labour Process', in Cole, M. and Skelton, B. (eds), *Blind Alley: Youth in a Crisis of Capital* (Hesketh, 1980).

Further Education Curriculum Review and Development Unit, *Day Release – A Desk Study* (FECDRU, 1980).

————, *Vocational Preparation* (Mansell Report) (January 1981).

Gabriel, Y., 'Feeding the Fast Food Chain', *New Statesman*, 12 April 1985.

Gamble, A., 'Mrs Thatcher's Bunker: the Reshuffle and its Consequences', *Marxism Today*, November 1981.

GLC, *Training in Crisis: The New Training Initiative 1981–1984: a Policy Review* (GLTB, 1984).

Gleeson, D., 'Privatisation of Industry and the Nationalisation of Youth', in Dale, R. (ed.); *Education, Training and Employment: Towards a New Vocationalism?* (Pergamon Press/Open University, 1985).

Goldstein, N., 'The New Training Initiative: A Great Leap Backward', *Capital and Class* 23, Summer 1984.

Gollan, J., *Youth in British Industry*, Left Book Club (Victor Gollancz Ltd, 1937).

Gould, K., 'YOPs Education Scheme Under-Used', *Times Educational Supplement*, 12 November 1982.

Greaves, K., Costyn, P. and Bonsall, C., *Off the Job Training on YOP*, Research and Development paper no. 12 (Manpower Services Commission, 1982).

Green, A., 'The MSC and the Three-Tier Structure of Further Education', in Benn, C. and Fairley, J. (eds), *Challenging the MSC on Jobs, Education and Training: Enquiry into a National Disaster* (Pluto Press, 1986).

Gregory, D. and Noble, C., 'Trade Unions and Special Measures for the Young Unemployed', in Rees, T. and Atkinson, P. (eds), *Youth Unemployment and State Intervention* (RKP, 1982).

Griffin, C., *Typical girls?* (RKP, 1985a).

———, 'Turning the Tables: Feminist Analyses of Youth Unemployment', *Youth and Policy* 14, Autumn 1985b.

Grimshaw, R. and Pratt, J., 'School Absenteeism and the Education Crisis', *Youth and Policy* 10, Autumn 1984.

Hall, S. and Jefferson, T. (eds), *Resistance Through Rituals* (Hutchinson, 1976).

———, Critcher, C., Jefferson, T., Clarke, J. and Roberts, B., *Policing the Crisis: Mugging, the State and Law and Order* (Macmillan, 1978).

Halsey, A. H., Heath, A. F. and Ridge, J. M., *Origins and Destinations: Family, Class and Education in Modern Britain* (Clarendon Press, 1980).

Hannington, W., *The Problem of the Distressed Areas* (Left Book Club, 1937).

———, *Unemployed Struggles: 1919–1936* (Lawrence & Wishart, 1977).

Hargreaves, D. H., *Social Relations in a Secondary School* (RKP, 1967).

Hayes, C., Fonda, N., Pope, M., Stuart, R. and Townsend, K., *Training for Skill Ownership – Learning to Take It With You* (Institute of Manpower Studies, 1983).

HMSO, *The Primary School*, Report of the Consultative Committee (Board of Education, 1931).

————, *Employment and Training: Government Proposals*, Cmnd 5250 (HMSO, 1973).

————, *Policy Making in the Department of Education and Science: Tenth Report from the Expenditure Committee*, House of Commons, Session 1975–6 (HMSO, 1976).

————, *A New Training Initiative: A Programme for Action*, Cmnd 8455 (HMSO, 1981).

————, *Fourth Report from the Committee of Public Accounts, Department of Employment, Manpower Services Commission, Special Employment Measures, Session 1983–4* (HMSO, 1983).

————, *Training for Jobs*, Cmnd 9135 (HMSO, January 1984).

————, *Employment: The Challenge to the Nation*, Cmnd 9474 (HMSO, March 1985a).

————, *Better Schools*, Cmnd 9469 (HMSO, March 1985b).

————, *Education and Training for Young People*, Cmnd 9482 (HMSO, April 1985c).

Hobsbawm, E. J., *Labouring Men: Studies in the History of Labour* (Weidenfeld & Nicolson, 1968).

Hoggart, R., *The Uses of Literacy* (Penguin, 1957).

Holland, G., 'Schools and the NTI: An MSC View', in *Schools, YOP and the new Training Initiative* (CRAC Publications, Cambridge, 1982).

————, *The Challenge of Long Term Unemployment*, address to the Stock Exchange (18 June 1984a).

————, *A National Perspective, Education and Training 14–18: Policy and Practice*, a national conference organised by the Careers Research and Advisory Centre and the National Institute for Careers Education and Counselling (Stoke Rochford, 10 December 1984b).

Horne, J., 'Youth Unemployment Programmes: A Historical Account of the Development of Dole Colleges', in Gleeson, D. (ed.), *Youth Training and the Search for Work* (RKP, 1983).

Horton, C., *Nothing Like A Job: A Survey of Unemployed School-Leavers (1983–1984) who could have gone on the Youth Training Scheme but did not* (Youthaid, 1986).

Hughes, J., 'Caught in the Squeeze', *Guardian*, 4 September 1983.

Humphries, S., *Hooligans or Rebels? An Oral History of Working Class Childhood and Youth 1889–1939* (Basil Blackwell, 1981).

Hunt, J. and Small, P., *Employing Young People: A Study of Employers' Attitudes, Policies and Practice* (Scottish Council for Research in Education, 1981).

Hutt, A., *The Post War History of the British Working Class* (EP Publishing Ltd., 1972).

IDS, *Youth Training Scheme*, Incomes Data Services Ltd, study 293 (July 1983).

————, *YTS: A Review*, Incomes Data Services Ltd, study 311 (April 1984).

IFF, *Adult Training in Britain*, A Survey carried out by IFF Research Ltd, for MSC (Manpower Services Commission, 1985).

ILEA, *Improving Secondary Schools*, Report of the Committee on the Curriculum and Organisation of Secondary Schools (ILEA, 1984).

ILO, *Young People in Their Working Environment* (ILO, Geneva, 1977).

Industrial Society, *Survey of Training Costs*, The Information Department, the Industrial Society, New Series no. 1 (1985).

IRR, *IRS Guide to the Youth Training Scheme*, *Industrial Relations Review and Report* (Industrial Relations Services, 1983).

James, A., 'Children's Experience of Work', in *Economic and Social Research Council Newsletter*, no. 51 (March 1984).

Jeffries, R., 'Going for a Song?', *Youth in Society* (NYB, 1982).

Jeffs, T., *Youthcall*, Youthaid Occasional Paper no. 1 1982.

Johnathan, R., 'Lifelong Learning: Slogan, Educational Aim or Manpower Service?' *Scottish Educational Review* 14 (2), November 1982.

Johnson, R., 'Educational Policy and Social Control in Early Victorian England', *Past and Present*, 49, November 1970.

Jones, K., *Beyond Progressive Education* (Macmillan, 1983).

Jones, L., 'Will Recycling TOPS Deliver the Goods?, *NATFHE Journal*, February 1984.

Kaufman, M., 'The MSC and a New National Training System', in Benn, C. and Fairley, J. (eds), *Challenging the MSC on Jobs, Education and Training: Enquiry into a National Disaster* (Pluto Press, 1986).

Keene, N., *The Employment of Young Workers* (Batsford, 1969).

Keil, E. T., *Becoming a Worker* (Leicestershire Committee of Education, 1976).

Labour Party, *Signposts for the Sixties* (Labour Party, 1963).

————, *Socialism in the 80s: 16–19 Learning for Life*, Labour Party Discussion Document (Labour Party, 1982).

Lacey, C., *Hightown Grammar: The School as a Social System* (Manchester University Press, 1970).

Lester Smith, W. A., *Education: An Introductory Survey* (Penguin, 1971).

Lewis, P., 'The Price of a Job', *Youthaid Bulletin*, no. 19 (December 1984).

LMI, *Labour Movement Inquiry into Youth Unemployment and Training, Bulletins 1–4*, available from Cllr Dave Morgan, Employment Department, Sheffield City Council, Palatine Chambers, Pinstone Street, Sheffield S1 2HN (1984/5).

Loveridge, R. and Mok, A., *Theories of Labour Market Segmentation: Main Report*, Commission of the European Communities, study no. 76/1, V/213/78-EN (1978).

LRD, 'YTS in Practice, Young Workers' Pay', *Bargaining Report*, no. 30 (December 1983).

MacLennan, E., *Working Children*, Pamphlet no. 15 (Low Pay Unit, 1980).

————, *Child Labour in London*, Pamphlet no. 22 (Low Pay Unit, 1982).

————, Fitz, J. and Sullivan, J., *Working Children*, Pamphlet no. 34 (Low Pay Unit, 1985).

Makeham, P., 'The Anatomy of Youth Unemployment', *Employment Gazette*, March 1980.

Mansell, J., 'Competence for all in UK Ltd', *Times Educational Supplement*, 25 January 1985.

Markall, G. and Finn, D. J., *Young People and the Labour Market: A Case Study*, Department of the Environment (HMSO, 1982).

————, *Cheap Labour? A Review of Work Experience on Employers' Premises in Central Liverpool*, Youthaid Occasional Paper no. 2 (1983).

Massey, D. and Meegan, R., *The Anatomy of Job Loss: The How, Why and Where of Employment Decline* (Methuen, 1982).

Mays, J. B., *Education and the Urban Child* (Liverpool University Press, 1962).

McLeish, M. and Mullin, W., *Programme for Opportunity: An Investigation into YOP in Fife* (Fife Regional Council and MSC, 1981).

McRobbie, A., 'Working Class Girls and the Culture of Femininity', in Women's Studies Group, CCCS, *Women Take Issue* (Hutchinson, 1978).

———— and Garber, J., 'Girls and Subcultures', in Working Papers in Cultural Studies 7/8, *Resistance Through Rituals* (CCCS, 1975).

Metcalf, D., *Alternatives to Unemployment: Special Employment Measures in Britain* (Policy Studies Institute, 1982).

Mills, I., 'Preventing Demoralisation: The Work of JICs', in *Youth and Policy* 9, Summer 1984.

Ministry of Labour, *Industrial Training: Government Proposals*, Cmnd 1892 (HMSO, 1962).

Moore, R., 'Education, Pedagogy and Production', in Gleeson, D. (ed.), *Youth Training and the Search for Work* (RKP, 1983).

————, 'Schooling and the World of Work', in Bates, I. *et al.*, *Schooling for the Dole? The New Vocationalism* (Macmillan, 1984).

Morgan, A. E., *Young Citizen* (Penguin, 1943).

MSC, *Annual Reports* (MSC, 1976–7; 1978–9; 1979–80; 1980–1; 1981–2; 1982–3; 1983–4).

———, *Reviews of First, Second, Third, Fourth Years of the Special Programmes* (July 1979, 1980, 1981, 1982).

———, *There's Work To Be Done*, Santosh Mukherjee (MSC, 1974).

———, *Towards a Comprehensive Manpower Policy* (MSC, 1976a).

———, *Instructional Guide to Social and Life Skills* (MSC, 1976b).

———, *Young People and Work: Report on the Feasibility of a New Programme of Opportunities for Unemployed Young People* (Holland Report) (MSC, 1977).

———, *A New Training Initiative: A Consultative Document* (MSC, May 1981a).

———, *A New Training Initiative: An Agenda for Action* (MSC, December 1981b).

———, *Youth Task Group Report: New Training Initiative* (MSC, April 1982).

———/TSA; *Vocational Preparation for Young People* (MSC, 1975).

———/YTB, 'Minimum Criteria for Schemes Starting in 1985', *MSC/YTB*, YTB/84/N11 (1984).

Musgrave, P. W., *Society and Education in England since 1800* (Methuen, 1972).

Musgrove, F., *Youth and the Social Order* (RKP, 1968).

NATFHE, 'Doubts about YTS, Progress with the Open Tech: National Conference on Education, Training and Development', *NATFHE Journal*, October 1983.

———, *The Great Training Robbery: An Interim Report on the Role of Private Training Agencies within the YTS in the Birmingham and Solihull Area*, Birmingham Liaison Committee, Trade Union Resource Centre, Birmingham (1984).

National Association of School Masters, *Discipline in Schools* (NAS, 1975).

———, *Retreat from Authority* (NAS, 1976).

National Joint Advisory Council, *Training for Skill: Recruitment and Training of Young Workers in Industry* (Carr Report) (HMSO, 1958).

National Union of Teachers, Executive Report, *Discipline in Schools*, NUT Conference Report (1976).

National Youth Employment Council, *Unqualified, Untrained and Unemployed: Report of a Working Party set up by the National Youth Employment Council* (HMSO, 1974).

NCPTA, *The State of Schools in England and Wales* (NCPTA, 1985).

NEDC, *Education and Industry* (NEDC, 1982).

———, *Changing Employment Patterns: Where Will the New Jobs Be?*,

Memorandum by the Chancellor of the Exchequer (NEDC, November 1983).

————/MSC, *Competence and Competition: Training and Education in the Federal Republic of Germany, the United States and Japan*, a report prepared by the Institute of Manpower Studies for the NEDC and MSC (1984).

Network Fact File, 'Employers Survey', in *Network* (MSC house journal) 12, August 1979.

Neuburger H., *Unemployment: Are Wages to Blame?*, (Low Pay Unit, 1984).

Newell, R., 'Rise of the MSC', *NATFHE Journal*, November 1982.

NFER, *The Youth Training Scheme and the FE Response: An Interim Report*, S. M. Stoney and V. M. Scott, NFER Research in Progress no. 7 (NFER, 1984).

Northcott, J. and Rogers, P., *Microelectronics in Industry: What's Happening in Britain*, Policy Studies Institute, no. 603 (1982).

Novak, T., 'Tory Job Creation: Lessons from the USA', *Social Policy Bulletin*, Winter 1985.

O'Brien, R., 'Industry, Education and People', The Josiah Mason Memorial Lecture (Birmingham University, 29 November 1977).

Orwell, G., *The Road to Wigan Pier* (Penguin, 1970).

Partridge, J., *Life in a Secondary Modern School* (Pelican, 1968).

Payne, J., *Changes in the Youth Labour Market 1974 to 1981*, Department of Social and Administrative Studies, Oxford University, unpublished paper (November 1984).

Pearson, G., *Hooligan: A History of Respectable Fears* (Macmillan, 1983).

Perry, P. J. C., *The Evolution of British Manpower Policy* (British Association for Commercial and Industrial Education, 1975).

Phillips, A. and Taylor, B., 'Sex and Skill: Notes Towards a Feminist Economics', in *Feminist Review*, 6, 1980.

Pope, R., 'Education and the Young Unemployed: A Pre-War Experiment', *Journal of Further and Higher Education* 2 (2), Summer 1978.

————, 'Adjustment to Peace: Educational Provision for Unemployed Juveniles in Britain 1918–19', *Journal of Social Policy* XXVII (1), February 1979.

Presdee, M., 'The Twilight Zone', *Youth in Society* (NYB, 1984).

Raffe, D., 'The Extendable Ladder: Scotland's 16 Plus Action Plan', *Youth and Policy* 12, Spring 1985.

Randall, C., *Manpower – Serving Whose Interests? A Report on Trade Union Involvement in the Manpower Services Commission*, CWW1, Centre for a Working World (Bath, 1986).

Rauta, I. and Hunt, A., *Fifth Form Girls: Their Hopes for the Future: A*

Survey carried out on behalf of the Department of Education and Science, OPCS Social Survey Division (HMSO, 1975).

Reeder, D., 'A Recurring Debate: Education and Industry', in Bernbaum, G. (ed.), *Schooling in Decline* (Macmillan, 1979).

Rees, G. and Rees, T., 'Juvenile Unemployment and the State Between the Wars', in Rees, T. and Atkinson, P. (eds), *Youth Unemployment and State Intervention* (RKP, 1982).

Roberts, H. and Kirby, R., 'YB on YTS: Why Not?', *Youth and Policy* 12, Spring 1985.

Roberts, K., 'The Developmental Theory of Occupational Choice: A Critique and an Alternative', in Esland, G., Salaman, G. and Speakman, M. (eds), *People and Work* (Open University, 1975).

————, *School Leavers and their Prospects: Youth and the Labour Market in the 1980s* (Open University Press, 1984).

————, Duggan, J. and Noble, M., *Unregistered Youth Unemployment and Outreach Careers Work – Final Report, Part One, Non-Registration*, Research Paper no. 31 (DE, 1981).

RPPITB, *Work and Learning: Proposals for a National Scheme for 16–18 Year Olds at Work*, Third Report of the Study Group on the Education/Training of Young People (Rubber and Plastics Processing Industrial Training Board, 1978).

Rubenstein, D. and Simon, B., *The Evolution of the Comprehensive School, 1926–66* (RKP, 1966).

Ryan, P., 'The New Training Initiative after Two Years', *Lloyds Bank Review*, April 1984.

Sanderson, M., *The Universities and British Industry 1850–1970* (RKP, 1972).

Schools Council, *Raising of the School Leaving Age*, Working Paper no. 2 (HMSO, 1965).

————, *Schools Council Enquiry I: Young School Leavers*, Report of an Enquiry carried out for the Schools Council by the Government Social Survey (HMSO, 1968).

Schools Council Welsh Committee, *Another Year – To Endure or Enjoy?* (HMSO, 1967).

Scott, D. and Wilding, P., *Beyond Welfare Pluralism?* Manchester Council for Voluntary Service and the Department of Social Administration (Manchester University, 1983).

Seale, C., 'Some Trends in YTS Curriculum Theory', in *A Critical Review of YTS Policy and Practice*, Further Education Staff College (Coombe Lodge, 28–31 March 1984).

Sheffield Trades Council, *Summary and Proposals to Economic & Employment Strategy Steering Group of Sheffield City Council*, Youth Opportunities Programme Working Party (Sheffield Trades Council, 7 April 1982).

Short, C., 'Mr. Tebbit's New Youth Training Scheme', *Unemployment Unit Bulletin no. 2* (February 1982).

Simon, B., 'Classification and Streaming: A Study of Grouping in English Schools 1860–1960', in *Intelligence, Psychology and Education: A Marxist Critique* (Lawrence & Wishart, 1971).

————, *The Politics of Educational Reform 1920–1940* (Lawrence & Wishart, 1974).

————, 'Breaking School Rules', *Marxism Today*, September 1984.

Simon, M., *Youth into Industry: A Study of Young People's Attitudes to Work at a Large Midlands Factory* (NYB, 1977).

SPB, *The Future Development of Special Programmes*, Director of Special Programmes, SPB/81/16, (Special Programmes Board/MSC, 1981).

Stafford, A., 'Learning not to Labour,' *Capital and Class* 15, Autumn 1981.

Stevenson, J., *British Society 1914–45* (Penguin, 1984).

———— and Cook, C., *The Slump: Society and Politics during the Depression* (Cape, 1977).

Tapper, T. and Salter, B., *Education, Politics and the State: The Theory and Practice of Educational Change* (Grant McIntyre, 1981).

Tawney, R. H., 'Keep the Workers' Children in their Place', in *Daily News*, 14 February 1918.

————, *Secondary Education for All* (Allen & Unwin, 1922).

————, 'Presidential Address to the English Section of the New Education Fellowship', in *New Era* 15 (2), February 1934a.

————, *Juvenile Employment and Education* (OUP, 1934b).

————, *The School Leaving Age and Juvenile Unemployment* (WEA, 1934c).

Taylor, A. J. P., *English History 1914–1945* (Pelican, 1970).

TD/MSC, *Training Division Planning 1984/85 – Resources and Issues – RD 83/84 Note by RAOI* (Training Division, MSC, 1983).

Thomas, D., 'New Ways of Working', *New Society*, 30 August 1985.

Thorpe, S., *Girls and Computer Literacy/Information Technology on the Youth Training Scheme* (Huddersfield Polytechnic, June 1984).

Tower Hamlets Trades Council, *Opportunity Knocks? Youth Unemployment and the Youth Opportunities Programme: A Discussion Paper for Trade Unionists* (1981).

TUC, *Statement on the School Leaving Age* (TUC, 9 January 1968).

————, *Training and Education of Young Workers: Report of TUC Consultative Conference held on 4 November 1975* (1975a).

————, *Day Release for Further Education; A Discussion Paper Prepared by the TUC* (1975b).

————, *Note of Comment on Training Services Agency Paper 'Vocational Preparation for Young People'* (1975c).

230   *Bibliography*

————/NEDC, *Where Are the New Jobs Coming From?*, Memorandum by the TUC, NEDC (83) 59 (24 November 1983).

TURC, *Unequal Opportunities: Racial Discrimination and The Youth Training Scheme*, West Midlands YTS Research Project (TURC Publishing, Birmingham, 1985).

————, *The Great Training Robbery Continues: A Follow-Up Investigation of the Role of Private Training Agencies in Birmingham/Solihull*, West Midlands YTS Research Project (TURC Publishing, Birmingham, 1986).

Unemployment Unit, *Chronology of Recent Unemployment Benefit Cuts*, Unemployment Unit Briefing no. 1 (March 1982).

————, *The Unacceptable Face Of Special Measures – A Critique of the Government's New Community Programme for the Long-Term Unemployed*, Unemployment Unit Briefing no. 4 (revised October 1982).

————, *Youth Wages and Unemployment*, Unemployment Unit Briefing no. 2 (revised May 1983).

van der Eyken, W. (ed.), *Education, the Child and Society: A Documentary History 1900–1973* (Penguin, 1973).

Vaizey, J., *Education for Tomorrow* (Penguin, 1968).

———— and Debeauvais, M., 'Economic Aspects of Educational Development', in Halsey, A. H., Flood, J. and Arnold Anderson, C., *Education, Economy and Society: A Reader in the Sociology of Education* (Macmillan 1961).

Veness, T., *School Leavers* (Methuen, 1962).

Watts, A. G., *Education, Unemployment and the Future of Work* (Open University Press, 1983).

————, 'Education and Employment: The Traditional Bonds', in Dale, R. (ed.), *Education, Training and Employment: Towards a New Vocationalism?* (Pergamon Press/Open University, 1985).

Watts J. (ed.), *The Countesthorpe Experience* (Unwin Education Books, 1977).

Waugh, C., 'Really Useful Knowledge?', *Schooling and Culture* no. 12, Cultural Studies Department, Cockpit Arts Workshop (ILEA, Autumn, 1982).

Webb, J., 'The Sociology of the School', *British Journal of Sociology* 13, 1962.

Welsh Office, *A Survey of the Youth Training Scheme in Further Education 1983–84*, Report by HM Inspectors Undertaken during Spring Term 1983–4 (Welsh Office, 1984).

Westergaard, J. H., 'Sociology: the Myth of Classlessness', in Blackburn, R. (ed.), *Ideology in Social Science* (Fontana, 1972).

———— and Rester, H., *Class in a Capitalist Society: A Study of Contemporary Britain* (Penguin, 1976).

Wickham, A., *Education Systems in an International Context*, Open University Course Unit, E353 (Open University Press, 1981).

————, 'Gender Divisions, Training and the State', in Dale, R. (ed.), *Education, Training and Employment: Towards a New Vocationalism?* (Pergamon Press/Open University, 1985).

Williams, R., *The Long Revolution* (Pelican, 1975).

Willis, P., *Learning to Labour: How Working Class Kids Get Working Class Jobs* (Saxon House, 1977).

————, 'Youth Unemployment: A New Social State', *New Society*, 29 March 1984.

Willmott, P., *Adolescent Boys of East London* (Penguin, 1969).

Woolcock, P., 'The Idiot's Guide to Work', *Guardian*, 10 May 1983.

Wrench, J. and Lee, G., 'A Subtle Hammering – Young Black People and the Labour Market', in Troyna, B. and Smith, D. (eds), *Racism, School and the Labour Market* (NYB, 1984).

Youthaid, *Quality or Collapse? Youthaid Review of the Youth Opportunities Programme* (Youthaid, 1981).

————, *An Income for Youth: Evidence to the Review of Benefits for Children and Young People* (Youthaid, 1984).

————, *The First Year: The Youth Training Scheme in London 1983–1984* (Youthaid, 1985).

————/National Youth Bureau, *Post-YTS Initiatives: A Review and Recommendation for Action* (Youthaid, February 1985).

Zimbalist, A. (ed.), *Case Studies on the Labour Process* (Monthly Review Press, 1979).

Index